WESTWARD LEADING

WESTWARD LEADING

William Barton Murdock

Library of Congress Cataloging-in-Publication Data

Murdock, William Barton, 1916-
    Westward Leading / William Barton Murdock.
        P. cm.
    Includes Bibliographic references
    ISBN 0-9745686-1-9 (pbk. : alk. paper)
    1.   West (U.S.)—History. 2. United States—Territorial expansion. 3. Transportation—West (U.S.)—History. 4. Transportation—United States—History. 5. Frontier and pioneer life—West (U.S.) 6. Frontier and pioneer life—United States. 7. West (U.S.)—description and travel. 8. United States—Biography. I. Title.

        F591.M925 2004
        978—dc22

                                              2004007709

Copyright © 2004 by William Barton Murdock
All rights reserved.

Photo credits:
Portraits of James Clinton, George Clinton, DeWitt Clinton and Sir Henry Clinton, artist: Benson J. Lossing, from *The Pictorial Field-book of the Revolution,* New York: Harper and Bros. Publishers, 1860.
Portrait of Brigadier General Fielder Jones used by permission of Potter County Historical Society.
Portrait of General George Wright used with permission of the Oregon Historical Society.
Portrait of Henry Villard used with permission of the Oregon Historical Society.
Portrait of Oswald Garrison Villard used with permission of the Oregon Historical Society.
Photo of Delilah F. Henderschott courtesy of Thae Reitzel Murdock.
Columbia River Locks photos courtesy of Julie Cole and the Tidewater Barge Lines.
1931 Phaeton photo published by Heritage Plantation, Hancock, Massachusetts.
Reo Tour Bus photo from 1927 travel brochure published jointly by the Chicago and Great Western Railways.
Photo of Henry E. Dosch's children used with permission of James Driscoll.
"Henry Dosch in His Office" used with permission of the Oregon Historical Society.
Cover artwork courtesy of Wells Fargo.

This book may not be reproduced in whole or in part, by electronic or any other means which exist or may yet be developed, without permission from:

Arnica Publishing
3739 SE 8th Avenue, Suite 1
Portland, OR 97202
www.arnicapublishing.com

*This book is dedicated to the women in my life—
Belle, Thae, Katharine, Linn, Kate, and Pam*

—Bart

TABLE of CONTENTS

— *Page xv* —
Preface
Why did people move west? Shall we stay where we are or go? The wanderlust versus community debate as highlighted in the Rolling Stone ballad. Changing concepts of the term the West.

— *Page 1* —
Chapter 1
Early Routes West
Water Routes West: The Ottawa River route. The Mohawk River route. The Pennsylvania Portage route. The Potomac River route. And in the south the James and Savannah River routes. With the completion of the Erie Canal in 1825, New York wins the transportation war!

The National Road is completed to Wheeling in 1818 and is extended to Vandalia, Illinois by 1852. Connecting roads lead south to New Orleans and north to Michigan. The Wilderness Road links Salisbury, North Carolina to central Kentucky and the Great Wagon road passes through the Shenandoah Valley, the Piedmont country of North Carolina to Augusta, Georgia.

Early Eastern Railroads include the Baltimore & Ohio begun in 1828, the Pennsylvania that connected Philadelphia with Pittsburgh by 1853, the Chesapeake & Ohio which made contact with Cincinnati and Cleveland and the Richmond, Fredericksburg & Potomac chartered in 1834.

Bridges, Ferries and Alternate routes. Early bridges were built at Wheeling in 1849 and Cincinnati in 1867. The marvel was the Eads Bridge built over the Mississippi 1867–74. The Golden Gate and Bay Bridge were built in 1936–37. Ferries are still to be found in areas such as Puget Sound in Washington, Coastal Alaska and the Great Lakes. The sea route west by way of Panama is the favorite of thousands.

— *Page 19* —
Chapter 2
The Clintons of New York

From 1743 with the appointment of a Clinton as the Royal Governor of the Province to the death of New York State Governor DeWitt Clinton, few were the years in which a Clinton was either at the helm in Albany or New York. During the Revolution Major General James Clinton and his brother George played major roles in Washington's overall strategy. George went on to become New York's first governor and later Vice President of the United States. Our principle interest is with DeWitt Clinton whose name will be forever linked with the creation of the nation's most successful waterway—the Erie Canal.

— *Page 39* —
Chapter 3
The Shermans and the Western Reserve

By the action of the Ordinance of 1787 Connecticut was still in possession of her western lands consisting of ten counties and a part of an eleventh in the northeastern portion of the new state of Ohio. Charles Sherman, the father of the famed Civil War General, was appointed by the General Assembly to oversee the distribution of land claims of those who had lost homes that had been put to the torch by the British during the Revolution. Judge Sherman moved his family to Ohio where he became a member of the Ohio Supreme Court. A second person associated with the Western Reserve was James Hillhouse. When his term was up in the Senate, he accepted the job of Commissioner of the School Fund. The tale of how he set as his goal to know and help every debtor, mark him as one of great public servants of our nation.

— Page 51 —
Chapter 4
The Annexation of Louisiana

Jefferson's Commissioners buy the ill-defined Louisiana Territory from France for fifteen million dollars. The first order of business is to define those borders. Zebulon Pike is sent north to establish the boundary with Canada. He then is sent on a second expedition to explore the headwaters of the Arkansas River and define the boundary with Spain. The President himself took an interest in the expedition to be headed by his onetime secretary, Meriwether Lewis and Lewis's one time commanding officer, William Clark.

— Page 63 —
Chapter 5
Dr. Eliot's Five-Foot Shelf

When gold "fever" broke out in 1848 the book on California that was readily available to many was Richard Henry Dana's *Two Years Before the Mast*. It was written while Dana was a student in Harvard Law School. The first edition by Harper's was issued in 1840. When Emeritus President Dr. Eliot issued his fifty-volume Harvard Classics he chose Dana's book as one of the 418 masterpieces to be included. It is without doubt one of the finest boys' books ever written and it remains to this day a book that can be readily found in any library.

— *Page 73* —
Chapter 6
Meadville and a Citizen Soldier

Meadville—a Rail Center, introduces George B. McClellan, later to become Commanding General of the Army of the Potomac, in his early role as a railroad superintendent. One of the Union's rare victories in the war can be attributed to his skill in moving troops by rail to the crucial point. After the war he resumed his railroad career and became president of the Atlantic and Great Western.

The Erie Railroad—the first to make the Hudson to Great Lakes connection. Together with the Atlantic and Great Western and three small regional railroads in Ohio, its rail bed was extended to Huntington, Indiana all the way to Chicago where it made connections with western railroads.

Allegheny College and Seymour, Indiana, produce a Citizen Soldier. After graduating from college, Fielder Jones studied law, was admitted to the bar, and then moved to Seymour, Indiana, where he became principal of a school. In 1861, after two years of teaching, he enlisted for three months and was elected Captain. Saw action at Cheat River, in western Virginia, completed his enlistment and then reenlisted, this time he was elected as a Lieutenant Colonel of what would become known as the 8th Indiana Cavalry. He served continuously for four years participating in the Battles of Stone's River, Chickamauga, marched with Sherman's force to Savannah and to Bentonville, North Carolina, for the final campaign in the Carolinas.

— *Page 93* —
Chapter 7
McCallum and Military Railroads

Daniel McCallum, an experienced railroad man, was appointed by General Grant as Military Director and Superintendent of Railroads in the United States. All military railroads came directly under his supervision. An important part of this command was the Construction

TABLE of CONTENTS v

Corps which repaired bridges, laid rail, repaired water towers and kept the flow of supplies moving from bases in the north to Nashville and Chattanooga. Over the length of the war 12,000 men served in the Construction Corps, included the author's grandfather.

— Page 105 —
Chapter 8
Sheridan in the West

One of the Union's greatest generals, Philip Sheridan, spent his pre-war years in the Pacific Northwest trying to get Indians to stay put on the reservations to which they had been assigned. The pay was poor and promotions were few. Many West Point graduates left the service to seek other work. Sheridan toughed it out, and when war came promotions came fast. He soon found himself a Major General and found favor with General Grant. When Grant went east to take over the Army of the Potomac he sent for Sheridan, who became his cavalry commander in the Shenandoah.

— Page 121 —
Chapter 9
Wright, Protector of the West

Wright was a very senior officer who served with distinction in the War with Mexico. After that war Wright was assigned to the Pacific Northwest as the Commanding Officer of the Ninth Regiment. The first task he faced was the protection of immigrants who had responded to the passage of the Donation Land Law of 1850. Over 7,000 had passed over the Oregon Trail to settle in the Oregon Territory. In 1861 Wright assumed command of the Department of the Pacific, a position he would hold until late in 1864. To his great credit, with largely volunteer forces, he was able to maintain the peace between pro-southern and pro-northern factions. He was drowned in 1865 having served in the west for fifteen tumultuous years.

— *Page 135* —
Chapter 10
The Stagecoach Era

    The New Hampshire Concord coach has become the icon of pre-railroad travel. Two eastern men with experience in handling freight shipments on the rapidly emerging rail lines of the East, Wells and Fargo announce the creation of a New York to San Francisco express company. Today Wells Fargo is a bank, but in the pre-railroad days it was both a bank, and in a limited sense, a carrier, carrying packages, mail bullion, and passengers. Its preference was to contract with other carriers to carry these items. Little by little, it became the colossus of the industry.

— *Page 147* —
Chapter 11
The Villards and the Northern Pacific

    Quite apart from his connection with the Northern Pacific, Henry Villard was a prototypical German immigrant. He came to America with at least the equivalent of a Junior College education. He worked for a time for a New York German language newspaper. He taught school in Pennsylvania, covered the Lincoln-Douglas debates in Illinois and became one of the foremost journalists covering the Civil War. After the war, representing Europeans who had invested in a railroad in the west, he soon found himself as the President of the Northern Pacific. His wife, Fannie Garrison, was a leading suffragette and his son, Oswald, a Progressive journalist, was editor of the *New York Post* and *The Nation* weekly magazine.

— *Page 169* —
Chapter 12
The Connectors

    The Chicago, Burlington & Quincy and the Kansas Pacific provided both the Northern Pacific and the Great Northern with means of reaching both Chicago and St. Louis. At one time there were no fewer than four railroads completing for the Seattle-Portland to Chicago business. For many years the combined rail service was known as the Burlington-Northern. Chapters 12 and 13 deal with railroad land grants, the means by which the federal government encouraged the development of rail service.

— *Page 179* —
Chapter 13
Promotion of Immigration

The settler coming West could claim a land grant directly from government or could purchase land assigned to the railroad. From the railroads' point of view, it really didn't make any difference how you bought your land. They wanted you to succeed. Their financial success depended on their ability to attract and serve settlers.

— *Page 185* —
Chapter 14
Gold Creek, Montana

Villard revealed himself as a first class showman as he arranged for the celebration of joining of the two sections of the railroad, east and west. Gold Creek, Montana, provided the backdrop and three sections of the train brought hundreds of dignitaries from New York, Washington and Europe. Villard chose William Maxwell Evarts as the Orator of the Day. He had recently served as Orator of the Centennial of the United States in Philadelphia. The miners and cowboys that showed up for the festivities seemed not to be impressed. They heard General Grant was on the train and they wanted to see and hear him.

— *Page 197* —
Chapter 15
Westward Journeys

Here's the story of two brothers who caught the gold fever, Asa and David McCully. It is a tale of gradual migration from Nova Scotia to Ohio to Iowa. The two brothers were in the mercantile business. In 1849 they went to California, made a considerable sum of money and returned by way of the isthmus. In 1852 they started on their second trip. This time a third brother, Samuel, their families, and relatives joined them. It would take them five months to cross the plains. The McCullys left their mark on the new state. Asa and David set up a mercantile business in Harrisburg and both brothers were instrumental in the founding of the People's Transportation Company.

— *Page 207* —
Chapter 16
River Transportation in the West

The Columbia River and its tributaries provide the northwest with a natural highway to the interior. Impassible rapids and falls required that portage be provided around these obstacles. Every load proceeding up or down the river had to be loaded on or taken off three times. Horse and wagons were first provided, followed by portage railways. By 1860 the Oregon Steam Navigation Company, with Captain J. C. Ainsworth as President came to be the dominant provider of river transport. About the time the company was organized, gold was discovered in Idaho and eastern Washington. Ainsworth and his partners operated their company until 1879 when they sold out to Henry Villard. The Corps of Engineers had been active on the river for over 130 years providing rock removal, dredging, embankment protection, and flood control. The first of the great dams built to generate electricity was built in 1937. Today, half the wheat grown in the nation moves to market over this waterway.

TABLE of CONTENTS

— Page 219 —
Chapter 17
The Automobile Era

The centennial of the automobile was observed in 1996. Here in the United States the first manufacturers were concentrated in Ohio, Indiana and Michigan. Cleveland, Indianapolis and Detroit would vie for recognition as the automotive capitol. Ohio became the home of the tire industry. Ford, Dodge Brothers and General Motors all settled in or around Detroit soon to be joined by Chrysler. All four of these companies had their eye on the low end of the market—cars that could be sold for less than $1,000. When the depression of the 1930s hit, many of the luxury cars and even a few mid-range price cars bit the dust.

— Page 239 —
Chapter 18
National Parks

One of the joys of rail travel in the 1920s was the travel bureau that the major railroads provided. The Union Pacific and the Chicago & Western put together a fourteen-day trip featuring two national parks, Yellowstone and the Rocky Mountain National Park starting and returning to Chicago. All expenses, rail and bus travel, hotel accommodation and meals cost two hundred dollars.

— Page 243 —
Chapter 19
Lewis and Clark Bicentennial

The Great Crystal Palace Exhibition held in London in 1851 triggered an explosion of expositions and world fairs. When the United States planned its Centennial in Philadelphia in 1876, it was opened by President Grant in the company of Dom Pedro II of Brazil. The crowning event took place in Independence Square where William Evarts was the orator of the day. The Colombian Exposition in Chicago followed this in 1893. In 1904 the Louisiana Purchase Exposition was held in St. Louis and the following year Portland, Oregon hosted the Lewis and Clark Exposition. Henry Dosch in his retirement years became the unofficial ambassador of good will. Thanks to his efforts, the exposition contained exhibits from all over the world. On the eve of the Bicentennial of the Lewis and Clark Corps of Discovery we pause to remember the difference one man made in the celebration a century ago.

— Page 269 —
Afterword and Acknowledgments

— Page 255 —
Endnotes

— Page 275 —
About the Author

ILLUSTRATIONS & PHOTOGRAPHS

2	Sioux City & Pacific Railroad Ad
32	Portrait of James Clinton
32	Portrait of George Clinton
32	Portrait of DeWitt Clinton
32	Portrait of Sir Henry Clinton
84	Portrait of Brigadier General Fielder A. Jones
113	General Sheridan's book cover, *Memoirs*
128	General George Wright
154	Henry Villard
166	Oswald Garrison Villard
198	Delilah Frances Henderschott
214	Columbia River Locks
238	1931 Phaeton
240	Reo Tour bus
249	Henry Dosch's Grown Children
251	Colonel Henry E. Dosch in His Office

Editor's Preface

In an effort to preserve the unique storytelling style of the author, Arnica Publishing is presenting to you the manuscript William B. Murdock originally wrote. Other than standard copyediting changes, Reverend Murdock's words come to you here just as he wrote them.

PREFACE

THE PEOPLE AND PLACES in this book have two things in common—all are in some way associated with transportation—all are in some way associated with the West. Whatever means of transport settlers used to travel from east to west are to be found here. The first came by ship. After their arrival on the shores of North America in search of land they might own, some pushed further west. They traveled by riverboats and canal, bridges and ferries, by stagecoach, rail, and automobile.

Wars intrude on the telling of this tale. Would France or England prevail in the struggle for domination? With that question settled, would this land maintain its ties with Great Britain or would it be independent? The war that followed split the country. British Empire Loyalists abandoned their lands and fled to Ontario and the Maritime Provinces. Those who had cast their lot with the thirteen original states formed a union, the United States of America.

CHAPTER ONE

Early Routes West

WHY DID PEOPLE MOVE WEST? The simple answer—the lure of free land.[1] The dreams of the first colonies established by France, England, Spain and The Netherlands were to become landowners. Because land ownership was confined to the nobility and the emerging merchant class, the landless mass figured that a chance at land ownership was worth the inconvenience of pulling up stakes and facing a month or so battling the rough Atlantic. The lucky ones brought some capital with them. Others brought their skills at trade or shop. And a few, in order to pay for the trip, indentured themselves for a given period of time.

For some of these early immigrants, leaving home meant leaving the place where ancestors had lived for centuries. In many cases they had followed the same occupation—father to son, father to son—years beyond counting. One might imagine that once they arrived here they would settle down and be content to pass the family home or farm from generation to generation. A few did. The vast majority moved with alacrity that contrasted dramatically with the habits of forebears who had felt themselves bound to family and to place. By the time the first continental railroad was completed the concept of home moved—and often.

In a later chapter the reader will be introduced to the Copp and McCully families. They began life in the new world in colonial Connecticut, and then moved to New Brunswick after the French and Indian War. Later they crossed the border, settled in Ohio, and then moved to Iowa before packing their worldly goods to join in a trek to Oregon and no northern California. Or take the Sherman family. Five generations in Connecticut before moving to Ohio. One son stayed put in Ohio and was rewarded with important elective positions. The other son graduated from West Point and lived wherever the Army sent him. The author's family traces its roots back to Massachusetts. Then it was a series of short moves, first to Connecticut, then Vermont and Delaware County, New York, Tioga County, Pennsylvania and finally after World War II the great leap to the West in the age of the automobile. In my own case the original Murdock, Robert was a joiner—one who built wooden ships or a carpenter. He made the trip from Scotland to Boston in 1688, and apparently was able to buy farmland within the year of arrival. As the years passed it is worth noting that his descendants—those in my

EARLY ROUTES WEST 3

lineage, at any rate—moved first to Connecticut, then to Vermont. After a few generations in Delaware County, New York, and a few more in Tioga County, Pennsylvania, the great leap was made to the West Coast in the automobile age.

Where is your home? How do you answer that question? On most occasions an appropriate response would be to give the place where you are presently hanging your hat. On other occasions the inquirer wants to know about your origins. My first home was on 238th Street in the Borough of the Bronx, New York City. The first four years of my life were spent in that two-story brick house. I haven't seen the place in over a half century. Nevertheless, that is *where I am from*. My parents moved seven times in the course of my journey from childhood to adulthood. As for me I seem to be repeating my parent's experience. Our present home is our seventh.

Before we leave the *where are you from* question, we should add that today many would answer that they were from Mexico, the Central American republics, the Caribbean Islands, South America and the Pacific Islands. Wars in Viet Nam and Korea served to augment migrations from Asia that date back a century and a half to the building of the railroads when Chinese laborers performed their miracles with pick and shovel. An often overlooked migration has been the arrivals of tens of thousands of Christian and Muslim Arabs along with other groups from the middle east. One of Oregon's recent governors traces his roots to Syria. The present governor of Washington traces his to China. A recent Lieutenant Governor of California was born in Trinidad.

However strong the lure of free land might be, there was always this debate—shall we go or shall we stay. The urge to pick up roots and move was matched by the desire to stay and maintain connections with neighbors and friends. In a sense, it was community versus wanderlust. This mental tug of war is captured in a ballad about moving found in a songbook published in 1803. The title is "Rolling Stone;" the husband begins:

> *Since times are so hard, I'll tell you sweetheart,*
> *I'm 'bout to leave off my plow and my cart.*
> *And down to Kentucky Genoa we'll go,*
> *To better our fortunes as other folks do,*
> *Whilst here we must labour each day in the field,*
> *The winter destroys all the summer can yield.*

To which the wife replies:

> *O Collin, I've seen with a sorrowful heart,*
> *You long have neglected your plough and your cart,*
> *O, your sheep now at random disorderly run,*
> *Your Sunday's new waistcoat goes every day on:*
> *Stick close to your farm or you'll suffer a loss,*
> *For the stone that is rolling can gather no moss.*

Is this the way it was, the husband eager to make a fresh start, the wife reluctant to leave a settled culture? In the early days, going west could well mean no schools, no roads, no drop-in visitors, no dependable mail service, and no weekly newspaper.

In the ballad's eleventh verse the wife reminds her husband that there are Indians still living in Kentucky:

> *Your house may be plunder'd and burnt to the ground*
> *Your wife and your children lie mangled around.*

That ends all talk of moving west. Collin replies:

> *Dear wife you've convinced me I'll urge you no more,*
> *I never once thought of you dying before,*
> *My children I love altho' they are but small,*
> *My dear wife I do value as much as them all;*
> *We'll stick to our farm and prevent every loss,*
> *For the stone that is rolling can gather no moss.*

The song book in which this ballad first appears was published in 1803. It probably was composed right after the Revolution. Settlers from the east had flooded into the region coming overland through the Cumberland Gap and by barge and boat down the Ohio River to Maysville. In 1792 Kentucky was admitted to the Union. To Collin and his wife, Kentucky was west. Their home was in a section of western New York—the Genesee some forty miles east of Buffalo and south of Rochester. Collin did not exaggerate. The winter howls out of Hudson Bay and sweeps across western New York "destroying all the summer can yield."

The ballad serves to introduce us to the changing concept of the term *The West*. To those who first arrived on the eastern seaboard anything a hundred miles inland would have been considered The West. Gradually, as the original thirteen colonies filled in, the region just over the Appalachian Mountain range would be the west. In the ballad, Kentucky was clearly understood to be the west, and across the Ohio there was a region known as the Old Northwest consisting of Ohio (1803), Indiana (1816), Illinois (1818), and Michigan (1837). Out of the lands south of Kentucky the states of Tennessee (1796), Alabama (1819), and Mississippi (1817) would be formed. The first major addition came during the presidency of Thomas Jefferson, the Louisiana Purchase in 1803. Florida was added during the years 1810 to 1819. Texas was annexed in 1845 and after the war with Mexico, California and the southwest were added. The Gadsden Purchase five years later expanded the southern boundary to the present line. During the War with Mexico, the Polk administration deemed it wise to settle a disputed border in the northwest. Thus the Oregon Territory became a part of the United States in 1846. An earlier agreement in 1818 had settled the northern boundary of the Louisiana Purchase at the 49th parallel.[3] The overseas expansion after the War with Spain had no immediate bearing on the settlement of the west, but the Purchase of Alaska was of paramount importance to the ports of Tacoma and Seattle. Hawaii, too, both as an independent kingdom and as a territory, looms large in the economy of all three Pacific coast states.

By the time of Seward's Purchase of Russian Alaska in 1867 the present boundaries of the United States were established and they permit us to shift our focus from geography to people in transit—how the settlers along the eastern seaboard, from the

Canadian Maritimes to Florida, gradually moved west. The term *The W*est was now applied to that vast region that stretched from the Mississippi to the Pacific Coast.

Water Routes

Long before the American Revolution there were three main routes these hardy pioneers took. The northern route was pretty much an all-water passage beginning at Montreal utilizing the Ottawa River westward by tributaries and portage to Georgian Bay, Lakes Huron and Michigan and the Illinois River to the fur trading center of St. Louis.

The second route was another all-water route beginning at New York, going up the Hudson River, west along the Mohawk River hence by portage (later canal) to Lake Oneida and the Oswego River to Lake Ontario. The third route goes back to the Colonial period when the British found it wise to fortify their western position at the Forks of the Ohio. This route west combined a water route as far as Cumberland, Maryland plus a road across the Allegheny Mountains that would connect the cities on Chesapeake Bay to what was variously called Ft. Pitt, Ft. Duquesne and finally Pittsburgh. The passage was named the Braddock route, after the British commanding officer, Major General Edward Braddock of the Coldstream Guards.[4] Assisting him was a young American officer, Col. George Washington, whose surveying and military skills had already been put to good use in the establishment of the first fort built in 1754. The Union Jack did not fly from the standard for long before it was replaced by the French tricolor, so essentially what Braddock's Expedition set out to accomplish was the recapture of a fort now firmly in French hands. Braddock, opting to utilize heavy cannon, moved up the Potomac to Fort Cumberland in the extreme western portion of Maryland. A road north to the Forks of the Ohio had to be cut for wagons wider and longer than the track Washington had hacked out just a year before. A trip that would take two

EARLY ROUTES WEST 7

hours today, took nineteen days. The result of the clash was a total defeat for the British and their American allies. Braddock was killed and Washington got away unwounded. What this route had going for it, from a British-American point of view, was that the Allegheny and the Monongahela Rivers joined to form the Ohio River, a gateway to the old Northwest. There were other water routes combined with overland passages that led west. The James River in Virginia and the Savannah River in Georgia were both found useful. But in every case the Appalachian-Allegheny mountain range proved to be a formable obstacle to water navigation. The French obstacle to transportation to the west as represented by their occupation of Ft. Duquesne was removed by the victory of British-American forces in the French and Indian War. To keep Americans humble John Keegan in his "Fields of Battle, the Wars for North America"[5] makes the point that the Seven Years War was won in Europe. By 1763 the French route based on Montreal and the Great Lakes was briefly in English hands, eventually Canadian, leaving two American contenders—let's begin by calling them by their new names—the Mohawk-Erie Canal and the Cumberland Turnpike soon to be called the National Road.[6]

As already indicated, one of the early waterways was the Hudson-Mohawk-Lake Oneida, Oswego system—which in its earliest years depended on portage at the Great Carrying Place just before entering Lake Oneida. A canal replaced this portage, but owing to its dependency on variable water supplies, it was never very satisfactory. In its place the Erie Canal was built. And the man to whom credit belongs was DeWitt Clinton, the governor of New York.[7] Massachusetts produced the Adams family, Virginia the Lees and in New York State the Clintons. George Clinton held the office of governor from 1777 to 1795 and again from 1801 to 1804 when he was elected Vice President serving in that office until his death in 1812. His nephew, DeWitt, followed his uncle to the Statehouse in Albany serving from 1817 to 1823 and again in 1825 till his death in 1828. The canal he sponsored was begun and completed during his governorship and for many of the early years was known affectionately as "Clinton's Ditch." Clinton had tried to get the Federal government to help in the cost of construction, but in spite of his influence in the nation's capitol was forced to look for funds at the state level and among New York City business interests.

The canal was a success from the very first. Scandinavians and Germans seeking fertile lands had been pouring into the region around the Great Lakes soon after the War of 1812. Yankee settlers from New England were settling the Western Reserve area in northern Ohio, which had been ceded to the new Ohio territory by Connecticut. Among them was the father of the Sherman brothers—John who was to become an influential Senator and William Tecumseh who was to make a name for himself in what northerners called the War of the Rebellion. These settlers needed a market for their goods, and the settled eastern cities provided that market. Before the Erie Canal opened in 1825 transportation costs by wagon over the Appalachians could cost as much as $100 per ton. Now with the canal the same goods could be shipped for as little as $4.00 per ton.[8] On the westward journey, manufactured goods were shipped at a fraction of the former cost. The travel time between New York and Buffalo was reduced from twenty days to less than a week. And many a migrant family made the initial part of its journey to the west by canal. The news that went out to the sister states of the young republic was that New York had won the transportation war! In a way, nature had favored the New Yorkers from the very first. To those who have lived most of their lives west of the Rockies, the Appalachian mountain range extending from Georgia and Alabama in the south to Maine in the north may seem modest by comparison. Reaching heights in excess of 6,600 ft. in the Great Smoky Mountains on the border between Tennessee and North Carolina, the range is broken only twice, first by the

EARLY ROUTES WEST

Hudson–Lake Champlain–Richelieu, essentially a north-south waterway and second by the Mohawk, Oneida, Oswego water route, an east-west waterway—and both of these in the same state. East of this natural watershed towers the Presidential Range with two peaks in excess of 5,000 and to the west, Mt. Marcy at 5,344. By contrast the canal height at Lake Erie was just 568 feet above the elevation at Albany. One of the immediate effects of the canal was to make New York the key city of United States. Philadelphia, which had long held that honor, began to suffer by the competition, and quickly moved to provide a patchwork combination of canals, inclined rail systems, to connect the one-time capitol with Pittsburgh. Alas, there were all those mountain ranges to pass, and the waterways—principally the Susquehanna—were in the main north and south routes that had figured prominently in the early days of settlement. The Pennsylvanians turned to inclined planes to transport wagons, crates and canal boats to get over the unforgiving Alleghenies. They called their route the Main Line or Portage Railway. The Main Line part was the rail bed from Philadelphia to Columbia on the Susquehanna. The whole distance between Philadelphia and Pittsburgh could be covered in ninety-one hours. In the first seven months of operation 19,000 passengers and 37,000 tons of merchandise were transported over this route,[9] impressive figures, but it was never a financial success and in the end the taxpayers of the state had to bail out the system.

Another unintended result of the Erie Canal was to make Chicago the key city of the mid-west. Once the barge traffic had reached the western terminus at Buffalo there was an all water natural route to the Midway by way of Lake Erie, the Detroit and St. Clair Rivers, Lake Huron and Lake Michigan. The demand for steam navigation on the Great Lakes grew and was met. By 1834 there was a weekly run between Buffalo and Chicago. By the end of the decade steamer traffic along this route played an important part in the settlement of the old northwest.

The 1830s can be called the age of the canals. With the success of the Erie as a model, the states of Ohio, Indiana and Illinois began ambitious tax supported plans. Ohio built the Ohio and Erie Canal connecting Cleveland with Portsmouth on the Ohio River in 1832. Toledo became the anchor point of two projects. The first was the Miami and Erie Canal finished in 1845. The second, a project of Indiana, the Wabash and Erie Canal was finished in 1842, followed by the Illinois and Michigan Canal built during the same decade that linked Chicago with the Illinois, the Missouri and the Mississippi Rivers.

The golden age of canal lasted just about a century starting first in Western Europe in the mid–18th century before spreading to North America. Before leaving the canal story, I'd like to add that while I've never traveled on the Erie I've flown over it on a clear day and can bear testimony to the fact that it still carries traffic. There is a museum in Syracuse featuring an honest to goodness nineteenth century barge worth turning off the freeway to visit. More and more vacationers are taking advantage of barge excursions on the Erie. In 1997 the Federal government pledged $137 million in loans and grants to restore the canal. Boats can be rented for excursions up and down the canal's 524 miles.[10] Where the Hudson is concerned, I recall with pleasure a trip I took during my newspaper days. It was a round trip from New York to Albany on the Hudson River Dayline with an overnight in a hotel on State Street, Albany and back the next day. A lot of history surrounds the Hudson River Valley. From the river you can see the military academy at West Point where several of the principals of this book spent their years of preparation, and where many heroes of the past are buried in the academy cemetery. The Bicentennial of the Academy was observed in 2002 with a commemorative stamp. Plan your next trip to New York during the months that the Academy is in session. Try to time your visit on a day when the Cadet Corps is on dress parade.[11]

Roads and Turnpikes

Several years before Clinton's Ditch opened, the National Road had reached Wheeling, at the time still a part of Virginia. Begun in 1811, the road utilized the old Braddock route, up the Potomac Valley to Cumberland in western Maryland, through southwestern Pennsylvania to Wheeling on the Ohio River. The choice of Cumberland as a jumping off place made sense. It was connected to Baltimore by an existing road. This effort was funded in large measure by the Federal government. It was twenty feet wide and paved with crushed stone. Bridges were built over the numerous rivers and streams that abound in the region. Development of the road was interrupted by the second war with England in 1812, but shortly after the termination, the road to Wheeling was completed in 1818. Federal help for the project was under attack as well. Increasingly citizens of the original thirteen states asked themselves why they should help to build a road that would compete with them in the market place and drain off needed population. So while western farmers and their representatives in Congress would continue to argue for "internal improvements," Madison, Monroe and their followers felt strongly that these improvements should be paid for by the states.

As a condition of its admission to the Union, the State of Ohio established a fund that would extend the National Road from Wheeling, through Zanesville and Columbus to Springfield between 1825 and 1837 and ultimately to the Indiana border. When the turn came for Indiana and Illinois to extend the road westward, there were diminished federal funds, no provision in the state constitution for special funds—only the tolls to provide for its extension. Wonder of wonder, by 1852 it was extended west as far as Vandalia, Illinois, on the Kaskaskia River some fifty miles short of the Mississippi River. By that time the case was being made that transportation needs could be met more cheaply by rail than by turnpikes.

The road west of Wheeling is today's US Highway 70. The section that had been built with federal funds was truly an all-weather road. The portion of the road through Ohio, with the support of those mandated funds, was an excellent road, macadamized from Wheeling to Zanesville, where a branch to the southwest known as the Maysville Turnpike ran through Maysville, Lexington, Nashville, Florence, the Natchez Trace, all the way to New Orleans. In Indiana the National Road intersected with a north-south route, the Michigan Road (named for the Lake, not the State). It was a 267-mile road leading from Madison on the Ohio River, through Michigantown, to the Wabash River crossing at Logansport, on to South Bend and Michigan City. Settlers from Pennsylvania, New England and the eastern states floated their goods and chattel in flatbeds, barges and rafts down the Ohio River to begin their northward journey at Madison. In the period before the opening of the Erie Canal, it is estimated that more than half of these settlers reached there by means of the Michigan Road. One of the workers on the National Road was an Irish emigrant named Sheridan who settled in Somerset, Ohio and whose son, Phillip would one day attend West Point and go on to fame in the Union cause.[12] In contrast the roads west of the Ohio-Indiana border with the dependence on tolls were poorly built for the volume of traffic that would use them. Of particular interest to the traveler with an interest in history is the region between Cumberland and Wheeling. One bridge and two tollhouses remain in the region of southwestern Pennsylvania. The annual National Road Festival that bills itself as the longest festival in the Country (in mileage) is observed each May along the old route from Cumberland to Wheeling. It wasn't until the Federal Road Act of 1916, a period well into the automobile age, that the principal of federal aid for interstate roads was reestablished. The great road builder of our own era was Dwight Eisenhower, whose personal knowledge of the importance of transportation to national defense prompted the building of the great interstate network we enjoy today.

Another road leading to the West, the origins of which go back to the pre-Revolutionary period, is the Wilderness Road. It followed an old Indian trail over the Appalachian Mountains beginning a bit north of Salisbury, North Carolina and led north and west to the Cumberland Gap into Harrold's Town, and Boonesborough—the area of Kentucky south of present day Lexington. It wasn't easy going this way! Mountain peaks to the north and south rose to elevations close to 6,000 feet. No sponsorship by a colonial government for this road! It was built by one of the great real estate speculators of the period, Richard Henderson, a colonial judge and founder of what was termed as Transylvania, which he and his fellow sponsors hoped would be the first trans-Appalachian colony. To that end he had long supported the annual expeditions of Daniel Boone. This window to the West was fed by another venerable road usually called The Great Wagon Road that extended from Philadelphia to Augusta, Georgia. This, too, was a crude extension of an ancient Indian trail. It passed first through Lancaster and York and then turned south in Western Maryland passing through the Shenandoah Valley of Virginia into the Piedmont region of North Carolina and the upcountry of South Carolina to the Savannah River. Towns like Hagerstown, Maryland, Winchester, Virginia and Salisbury in North Carolina became key supply points along this emigrant's trail. The inflow of immigrants, coming chiefly from Northern Ireland, Scotland, England and Germany seemed to those living in the area to be a veritable stampede.[13] The population of these southern states was doubling every eight years, and entrepreneurs were eager to open up the land across the mountains.

Early Eastern Railroads

The Baltimore and Ohio was the first railroad in the United States to be chartered as a common carrier of freight and passengers. The founders of this road had a sense for the historic occasion. They dedicated their railroad on July 4, 1828, when Charles Carroll of Carrollton, the sole surviving signer of the Declaration of Independence laid the "cornerstone." With Baltimore as its base, the line reached Harper's Ferry by 1834, Wheeling by 1852. By acquiring other rail beds it eventually reached Chicago, St. Louis, and the Great Lakes. As the reader will note, this route roughly follows the Braddock or National Road over the principal obstacle, the Allegheny Mountains. And along the Erie Canal another important railroad emerged. The Mohawk and Hudson, predecessor of the New York Central system, connected Albany with Schenectady by 1831. In short time the railroad would connect New York with Buffalo and beyond. The great Pennsylvania Railroad would connect Philadelphia with Pittsburgh by 1853. The Chesapeake and Ohio, chartered in 1836, ran a rail bed through the coal region of western Virginia making connections with Cincinnati and Cleveland. All these early routes were east to west, a circumstance that would become important with the outbreak of the Civil War in 1861.

In the South the Richmond, Fredericksburg & Potomac was chartered in 1834. The RF&P connected the nation's capital with what would be the capital of the Confederacy. The "vertebrae of the confederacy," as it was called by knowledgeable railroad men, led eastward from Memphis, through Corinth and Tuscumbia to Chattanooga, where it branched south and east to Atlanta, Charleston and Savannah, with the northern branch proceeding through Knoxville and Lynchburg to Richmond. The importance of defending Chattanooga at all costs required President Jefferson Davis and the Confederate high command to strip the Army of Northern Virginia of Longstreet's two divisions and send them by rail to support the Gen. Bragg force defending Chattanooga. How the battle went is a bit beyond the scope of our limited objective, but the ability of commanders to move large bodies of men swiftly and efficiently from one theater of the war to another, was to be repeated often during the four long years. On the Northern side it is worth noting that Gen. George B. McClellan commanding the Army of the Potomac, was a president of a railroad company before rejoining the army at the time of the conflict. A brief review of the early railroads can easily overlook the fact that many of these roadbeds were first local or regional roads, joined later to meet market needs. Others were state supported. South Carolina laid a roadbed from Charleston to Augusta. When it came to the Georgia line, that was the end of that expansion. Georgia had its own plans to take its rail traffic to their own port at Savannah, and they were not about to let South Carolina poach on their turf!

In the decades preceding the Civil War the era of the canal was fast being supplanted by the era of the railroad. Using 1840 as a base, there were approximately three thousand miles of steam railroad operating in the United States. Roughly half of this total operated in the middle states with Pennsylvania out in front. By 1850 the total mileage had tripled to nine thousand miles, and the leaders now were New York, Pennsylvania and Massachusetts. And the division, north and south, reveals that the northern roads led by about a three-to-one ratio. In the 1850s Chicago was on its way to becoming the rail center of the country. Soon railroads were pushing west of Chicago. The Chicago, Rock Island and Pacific was the first to link up with the Mississippi in 1854, and the first to bridge that river. The Chicago, Burlington and Quincy reached the Mississippi five years later and would become, along with the Union Pacific, the Southern Pacific, and the Northern Pacific, major players in the post-Civil War expansion.

Bridges, Ferries and Alternate Routes

Every river and lake of any size was an obstacle to the wagon or the stage. There were three ways of crossing such rivers—the first, primitive in the extreme—swim the livestock across the stream, float the wagon, and raft the passengers. The second would soon emerge if there was traffic enough to support it, a ferry. It might be a small raft-like contrivance just large enough for a few wagons, and pulled across by pulley and horse power, or if it were in one of the important crossing places, like St. Louis, terminals would be erected on both sides of the river. Before the engineers learned to build permanent bridges over rivers like the Mississippi and the Missouri, ferries large and small dominated the transportation scene—both road and rail. Some of the early bridges that emerged along the principal arteries highlighted are two across the Ohio, one at Wheeling (1849) and the other at Cincinnati (1867), both suspension bridges and both with spans over 1,000 feet. One of the great engineering feats of the period was the Eads Bridge that spanned the Mississippi at St. Louis. It was completed in the post Civil War period, 1867–74 and was important because of the difficulty in building the supporting pier in mid-stream and because it was the first major bridge to be built by the cantilever method. The age of bridges has lasted for centuries and is likely to last for centuries to come. The Missouri River was crossed at Omaha, Nebraska in1893. The Columbia River was bridged by 1930, the Willamette by 1908. The Golden Gate and the Bay Bridge in San Francisco date from 1936–37. For a time after their construction the Ferry still ran between Oakland and San Francisco, as many a G. I. from the Pacific War Theater will recall. Take the Ferry from Oakland and it would deposit you at the terminal at the foot of Market Street, where you could hop a streetcar or a cable car and "do the town."

One last mention of a route west—a route that moves the focus from land to sea. It was by ship from one of several East Coast ports to Panama. Cross the isthmus, Colon to Balboa, by rail, and then book passage on a ship sailing north to Monterey or San Francisco. Richard H. Dana, Jr. took this route on his second visit to California. If your destination was the northwest you had to change ships a final time for a trip north to Astoria, Portland, Tacoma or Seattle. Before the French completed the rail passage across the isthmus, travelers could be in for a trip featuring mud, slides, rain and insects. Before the rail routes traversed the continent, for those with sea legs, this route did have its appeal. When Army and Navy officers serving in the west sent for their wives and families to join them, this was the preferred route. Least preferred was by ship around the horn, the way Dana made his first trip to California. It was a trip definitely not for the faint hearted.

So there we have it, the transportation picture in brief, a choice of travel by road, rail, canal or sea. A choice of a Northern route through New York's Erie Canal, New York Central or Pennsylvania Portage rail connection, or the middle states Cumberland-Wheeling route that supported both the National Road and the Baltimore & Ohio Railroad, or the southern route, Richmond to Atlanta to Chattanooga to Memphis. Or the trip west by way of Panama. And yes, there were other routes as well. Some of these routes depended on the size of your bankroll. But in the main, as we view this vast migration, we agree with John Ross Buchanan, the General Passenger Agent for the Elkhorn Valley line.[14] The reason was land. "Free homes for millions" was a slogan that sums it up. The most absorbing topic in America was land, its ownership, sale and settlement. It lay at the root of feverish speculation characterizing this huge hinterland that doubled its population with each census. Whether you were an immigrant recently arrived on these shores or a settled farmer in one of the Atlantic seaboard states, if you could sell your land for thousands of dollars and buy another for a few dollars an acre, the temptation to move west for free land was enormous. The sense of vastness, newness, and the hope of material reward moved many to follow Horace Greeley's advice, Go West!

CHAPTER TWO

The Clintons of New York

A TIME-HONORED RITUAL of late spring and early summer is the annual gathering of the alumni and the granting of degrees. The orator of the day may be a graduate of the institution, a distinguished scholar, a prominent member of government, a jurist, an eminent divine, the President's wife, and even, on one memorable occasion, the Prince of Wales. For the occasion the faculty is all turned out in their academic caps and gowns. It makes for an unforgettable and colorful occasion. For their efforts the commencement speaker is awarded an honorary degree. The graduates have earned their Bachelor of Arts or Science degrees together "with the rights and privileges pertaining thereto." It may take a lifetime to discover what these rights and privileges are. As David McCullough told the Middlebury class of 1886, "Grow with confidence. Prize tolerance and horse sense. And sometime, somewhere along the way, do something for your country."

Turn now to a not dissimilar scene held at Columbia College, New York, in late May 1827. The speaker on this occasion is the Governor Dewitt Clinton, one of the very first graduates of the institution under its new name. The college prior to the Revolution had first been chartered as King's College in 1754. It was in a sense an appendage of Trinity Church at the head of Wall Street and whose Rectors served as members of the faculty. King's College lasted just eighteen years when its principal edifice was turned in to a medical hospital for the British armed forces. During its brief existence the student body included luminaries such as John Jay, our first Chief Justice, Robert Livingston, a member of the committee that drafted the Declaration of Independence, Gouvernor Morris, who helped to write the State Constitution, and Alexander Hamilton, who was a student at the institution when it was terminated. Clinton tells a story about the last days of King's College. The faculty, which had been recruited from the principal Scottish and English universities, was largely loyalist in their sympathies. The president of the college, Dr. Cooper, had publicly opposed those seeking to sever ties with the mother country, and an enraged mob descended on the school intent on doing Dr. Cooper physical harm. Hamilton, placing himself between the people and his learned friend and mentor, had managed to distract them long enough to allow the latter to make a narrow escape.

The city of New York was under British control for most of the war, 1776–1783. As soon as the War for Independence had come to an end the attention of those new in authority turned quickly to the need for a sound educational system. On 1784 Columbia was established. To insure that the applicants met the high standards laid down in the incorporation, the Regents examined each candidate. DeWitt Clinton, in his talk to the alumni some forty-three years later, recalled that he was the very first student to be examined, and numbered among those in the very first graduating class.[1] One by one he fondly recalls the members of the faculty. The first degrees were conferred in 1786. At the time the population of the city was 24,000. By the time DeWitt Clinton spoke to the alumni in 1827 the population had increased to 180,000. Today, the most recent census credits New York with seven and a half million. This would come as no surprise to the Governor. "Unless some extraordinary visitation of calamity, distracts and deranges the natural current of events, and blights the prospects of greatness, this city will, ere the lapse of a century, extend itself over the whole island (Manhattan), and cover the shores of the adjacent rivers and bays with an exuberant population of more than a million."[2] True, he missed the mark by several million. Remember when Clinton spoke of the city he was thinking in terms of "the island"—Manhattan. Brooklyn was another city. His guess based solely on Manhattan probably was right on the mark.

Let's have an in-depth view of this Columbia College graduate. By the time the governor gave his talk to the alumni in 1827 the family had been in America for a century. The first of the line was Charles Clinton who led a party of immigrants to the New World from Ireland where has family had fled during the time of Cromwell. He founded a settlement in Ulster County, New York, where he set up as a surveyor, a farmer, and a land speculator. He was appointed as a lieutenant colonel serving with distinction under General Bradstreet in the French and Indian War. He later served as a judge of the Court of Common Pleas in his county. While still in Ireland he married Elizabeth Denniston. The couple had four sons, Alexander, Charles, James, and George. The older ones were physicians, Charles having served as a surgeon in the British Navy. The two younger sons were destined for fame in the new nation. George was the first governor of New York State and later was Vice-President of the United States. James was a Major General in the Continental Army. James was born at the family farm in Ulster County in 1736. From 1758 to 1763 he served in the provincial army engaged in border skirmishes and guarding the border. He continued in the army during the French and Indian War at the close of which he returned to his family farm and married Mary DeWitt, whose Dutch ancestors were among the earliest of European settlers in the Hudson River Valley.

James and George were early adherents of the Revolutionary cause. In recognition of his years of service in the provincial army, James was appointed a Colonel in 1775 and a Brigadier General the following year. After a failed attempt to attack Quebec, he was stationed at Ft. Clinton in the Highlands of the Hudson where he strengthened the defensive works. In October 1777 the British forces under Sir Henry Clinton made a concerted effort to link up with Burgoyne's expedition coming south from Canada. Here it was Clinton versus Clinton. Sir Henry Clinton's forces won the battle and captured both forts, Clinton and Montgomery. James and his brother fought side by side in this battle—both were wounded in a British bayonet charge, but managed to escape capture. In a strategic sense the Americans had lost the battle but gained an objective—to slow down the British northern advance. The link up between the two British forces was further delayed by the American victory at Saratoga.

Some months later James Clinton, operating under orders from General Washington, moved troops into western New York where Tories and their Indian allies had been ravaging the countryside. Another American force under General Sullivan marched west through Pennsylvania and the two commands joined forces near present day Elmira where the Tories and Indians, led by Brant [3] and Butler were routed. James Clinton was posted to Albany as head of the Northern Department until 1781 when Washington and his French counterpart, Rochambeau, completed their plans for ending the war in the southern colonies. Clinton and his forces joined that army and participated in the siege of Yorktown. At the battle's conclusion General Clinton was given the honor of receiving the surrendered colors. This was the father of DeWitt Clinton, who spent much of his life in uniform.

When the war was over he returned to his farm where he and Mary DeWitt could enjoy the peace and quiet of the Catskills. He and Mary had reason to be proud of their four sons. Alexander was private secretary to his uncle George during his governorship. Charles was a lawyer in Orange County. DeWitt whom we have already met, and still another George who was a lawyer and a onetime member of Congress.

His brother George Clinton was three years younger than DeWitt. He studied for the law under William Smith of New York and in 1768 was elected to a seat in the Provincial Legislature. He was a member of the Continental Congress, like his brother was appointed a brigadier general and was active throughout the war. He was wounded in action along side his brother at Forts Clinton and Montgomery. George is not remembered for his military skills so much as for his personal skills. He was a leader who inspired confidence. On the national scene Governor George Clinton found himself aligned with Jefferson's anti-Federalists. He won six two-year terms as governor. Out of office for a brief time, he returned for a seventh term and then was elected Vice-President of the United States twice, first with Jefferson in 1804 and second with Madison 1808. In three national elections 1792, 1796, and 1808 George Clinton received electoral votes for President. The election of 1792 is of particular interest. Washington, running for a second term under the Federalist banner, received 132 votes. His running mate, John Adams, received 77 votes and George Clinton, an Anti-Federalist received 50 votes. Clinton died in office before the expiration of his second term as Vice-President.

DeWitt Clinton, the best known of this formidable family, was a graduate of Columbia (formerly King's College) in 1786 following which he studied law using his training mainly in land transactions in western New York. He served as a private secretary to his uncle in Albany replacing his brother Alexander in that post. When his uncle declined to run for reelection in 1795 young DeWitt used the time for advanced studies in natural science. In 1796 he married Maria Franklin, the daughter of a well-to-do merchant, Walter Franklin. In 1797 he was elected to his first public office, the State Assembly and a year later to the State

Senate. Like his uncle, DeWitt threw in his lot with the Anti-Federalists, now called Democratic-Republicans, and in 1802 at the age of thirty three, he was appointed a U. S. Senator. While there, he was among those who formulated the Twelfth Amendment dealing with the manner of electing Presidents and Vice-Presidents. He resigned that post and served as mayor of New York City for all but a year or two of the period 1803–15. As mayor he was highly visible like some of his more recent successors, attending fires, inspecting markets, and supervising harbor defenses. He had a keen sense of history and is numbered among the founders of the New York Historical Society serving as its president in 1817. Twice was elected governor of the state, first 1817–23 and then again 1825–1828. As Governor he was responsible for having the Dutch archival records translated.

In addition to his interest in his alma mater, Clinton was an avid supporter of both public schools and normal schools for the training of teachers. By 1827 the State of New York had four colleges with 437 students, thirty-three academies with 2,440 pupils, 8,144 common schools with 431,601 enrolled.[4] Truly a remarkable record. In the course of time the New York City School Department named one of its schools for the governor—DeWitt Clinton High School—an honor he would have relished.

Mention has been made of Clinton's move from the Senate to the office of Mayor of New York. He held this post, with the exception of one or two years, for the period of a dozen years or so. Why would a person wish to move from the Senate to Mayor of a city? Today it seems like a retrograde step. The answer is simple. First, the pay was higher. As Henry James puts it "the Senate was not yet a favorite place for party leaders to fortify themselves in power; its debates were rarely reported, and a public man who quit the House for the Senate was thrown into the background rather than into prominence."[5]

The same year that Clinton resigned, Theodorus Bailey resigned the other Senate seat in order to become postmaster of New York.

At the time Clinton accepted the position of mayor, the office carried with it judicial powers which brought large emoluments to the incumbent. For much of the term he served as both mayor and State Senator, and in the latter position he was named as one of the Canal Commissioners. The year was 1810. He and his fellow commissioners were authorized to examine the Mohawk Valley and the western part of the state for the purpose of learning the practicability of constructing a canal from the Hudson to the Great Lakes. His fellow commissioners were Governeur Morris, Stephen Van Rensselaer, General William North, Thomas Eddy and Peter B. Porter.[6] Three young men identified as "Mr. Eddy's son, and a son and nephew of Mr. Osgood" came along perhaps for a lark, but as events unfolded we find that many a time they had to handle the poles to guide the boats through shallow waters. A surveyor was hired and the party left Schenectady on July 4, 1810. A few of the members preferred to travel overland by stage. Most of the party, Clinton included, opted for the canal boat travel. There were two boats, one for the passengers and another for the baggage. The westward route took them to Utica, Rome, Ft. Stanwix, Oneida Lake and finally Oswego, on Lake Ontario, a one time great fur-trading center.

DeWitt Clinton always resisted his identification as the father of the Erie Canal. He felt that the canal had been thought about, discussed, and plans already in operation long before the State began its efforts. By way of example there was the Inland Lock Navigation Company incorporated in 1792. It had five locks at Little Falls, two at German Floats and two at Rome. Another company was the Western Inland and Lock Navigation. These and other small canal companies tried, by the erection of dams, to control the flow of water. During the spring thaw various shoals, rifts and rapids rendered their work useless on a seasonal basis. In most cases, what was lacking was adequate financial resources, something that only the state or federal government could provide.

Clinton kept his notes in the form of a personal diary and it makes interesting reading. At Buffalo, which in 1810 contained forty to fifty homes, he notes "all persons that travel to the Western States and Ohio, from the Eastern States come this way." Salt was the number one product transported on the waterways during this early period. Produced at Salina (south and west of present day Syracuse) Clinton gives a detailed picture of the salt production. At the time he visited, 807 kettles containing 61,000 gallons were housed in salt houses. The product was sold by the barrel for $2.50 in Oswego. By the time that same barrel of salt reached places such as Pittsburgh or Presque Isle (present day Erie, PA) the price doubled and tripled.

The party returned by way of Batavia, Canandaigua, and Lakes Seneca and Cayuga. The commissioners were back in Albany by August 31. Clinton had become acquainted with the most interesting part of the State. He knew where the best peaches grew, where the best grade of wheat was grown, the source of Seneca oil (down near the border with Pennsylvania, near Olean). He learned sources of soda and gypsum.

The report of the commissioners was favorably received, but the second war with England intervened. The War of 1812 was not popular in the northern states. It was opposed by the manufacturing and maritime interests that dominated New England politics. The war in these states was derisively called Mr. Madison's war. DeWitt Clinton, a long time adherent of the Democratic-Republican Party, the president's party, edged closer to the Federalist position. By 1812 the much-weakened Federalist Party was willing to settle on Clinton as their nominee. When Madison had run in 1808 he crushed the Federalist candidate. The old party of Washington and Adams had been reduced to being a moribund regional party, with little clout outside of the New England states. The party studiously avoided naming a nominee in 1812. In August of 1812 a group of prominent Federalists met in New York and drew up "An Address to the American People."

"The state of New York has now, for the first time, put forward its claim, and examine, we request you, whether some considerations do not strongly mark the propriety of its giving the next president to the union. The state of Virginia has, for twenty of the twenty-four years of our present government, enjoyed that honor; she seems desirous of possessing it for another term, and perhaps for as many more as the patience of her sister states will permit. The nomination of DeWitt Clinton for the presidency, by the state of New York, proposes to the Union, as we firmly believe, a relief from the evils of an inefficient administration, and of an inadequately conducted war."[7]

War against the mother country had been declared on June 18, 1812 and was keenly supported by the new states and territories west of the Appalachians—Ohio, Indiana, Kentucky, and Tennessee. Harrison's victory at Tippecanoe on November 7, 1811 over a northwestern Indian League organized by Tecumseh, probably aided by the British, whetted the frontier appetite for an invasion of Canada. So the backers of the Clinton candidacy had to tread carefully lest they be called traitors or worse. Many of the hybrid party's backers in New England were called the "Peace Party," and while that might play well in Quaker Philadelphia, it was deemed wise to accuse the President of inefficient administration and prosecution of the war. With the election coming just five months after the war's beginning, the outline of the Clinton campaign emerges: Play the states' rights card—Is Virginia going to continue to dominate national elections? Play up Clinton's success as a mayor and governor. His qualities have been proved over a long period in public life. Play up his support of the commercial interests of the Union. A Clinton administration would aim at reviving an almost expiring commerce. Clinton has a pro-business record. Play up the record of his venerated uncle, George Clinton, Vice President of the United States. This is a family you know and can trust.

It was a powerful argument and it played well in settled states of the northeast. Clinton carried every New England state except Vermont. He carried his home state of New York, he carried

Delaware and gained a split vote in Maryland, but in the South and West not a single electoral vote. The electoral votes were 128 for Madison, eighty-nine for Clinton. Had Pennsylvania voted for its northern neighbor Clinton would have been president. The fact that he had consorted with the Federalists didn't set well with some of his supporters in New York.

He was denied renomination as Lieutenant Governor and was ousted from the mayor's post in 1815. As a final indignity, he was removed as a member of the Canal Commissioner. As a result Clinton, the skilled practitioner of the political arts vanished, and there arose from the ashes a statesman. His comeback was quick and startling. In two years time he was elected as Governor on the ticket of his old party.

His constant theme during the post war period was internal improvements. This was the binding theme to hold together the emerging Whig party. For Clinton this meant the building of the canal long delayed by the second war with England. On April 15, 1817 a bill was passed in the State legislature committing the State to the construction of the canal. On July 4th of that year the work began. His wife Maria was able to share this moment of triumph, but she would not survive to see its completion. She died in 1818. A year later the governor wed Catherine Jones who presided over the social affairs of the office during the final years of his administration. The hope of getting help from the federal government to assist in this project had been actively pursued by the private financial interests of the City for years. President Madison was unyielding in his opposition, feeling that if an exception were made in New York, soon every state would be knocking at the doors of Congress asking for largess.

The canal scheme had its detractors from the first. Judge Jonas Platt, then a State Senator, recalls a scene in the legislature when the bill to approve the canal was being debated. "General Schuyler and Mr. Weston," John Taylor, the Lieutenant Governor, stated, "were as wise and skilful as any of the new projectors. We know, and the fact is on the record, that all their calculations of expense and of tolls were not only erroneous, but they erred more than 200 percent in their estimates. What confidence, therefore, can we place in the opinions and estimates of the new projectors, who recommend a canal over mountains and valleys of 360 miles in extent?" The older company General Schuyler headed had not produced the results promised and was unable to pay out dividends. Instead of facilitating the building of a State-owned canal, the experience of these earlier companies actually served as an impediment.

Clinton's view of State support can be summarized in the words he chose to urge support for the State Historical Society. "The State is rich in funds, rich in credit, and rich in resources, and so ought to be rich in liberality and public spirit." In seven years time he could announce to the legislature the completion of water communications between the Great Lakes and the Atlantic Ocean. Begun July 4, 1818, the canal from Lake Erie to New York City was completed October 26, 1825. The canal was 393 miles in length, forty feet wide, four feet deep with a maximum displacement of seventy-five tons. There were seventy-seven locks, ninety feet by fifteen feet and the expense of the project came to $9,130,373.80. The energies and the resources of a single state, chiefly directed by the governor, had united the waters of the inland lakes with the waters of the Atlantic.

From 1810 until 1824 he retained his position as one of the Canal Commissioners. He was narrowly reelected in 1820 and did not campaign for reelection in 1822. Martin Van Buren's Albany Regency reigned supreme and decided to removed him from a position he greatly cherished. It angered the public who forthwith returned him to the governor's office in 1824 and again in 1826, so he had the pleasure of finishing what he had helped to start. For all of his intellectual attainments he offended many by his distribution of patronage. He talked much of internal improvements, but backed only those he favored. He was slow to praise others. Like his uncle, he was a states-rights man. He was a prominent Mason in an age of anti-masonic feeling. People voted for him because they saw him as a man of vision and administrative competence. The writer of the *Life and Writings of DeWitt Clinton*, William Campbell, adds a personal touch to the book published in 1849. He had just entered Union College in the fall of that year. He stood with his college companions on the banks of the canal when Governor Clinton's boat, making the first trip on the just completed Erie Canal landed at Schenectady. Commemorative medals were struck and sold to an adoring public.

The canal was a success from the very first. Its effect is best summed up in economic terms. It expanded an already developing trade route. The agricultural produce of lands of western New York, Ohio, Indiana could be shipped at nominal cost to the principal markets of the East. The manufactured goods of the east were readily available to willing buyers in the west. Passenger transportation was available. When Cadet Philip Sheridan went from his home in Ohio to West Point part of his travel was by way of the canal.

For all the talk about his offending people, when it came time to dedicate the canal he went down through the list of everyone who had anything to do with its origins and support, writing a note honoring their services in initiating and promoting the great system of internal navigation. He invited them to the celebration. Some of the letters were further personalized urging the recipient to put down in writing for posterity the remembrance of their participation. David Hosacks *Memoir of DeWitt Clinton*, published shortly after Clinton's death contains an appendix indicating that a huge proportion of the recipients responded.

On January 1, 1828 Governor Clinton delivered his last message to the Legislature. "Peace, plenty, and health have presided over our land; war is a stranger; famine and the pestilence that walketh in darkness are never experienced; instead of scarcity, there is generally a superabundance of subsistence, an excess of production. The cordial anxiety of Henry IV of France, that every peasant in his kingdom might have a fowl in his pot; and the benevolent prayer of a sovereign of Great Britain, that his poorest subject might have an education sufficient to read the Bible, were, at the times they were uttered, considered chimeras of the imagination. In this fortunate land they are realized, so far as they apply in the fullest latitude, and to the utmost extent; these distinguished dispensations of Divine Providence ought, indeed, to fill our hearts with gratitude, and our lives with devotion to the Author of every good and perfect gift."

On February 11, slightly more than a month later, the Governor died. Clinton was married twice, had ten children, seven of whom survived him. His funeral was the occasion of an effusive letter from the Marquis deLafayette, who outlived practically all of the great figures of the Revolutionary period.

As for a memorial, let Grant have his tomb on Morningside Heights, New York City. Let Jefferson have his Monticello and his University at Charlottesville, DeWitt Clinton's memorial would be the Erie Canal, America's new Main Street. Along its banks would spring up industries turning hamlets into cities. Of course the age of rail hastened this development, but the beginnings were in place as the towering figure backed off the stage—just shy of his sixtieth year.

Others deserve mention before we close the book on the governor. David Bates began work as the assistant engineer under Benjamin Wright in 1817 and served continuously until 1884. That isn't quite as long as Victoria's reign, but it's close! He built the aqueduct over the Genesee at Rochester and the locks at Lockport. Another assistant during the canal's construction was Canvass White. Where did his parents dig up that first name? It was White who discovered and patented hydraulic cement. The growth of the cement industry in the United States traces its beginning to the use of this product in the building of the canal.

Before taking leave of the Clintons of New York mention should be made of two other Clintons, major figures in the history of the period, who served the king before and during the Revolution. They are, as described by Campbell, two branches of the same family. The first, another George Clinton, was governor of the province 1743 to 1753. He spent his entire career in the Royal Navy eventually attaining the coveted rank of Admiral of the white, the highest rank in the Navy. While still a captain he lobbied for this position ashore believing that he might relieve himself of heavy debts he had incurred. How well he did on that score we are left to guess. He died in 1761 survived by his son, Henry, who succeeded Sir William Howe as supreme commander of British forces after 1788. Although active in the field in Virginia and South Carolina, Sir Henry's headquarters were in New York City until he left in 1782.

Mention has already been made of the Clinton versus Clinton battle that took place at Forts Montgomery and Clinton in the Hudson River Valley in October of 1777. The British plan of action during that ill-fated campaign was simple. They would send Burgoyne's forces south from Quebec by way of Lakes Champlain and George. Send Sir Henry Clinton's forces based in

JAMES CLINTON

GEORGE CLINTON

DEWITT CLINTON

SIR HENRY CLINTON

New York up the Hudson Valley, and lastly send St. Leger's force from Oswego down the Mohawk on a diversionary thrust to draw off American troops from the main theater of action. Benedict Arnold, still serving the American cause, made short work of St. Leger. Ticonderoga fell to the British in early July. But then the trouble began. General Schuyler was able to obstruct Burgoyne's advance by felling trees and wrecking bridges. Forty bridges had to be repaired in the march south. What was worse, volunteers were joining the Americans and the British were experiencing desertions and supply problems. A party of foragers detached by Burgoyne was defeated at Barrington. In what seemed like a defeat, the action of the two Clinton brothers James and George, at least made Sir Henry worry about his ability to keep open his own supply lines. His force fought its way to Kingston. Eighty miles separated the two British forces. Close the link and the Americans have their communication between New England and the mid Atlantic severed. That was the plan, and by October it was fast unraveling. St. Leger's diversion was unavailing. The highlands of West Point had been stoutly defended by James Clinton. To risk a trip up the river seemed foolhardy. At Saratoga the British general surrendered on October 17, 1777. Burgoyne's force that once numbered 6,000 had been reduced to 3,500 and was facing starvation. It was one of the great victories for the American side.

The following May, Sir Henry Clinton assumed command of British forces in North America. He was succeeding the Howe brothers, William of the Army and Richard of the Navy, both of whom had additional powers as peace commissioners and were authorized to restore any colony or portion thereof to its former style of government once the rebels were defeated or dispersed. Soon after the Howes were appointed to their North American posts, New York City was restored to British rule. One of the reasons for appointing General Robertson as governor of the province was to restore the city and county to His Majesty's protection and peace.[8] The Howes were not enthusiastic to this petition, feeling that it diminished their military powers, a view Sir Henry would come to share.[9]

The year 1778 proved to be a turning point in the American Revolution. Up until that time the British had been content to fight an unhurried war, minimizing the cost to the British taxpayers by the employment of limited land forces and relying on the navy to hinder American commerce thus bringing the rebels to their knees. But with the entry of France into the contest, the war was transformed into a global conflict. The face of the war would extend far beyond the confines of the wayward North American colonies, to the West Indies, to India, to the Mediterranean, to the defense of the homeland itself. The government in London pushed hard for conciliation. More and more they chose to use their already close ties with native-American allies, loyalists and mercenaries. Britain chose to fight the war in America on the cheap.

That was the military situation when Sir Henry Clinton's destiny in the new world played out. He was forced to serve with a very senior Scottish officer, James Robertson, who had spent twenty-seven years at various posts in North America.[10] In correspondence to his friends back home, Clinton would constantly refer to Robertson as "the old gentleman." Actually Robertson was 62 when appointed as provincial governor. By modern standards, this was hardly old enough to be eligible for a pension. But this was an age when only two percent of the population lived to age 65.

Clinton's naval commander was Admiral Marriot Arbuthnot. Happy campers, these top English commanders were not! Clinton was irritated by the presence of Robertson whose service under Lord Jeffrey Amherst in the French and Indian War gave him a personal pipeline into the highest levels of government back home. To get along with this officer who would eventually be appointed Lieutenant General required tact, flexibility, understanding and willingness to compromise. Unfortunately Sir Henry possessed none of these virtues. He was always supremely confident in his own ideas and plans. He is said to have been quick to blame others when operations failed. He quarreled frequently with his naval commander, another of his "old gentlemen," and whose authority was equal to his own. He called Arbuthnot's appointment "an unbelievably bad choice." Within months of his arrival on station, Sir Henry was bombarding his London friends to recall Arbuthnot. "Send out another Admiral or send me home."[11]

To be fair to Sir Henry, there were other critics of the Admiral. In time Clinton's efforts bore fruit. Arbuthnot was relieved, Rear Admiral Thomas Graves was in charge for an interim period while the successor, Admiral Robert Digby arrived with four ships of the line including the new ninety-gun Prince George. The time was fast approaching when the Royal Navy had decided to have it out with the French fleet gathering in the West Indies. The numbers on both sides tell the story. With the new arrivals under Digby the English could muster thirty-seven ships and frigates. The French had Barras's modest squadron of seven ships based on Rhode Island plus another twenty-eight ships under De Grasse in the West Indies.

On August 31, 1781 British Admirals Graves and Hood with nineteen ships of the line, six frigates and one fire ship were stationed off Sandy Hook, New Jersey, some ten miles south of New York harbor. Learning that Barras had moved south to join De Grasse they sailed after him to the Chesapeake Capes believing that they had overwhelming superiority. On September 5 the British found not only Barras but also De Grasse with his huge fleet of twenty-four ships (four others having been detached to block the mouths of the York and James Rivers). In the engagement that followed the British fleet was badly mauled; the seventy-four-gun *Terrible* was damaged so severely that it had to be destroyed; Graves flagship, the ninety-gun *London* lost all of its masts; and the frigates *Iris* and *Richmond* were captured. The two fleets maneuvered for the next few days and on September 14, the British left the Virginia coast, allowing the French to control the Chesapeake Capes and thus bar any naval reinforcements that might be sent to assist Cornwallis. "Britain had conceded command of the sea at the decisive point to the enemy, an almost unprecedented and rarely to be repeated lapse of strategic grip by the Royal Navy. The concession was to spell the end of the six-year long effort to reimpose rule over the American colonies."[12]

It should be added that Sir Henry did get his troops to Virginia on October 24. He learned that Cornwallis had surrendered five days earlier. He forthwith turned around and returned to New York. The war did not end with Yorktown. The British still retained their New York stronghold. The Carolinas and Georgia still had a strong British presence. Virginia was a disputed territory. The Americans controlled Boston, Rhode Island, the entryway to the Chesapeake and Baltimore, and the back-country entry points of the Mohawk and Upper Hudson. There was brave talk about taking the offensive and continuing the war. And then there was the report of a battle down in the West Indies where on April 12, 1782 in the passage between Dominica and Guadeloupe, in the Battle of the Saints, the Royal Navy met and defeated the French fleet with De Grasse himself captured. There was great rejoicing in New York when this news was received and the Governor issued a special service of thanksgiving to be observed.

The British hung on to Savannah until July 11, 1782, Charleston until December 14 of the same year and New York until November 25, 1783. In the west Detroit would stay in British hands until 1797. By that time Sir Henry Clinton, General Robertson and Lord Cornwallis had moved on to other assignments—or to retirement where they were at pains to explain to the world why they were right and others were wrong.

Thus we bring to an end the Clintons of New York. From the arrival of Admiral George Clinton as Provincial governor in 1743 to the last of DeWitt Clinton's period as Governor of New York State in 1828, a Clinton was at the helm either at Albany or at New York or in Washington as a Senator or Vice President for most of those years. Although the lineage of the American branch of the family traces back to England and Ireland, they had the good sense to marry into some of the already established Dutch families.

As we proceed along the trails, rails, and canals to the West we will note again and again the truth of Clinton's assertion that New York, situated at the confluence of all the great navigable communications, from the shores of the Atlantic to the western lakes, is where all the great monied and commercial operations of American are centered. "Where, in short, every man that wishes to buy or to sell to advantage, will naturally resort."[13]

CLINTON FAMILY GENEALOGY

Charles Clinton - *Elizabeth Denniston*
Led a party of emigrants to Colonial America in 1729; settled in Ulster County Province of NY, commanded a Regiment in French and Indian War.

b. 1690 Ireland   d. 1773 Orange County, NY

∨

Alexander	Charles	James - *Mary DeWitt*	George - *Cornelia Tappen*
Surgeon	Surgeon, Royal Navy	Major General in charge of Northern Department during Revolution	First Governor of New York and Vice President of the U.S.
		b. 1736 d. 1812	b. 1739 d. 1812

∨

Alexander	Charles	DeWitt - *Maria Franklin* *Catherine Jones*	George
Private Secretary to his uncle, Gov. Clinton	Lawyer, Orange County, NY	Senator, Mayor of New York City, Governor of New York. Maria Franklin died in 1819. She and DeWitt had ten children.	Lawyer, Member of Congress
		b. 1769 d. 1828	

Admiral George Clinton, who served as Governor of the Province of New York 1743–1753, and his son, Sir Henry Clinton, commander of British Forces in North America after May 1778, while distantly related to the Clintons of New York, are not included in this genealogical chart

CHAPTER THREE

The Shermans and the Western Reserve

WILLIAM TECUMSEH SHERMAN was born in Lancaster, Ohio, February 8, 1820. He was the third son of Charles Sherman, who had been a circuit riding Judge of the Ohio Supreme Court Two older brothers, Charles and James, do not concern us, but the Connecticut born father who came west at the urging of his state most certainly does. So first let's look at the events that conspired to send Charles Sherman to what was known as the Western Reserve.

In 1662 King Charles II gave to Connecticut "all of the territory of the present state and all the lands west of it, to the extent and breadth, from sea to sea." This codicil gave to the state, aside from the home region in New England, the upper third of Pennsylvania, about a third of Ohio and parts of what has come to be Indiana, Illinois on west to the Pacific Ocean.

The Ordinance of 1787 provided for a government in the Northwest Territory.[1] It prohibited slavery, provided for religious freedom and for the establishment of schools. A court, organized by these articles, sat at Trenton, New Jersey and settled the dispute between Pennsylvania and Connecticut in favor of the former. Connecticut, by her charter, also had claims on New York but Charles had given those lands to New York. The monarch's view of lands in the new world was a bit hazy. The two provinces settled their differences long before the Revolution. When the war with the mother country was over, by the action of the Ordinance, Connecticut was still in possession of her lands consisting of the following Ohio counties: Ashtabula, Trumbull, Geauga, Cuyahoga, Summit, Lorain, Medina, Portage and the northern part of Mahoning plus two known as Fire Lands, Erie and Huron. Present day cities of Cleveland, Akron, Warren and Youngstown all are located in this region, bounded on the north by Lake Erie, on the east by the Pennsylvania line, and the south by the forty-first parallel and on the west by a line 120 miles west of the Pennsylvania line. The lands totaled 3,366,921 acres. The problem back in Hartford became, now that we are in possession of these lands, what shall we do with them?

In 1786 the General Assembly appointed a committee of three to dispose of western lands. The price of fifty cents per acre was determined upon. The lands were to be divided into townships of six square miles apiece. It was further agreed to make a grant to each purchaser, his heirs or assigns, and to reserve five hundred acres of good land "for the support of the schools forever, and two hundred forty acres in fee simple to the first Gospel minister who shall settle in such town."

There was a further problem to be resolved. What should the State do about all the claims that had been filed by residents whose property had been damaged or destroyed by enemy action in the late war? During the Revolution there were two British forces, one under Benedict Arnold (after he made the switch) and the other under William Tryon (a one-time governor of New

York), who had put to the torch lands and property owned by persons believed to be disloyal to the crown. Danbury, Norwalk and New Haven were the chief centers of this vindictive action. In 1791-92 500,000 acres of land were set aside to satisfy these claims. The lands were designated, appropriately enough, as the Fire Lands. In a short time the Hartford planners decided the wisest course was to dispose of this White Elephant and let someone else oversee its development. Thus it was that the bulk of the still unclaimed lands were sold to the Connecticut Land Company for the sum of $1,200,000 all of which was to be put aside in perpetuity as a school fund. Sherman's father, Charles R. Sherman, was appointed by his state to oversee the claims of these settlers who had suffered loss during the Revolution. For his services he received title to two sections of land. He stayed on after the Western Reserve and Fire Lands became part of the new state of Ohio in 1802, eventually becoming a Judge of the Ohio Supreme Court. During much of that time Judge Sherman traveled from county seat to county seat holding court in whatever building was available.

Before the migration to the west the Shermans had lived in and around Woodbury, Connecticut for six generations. The Town Historian, Frederick Strong, in a recent letter to the author outlined the Sherman genealogical line complete with a picture of the Sherman House built in 1696. The builder of this still standing house was known as "Captain John." He took up about 600 acres of woodland and erected his home on Hurd's Hill setting aside other building sites for his children. The first names of the Sherman ancestors residing in Woodbury were, John, John Jr, Daniel, Daniel, Taylor and Charles many of them both lawyers and judges.

Charles was named to the Ohio State Supreme Court and took residence in Lancaster, some fifty miles from the new capitol, Columbus. Here both William and John, a future Senator, were born. In 1829 the judge died leaving his widow and several young children. William, just nine years old, was raised by the Judge's close friend, Thomas Ewing, a onetime senator from Ohio and a member of the national cabinet during the Taylor Administration. Ewing chose a profession for young Cump and had the boy enter the United States Military Academy in 1836. Although someone had chosen this career for him, he found he liked life at West Point and graduated near the head of his class accepting a commission as a Second Lieutenant four years later. It is not the intention here to trace the military career of the future general. While his record before the Civil War is perhaps not well known, his record during and after that struggle is part of the nation's history. We shall encounter him as a civilian in California before the war and during the war as he depended on the Railroad Construction Corps to supply his troops en route to Atlanta. A younger brother John Sherman, whose main claim to fame is the Anti-Trust Act which bears his name and was signed into law under President Benjamin Harrison June 26, 1890, has been the cornerstone of all anti-trust legislation to this day. In presenting this bill the Ohio Senator declared: "This bill...has for its single object to invoke the aid of the courts of the United States to deal with combination when they affect injuriously our foreign and interstate commerce and our revenue laws. It is to arm the federal courts within the limits of their constitutional power, that they may cooperate with the state courts by checking, curbing, and controlling the most dangerous combinations that now threaten the business, property, and trade of the people of the United States."[2] In a few years time when Teddy Roosevelt was in the White House and the Rockefeller-dominated Standard Oil Company was chewing up its competitors one by one, this law was the tool the litigators used to break up what was threatening to become a monopoly.

The Ohio senator, whose first job was working on the Ohio Canal as an engineer, had a long and eventful career in the House, the Senate. Then, as the Secretary of the Treasury in the Hayes

Administration, his efforts were directed to the interest of sound money and protection—a nineteenth century code word for tariff. More than once his name was seriously considered for the presidency in both 1880 and 1888.

Here are two brothers, one would have loved to have been the standard bearer of his party, the other who for twenty years kept saying variations of the same text: "I will not accept if nominated and will not serve if elected." John would have made an excellent chief executive; the General, while always colorful and blunt, was right. He said that there was no reason to believe that military men had any special qualifications for the presidency. And so he persisted in saying no. His Republican admirers finally got the message and left him in peace. He seems not to have been able to steer them to his brother. Towards the end of his life John served as President McKinley's Secretary of State. In all John Sherman served his country for over forty-four years. Throughout that time the two brothers maintained a steady correspondence and much of what we know about the inner thoughts of both men trace back to this source.[3]

A contrast in the public relation style of the two brothers is presented in the story of a trip the two brothers made to the home of their ancestors in April of 1887. They were both in New York at the time and decided to visit Woodbury, Connecticut, where their forbearers had lived for nearly two centuries. They advised the town historian of their intention and that gentleman informed the press. When they arrived in Waterbury they discovered their visit was known. "Several gentlemen met us at the depot and conducted us to the hotel, some of them having served with General Sherman in the Civil War," John Sherman wrote. "We explained to them that we were on our way to Woodbury, had no plans to execute, intended to erect no monuments, and only wished to see where our ancestors lived and died."[4] The General's comment was true to form. He admired the scenery but added, "I cannot see how this rocky country can be converted into farm lands that can be made profitable." And then to compound any injured feelings he may have caused he added, "I am pleased indeed to think that my ancestors moved from this region to Ohio in 1810." Yet all seems forgiven by the present generation of Woodbury residents who are proud of the town's connection with the Sherman family.

A second Connecticut Yankee affected by the state's claim on the Western Reserve and Fire lands was the more prominent James Hillhouse, 1754–1832. Hillhouse first comes to our attention during the invasion of Connecticut by Governor Tryon in the summer of 1779. The British having tried the olive branch diplomacy of Sir William Howe switched to a predatory war policy. While the change in policy came from the ministerial level in London, Sir Henry Clinton found himself in the role of its executor. A force of twenty-six hundred men under the command of Governor Tryon were placed in two warships, the Camellia and the Scorpion, with forty-eight transports and tenders, commanded by Commodore Sir George Collier. Towards the evening of July 3rd they passed from New York Harbor to Long Island Sound. On the 4th, while the Patriots were celebrating the adoption of their Declaration of Independence, the two commanders drew up their proclamation and address to the inhabitants of Connecticut, inviting them to return to their original allegiance.

Collier's fleet sailed in to New Haven Bay on the night of the 4th and early the next morning landed two divisions, one at East Haven and the other at West Haven. The first opposition to the intruders was made by twenty-five of the inhabitants, many of whom were Yale students, under Captain James Hillhouse of the Governors Foot Guard. Although they were small in number they managed to drive back an advanced party. The British were not deterred from their plans to put New Haven to the torch. After they had done so they reassembled their landing force and sailed back to the safety of New York. After the war Hillhouse was elected to the state General Assembly, 1780–85, and then served in the 2nd and 3rd Congress as a Federalist, 1791–96 when his Senate term began. He served in the U.S. Senate through 1810. During the year 1801 he had been elected by his fellow Senators as President Pro Tempore of that body. Near and dear to his heart during all of this time of public service Hillhouse was also Treasurer of Yale College, a position he held for half a century, 1782 to his death in 1832.

When he returned to his New Haven home after the session of 1810, he was waited upon by a delegation of citizens who urged upon him an appointment as Commissioner of the School Fund. He considered this task of such importance that he resigned from his Senate seat and accepted the responsibility. A while ago we marveled that DeWitt Clinton would give up a Senate seat to accept the office of Mayor of New York. His reason made good practical sense—there was more money to be made. Now in this second example of leaving the Senate it wasn't the money. His yearly stipend was to be $1,000. There may have been other reasons. The Federalists by 1810 were the minority party. Washington was a raw new city and did not have the cultural attractions of either of the previous capitols, New York and Philadelphia. For whatever reasons Hillhouse accepted this new appointment, resumed his private practice of the law, and took on the task of becoming a bill collector. Yes, a bill collector. Theoretically the Western Reserve lands had been sold to the Connecticut Land Company for $1,200,000. The Board of Managers of the Land Company was to pay to the state six percent interest beginning in 1797. When the first $72,000 became due, the land company was still paying out money on surveys. They had not resold much of the land and were unable to repay the money due. They fell in arrears and during the first thirteen years only about half the amount due was actually paid The state, having passed a resolution to create a fund to support schools in perpetuity, was unable to follow through. By 1809 it was evident that both the Land Company and the settlers were in grave danger of going bankrupt.

Desperate times call for desperate measures. The Board of Managers of the Land Company was discharged. The entire authority and responsibility for managing the fund was vested in one man. His title was Commissioner of the School Fund. Whether or not there would ever be a school fund to administer now rested squarely on the shoulders of James Hillhouse. His devotion to his state, to the aims of the fund, required great personal sacrifice.

This was not a job that could be run from a desk in New Haven. He set as his goal getting to know every debtor the Land Company had deeded land to. This meant travel from New Haven to the farmlands of the Western Reserve strung out along the shores of Lake Erie. In 1810 the Erie Canal was still a dream. His probable route would be by stage down the Boston Post Road to New York, by boat to Albany, west by barge on the Mohawk to Oswego on Lake Ontario where he had the choice of travel by boat or stage down the Genesee valley then west to Lake Erie where the Indian route known as the Lake Trail could take him south and west to the Reserve Lands. It probably took the better part of a week to make this trip. Rail service from New York through Albany to Buffalo would not be available until long after his death. The Erie Canal was completed in the final year of his service as a Commissioner.

From the first, Hillhouse took a wise paternal course with the Western Reserve settlers. He called on them in the sense of a wise counselor going over their affairs and advising them in ways that might improve their condition. For fifteen years he avoided litigation entirely. The people he dealt with might easily have come to fear and dislike him. These were the days when people could still be imprisoned for debt, and often times were. Instead they came to look upon him as their own personal attorney. There were times when they loved this man, trusted him and admired him for the work he was doing. Leonard Bacon, who wrote the definitive book on Hillhouse in 1860 put it this way, "No young immigrant making his way into the wilderness to lay there the foundations of future wealth, ever encountered hardships, fatigue and peril, more patiently or cheerfully than he. Unattended he made long journeys westward, year after year, at all seasons, and with all sorts of hazards, in his sulky, at the heels of the fleet and hardy little mare that was his chief locomotive power for the first six to eight years of his commissionership. Once he came near death by freezing in a winter drive; twice by fever caught in miasmatic regions which his duty caused him to explore, once arrested as a criminal at the instigation of a malicious debtor, it seemed no difficulties could stop him."[5]

Two stories are told how he helped the Phelps and Granger families out of hopeless financial situations. Phelps was one of the Committee of Eight appointed to sell lands in the Reserve. He was one of the heaviest investors with $168,185 of his own capital and another $80,000 invested in association with Granger. Hillhouse did not arrive on the scene soon enough to save Phelps. He had been imprisoned and died there in debt. He owed the Land Company, inclusive of unpaid interest, $300,000. Hillhouse worked on case the night and day and negotiated sales, payments and settlements. He slowly threaded his way through the record of investments, sales and mortgages. He managed to clear up every title, to settle the accumulations of debt that had sent Phelps to prison and to pay the claim in full to the School Fund.

Charles Sherman, a fellow Connecticut Yankee who had come west to oversee the Fire Lands, and at the time a member of the Ohio Supreme Court, wrote, "So much were the family of Mr. Phelps benefited by the services which he rendered them, beyond what the interests of this state required, that besides paying all the expenses incident to the operation in searching records, foreclosing mortgages, defraying taxes, paying agents, they allowed compound interest on the School Fund debt, which exceeded more than $14,500, the amount which could have been recovered by law."[6] The family, rescued from poverty, gave Hillhouse $6,000 for his personal service. He accepted the check and immediately endorsed it to the School Fund. The same story was repeated with the Granger family. When they responded with a $2,500 check for personal services, it was forthwith put in the School Fund. He declined retaining a donation with those whom he dealt with as a public agent.

Hillhouse retired as Commissioner in his seventy-first year, with his crowning glory—the School Fund—fully funded and operative. Not only had he restored the fund to its original sum, but he had added another half-million to it. He lived to see the completion of a canal across Reserve lands that linked it to the markets of the world. The Commissioners of this proposed Ohio canal wanted assurance about the prospects for the canal that would connect Cleveland on Lake Erie with Portsmouth on the Ohio River. And who do you suppose they turned to? To "Mr. Canal" himself, the Governor of New York, DeWitt Clinton. He replied on November 8, 1823 that the projected canal between Lake Erie and the Ohio River, would, in connection with the New York canals, form a navigable communication between the Bay of New York, the Gulf of Mexico, and the Gulf of St. Lawrence. Clinton further predicted that the Ohio canal would embrace within its influence, the greatest part of the United States and of Canada. He even made a rough guess that the cost of the project would not exceed $2,500,000. Obviously this was exactly what the Ohio commissioners wanted to hear. Work was begun in 1825 and completed by 1832. With these new markets the future of the settlers was assured.

As for Hillhouse, whose life span reached from the Revolution to the canal age, he spent the last years of his life as the treasurer of his beloved alma mater. As his biographer put it: "He was dignified with his coat off and with a scythe in his hands, leading the mowers across the field, and cutting the widest swath of all, as when he stood conspicuous and honored in the Senate, or on a Sabbath morning walked to the house of prayer with patriarchal grace, beneath the stately elms which his own hands had planted."[7]

His memory is perpetuated by Hillhouse Avenue in New Haven and by his mansion and grounds now a part of Yale University.

CHAPTER FOUR

The Annexation of Louisiana

As WELL KNOWN AS THE annexation of the Louisiana territory is, the story of why Napoleon would be willing to consider its sale bears retelling. The truth is that the French colonial effort in North America was brought to its knees by a rising of the slave population in the island of San Domingo.

The news reached Paris in the early days of 1803. The French governor LeClerc was dead and his army was annihilated. The colonial system of France centered on San Domingo. Of what use was the rest of the system if the head was cut off? To save the existing government Napoleon must send at least thirty thousand troops to ensure its safety. The First Consul had other plans for thirty thousand troops. Perhaps this was the time to unload a failed experiment. Into this situation two American commissioners appeared interested to annex West Florida and New Orleans. Suddenly they are presented with the question, "What will you give for the whole?"

The two American commissioners were Robert Livingston, the Minister to France, and James Monroe, Jefferson's minister plenipotentiary, having just arrived from America. For France, the negotiations were carried out by Talleyrand and Barbe-Marbois. All realized that a momentous decision had been achieved. Of the pact, Livingston said, "The annexation of Louisiana was an event so portentous as to defy measurement. It gave a new face to politics, and ranked in historical importance next to the Declaration of Independence and the adoption of the Constitution, events of which it was the logical outcome, but as a matter of diplomacy it was unparalleled, because it cost almost nothing." Actually the sum paid was $11,250,000 to France and another $3,750,000 to assume claims against the former colonial power, but in view of its eventual worth, Chancellor Livingston is entitled to his exaggeration.

Napoleon reflected on what he had done and remarked to Barbe-Marbois: "The accession of the territory (by the Americans) affirms forever the power of the United States, and I have just given England a maritime rival that sooner or later will lay low her pride." As one wag saw it at the time, the commissioners had been sent to buy the east bank of the Mississippi (Florida and New Orleans), and instead they bought the west bank. For the time Spain still clung to Florida, but Jefferson's commissioners had given the young country a third of all the lands it would ever possess. The extent of the new territory for the most part was ill defined.

Did the president have the power to conduct such negotiations? The Senate quickly disposed of that issue, fearing that Napoleon might change his mind, approving the treaty with France by a 24–7 vote. The result of the debates in the Senate and the House decided one point without equivocation. All agreed, Federalists and Republicans alike, that the government had the power to acquire new territory either by conquest or by treaty, as in this case. The only difference of opinion regarded

THE ANNEXATION of LOUISIANA

the disposition of the territory after acquired. Did it belong to the central government at Washington? The dominant Republicans took the view that the new territory would become a part of the general territory mentioned in the Constitution and eventually be admitted as states. The Federalists were in agreement with the position provided that the consent of the existing States was obtained for each new entry. Two Connecticut Senators (one of them was James Hillhouse), plus two Delaware Senators and one from Massachusetts voted the Federalist position and lost the point by a 26–5 tally.

To initially govern this vast new territory the President naturally turned to the military, and in due course General James Williamson was appointed governor of all the territory north of the 33rd parallel (the present day boundary between Louisiana and Arkansas) with headquarters in St. Louis. Wilkinson, a veteran of the Revolutionary War, would eventually prove to be a frail reed to lean on. He had what might charitably be referred to as a checkered career, which included a trial, by court martial. Charges included: accepting a pension from Spain, engaging in treasonous conspiracy, being an accomplice of Aaron Burr, insubordination, wastefulness and corruption. The court acquitted him but President Madison, acting as the convening authority, inserted in the general's file a personal reprimand. Wilkinson's record in the War of 1812 resulted in a failed attempt to take Montreal. But all of that came later and as a governor of this territory it is fair to record he did an acceptable job.

The first order of business was to define the boundaries. In 1805 Wilkinson ordered Lieutenant Pike, a young officer in the First Infantry, to take a sergeant, a corporal and seventeen privates to ascertain the true source of the Mississippi. Pike worked his way upstream from St. Louis. By October 16, 1805 he reached a point 223 miles above the Falls of St. Anthony and there stopped to establish a winter camp. By December 10 he was on the move again traveling with sleds until he reached a British trading post on Sandy Lake. His trip was an act of formal authority rather than a voyage of exploration. He notified the British and the Indian tribes along the way that they were under the jurisdiction of the United States.

General Wilkinson was so pleased with the results of the operation that he immediately ordered Pike to lead another expedition—this time to the head waters of the Arkansas and Red Rivers as far west as the Spanish settlements in new Mexico. On July 15, 1806 Pike again set forth with about the same sized contingent. By September 1st he had reached the Osage towns on the Missouri River. Striking across the prairie, he marched through the country of the Pawnee reaching the Arkansas and ascended its branches. He left a permanent reminder of his presence as he reached Pike's Peak in Colorado. Turning south and west he entangled his contingent in the mountains and after suffering in the ice and snow on February 26, 1807 was stopped by the Spanish authorities at Santa Fe, who sent him to Chihuahua, and eventually he was allowed to return to the United States by way of Texas.

Both of these expeditions were subordinate to the Lewis and Clark explorations that President Jefferson himself helped to organize and in which he took a deep personal interest. The President's private secretary, Captain Meriwether Lewis had been sent to Philadelphia to study natural history some months before the purchase of the territory. Lewis asked Jefferson to appoint his friend and former commanding officer, William Clark, as a co-captain. On May 14, 1804 the Corps of Discovery, as it was called, set out with a contingent of thirty-eight men, including Clark's slave York and an Indian interpreter. They had a 55-foot, 22-oared keelboat plus two flat bottom pirogues that they let down in the Mississippi at Wood River, rowed downstream to the Missouri with its serpentine twists and turns which was to be their nautical highway to the west. Occasionally they would

THE ANNEXATION of LOUISIANA

meet white traders returning to St. Louis with their furs. Experienced traders had advised them that it would be wise to pay tribute to local Indians. Beyond the mouth of the Platte they regularly hunted for meat—deer, elk, and buffalo. By November they encountered their first snow and built winter quarters at Mandan. It was here that Lewis hired Toussaint Charbonneau, a French Canadian trapper who had lived for years among the western Indians, as an interpreter. A week later his pregnant wife, a Shoshone, named Sacagawea joined them. Winter loosened its grip. By April Lewis and Clark sent the keelboat, under Corporal Warfington and a small group, back downstream with specimens and a letter for the President.

The rest of the group set out from Mandan on April 7, 1805 in boats and canoes they had fashioned during the winter months, to find the head waters of the great Missouri. The journey proved to be full of labor but remarkably free of danger. Rattlesnakes and bears were the most troublesome. By August 11 the contingent had run out of river and found themselves at the base of the mountains that divide the waters of the Missouri from those of the Columbia. For two hot weeks the contingent pulled their boats up steep slopes. Through rain, hail and snow showers they hiked across the Bitterroot Range of the Rockies and along an old Nez Perce trail and the Lolo Pass. They took to the waters again and on the Clearwater, the Snake and the Columbia, reaching its mouth on November seventh when, as Henry Adams puts it, they "saw at last the ocean which bounded the American ambition. There they were forced to pass the winter in extreme discomfort...until March 26, 1807, they could retrace their steps."

The explorations of Canadian fur traders Simon Fraser and David Thompson spread over a six-year period, 1805 to 1811. Working at times for the Hudson Bay Company and the better resourced North West Company, Thompson explorations took him south of the 49th parallel (the eventual boundary between

Canada and the United States) where he traversed the maze of mountains and rivers in Idaho and Washington en route to the mouth of the Columbia which he reached July 14, 1811 only to find the American flag flying over Fort Astoria.

Earlier expeditions, based on New Spain, had reached San Diego, Monterey and San Francisco by sea. Portola reached Monterey by land and then pushed north where he stumbled onto the great bay of San Francisco. By March 1776, the year that the United States declared its independence from Great Britain, the de Anza expedition of settlers, soldiers and mule drivers had established a mission and a presidio in the city by the Bay.

Two others deserve mention in this section on trail blazers, the first surveys conducted by Lieutenant John Charles Fremont in the late 1830s and the 1840s and the second a group of engineers searching for the best rail route from east to west conducted under the title of the Great American Railroad Surveys during the years 1853–55.

First the Fremont surveys. Fremont was the son-in-law of Thomas Hart Benton, a powerful figure in the United States senate who was determined to secure the Oregon Territory for the United States. In 1842 Benton persuaded his fellow senators to provide funds for a topographical survey of the vast western region to be conducted by the Army Corps of Engineers. Fremont, in the company of Joseph Nicollet, a French born scientist, had already explored the Cherokee country in 1836–37 and had led a survey of the Des Moines River area in 1841. Late May 1842 Fremont's party headed up the Missouri by steamboat, meeting Kit Carson who would be both a scout and a lifelong friend. Instead of taking the trail Lewis and Clark had blazed, he used the North Platte River route, which took him west by way of Fort Laramie and by what we have come to call the Oregon Trail. Along the trail he climbed the Fremont Peak in the Wind Mountains in Wyoming where he planted the American flag.

Fremont, ever the showman, can be accused of copying Zebulon Pike, for in no time the artists rendering of this feat was published in the papers and magazines back East. (He had the foresight to include artists in his table of organization for the survey.) He explored the Great Salt Lake and then pushed on to the Columbia River and Oregon. At The Dalles, Fremont's party turned south for California. He soon learned that the Sierras are a bad place to be in mid-winter. For thirty days, his men, now deserted by frightened Indian guides, finally found Truckee and the Donner Pass and picked up a trail that took them to the central valley's settlement of Sutter's Fort. Fremont was greatly impressed with California and one day would return with his wife to live there. In 1845 Fremont received orders to survey the Red River (the boundary between Oklahoma and Texas). Instead he wandered out to California where he became involved in the Bear Flag Revolt, an action for which he was later court marshaled. He resigned from the army in 1848 and for a time was employed by private interests seeking a central railroad route. Both ended in disaster. During the first survey some of his best men perished in mid-December snow of the San Jean Mountain range in southwestern Colorado. Much of Fremont's lasting fame rests on a map of the entire west drawn by his cartographer, Charles Preuss. For emigrants traveling to the west on the Oregon Trail this was exactly what was needed. His friendship with Kit Carson, his chief scout, did him no harm. Kit was one of the early folk heroes of the West. When California held its first election as a part of the United States, Fremont was one of the two selected for the U.S. Senate. Unfortunately he drew the short term and served in that body from September 1850 to March 1851. Fremont's nomination for President by the newly formed Republican Party in 1856 pitted an anti-slavery South Carolinian against a let's-not-rock-the-boat stand-pat Democrat, James Buchanan. Fremont made a credible showing considering that the party that had nominated him was making its first try at the presidency. The electoral vote was Buchanan 174 to Fremont's 114. In no way did his reputation depend on his military record. His major at the College of Charleston was in mathematics and his earliest employment was in the engineering field. When the Civil War came he was reinstated in the army, this time as a Major General in charge of the Western Department based in St. Louis. The task of organizing an effective army with insufficient arms and supplies with a few thousand untrained troops proved too great a task for Fremont's limited military skills and he was blamed for several distressing defeats early in the war. One of those defeats was at the hands of Stonewall Jackson. Fremont could at least claim that he was in good company on that score. Jackson, with an inferior force, never more than eighteen thousand, had to face two large Union armies, Nathaniel Banks in the Shenandoah, and Fremont's across the mountain in West Virginia. When his command was placed under John Pope, and old foe from his days in Missouri, Fremont resigned his commission. During the dark days before Sherman captured Atlanta, when it seemed to some in the North, that the country had tired of war and would surely vote Lincoln out of office, Fremont emerged as a possible Republican nominee for the 1864 election. After the exultant Union victories in Georgia and the Shenandoah, Fremont withdrew, but not before he got in one last dig at the Lincoln administration, which he claimed had been a failure militarily, politically and financially. After the war was over Fremont made a fortune in California, gold having been discovered on his Mariposa estate and then lost a fortune in railroad investments. In 1878 he was appointed governor of the Arizona territory. His final days were spent in New York where he died in 1890.

    The surveys sponsored by the government to find the most practical rail route to the Pacific Coast were conducted during the years 1853–55. Over one million dollars was spent by the federal government on these surveys. Isaac Stevens, the new governor of the Washington Territory, and a former topographical engineer, explored a route between the 47th and 49th parallel. The chief sponsor of this route was the Senator from Illinois, Stephen Douglas. Eventually the Northern Pacific and the Great Northern would serve this route. Lieutenants Gunnison and Beckwith explored a route along the 38th parallel. Gunnison and seven members of this party were killed by the Utes in Utah, at which point Beckwith completed the survey to California. In future years the central route would see both the Union Pacific and the Western Pacific utilizing this terrain. The chief sponsors for this route would be congressional delegation from Missouri. The Secretary of War during the Pierce administration was none other than the future president of the Confederacy, Jefferson Davis, who favored a southern route along the 32nd parallel. The route was surveyed by Lieutenant Amiel Whipple and Captain John Pope. Valuable as some of these surveys may have been, in truth none of them were entirely followed. Eventually professional railroad men back by private capital and land grant subsidies would determine the route.

The Lewis and Clark Expedition

Note well the title chosen for the expedition—The Corps of Exploration. At first glance we are apt to think of it as referring to geographical exploration. But that is far too narrow a meaning. With this President himself an avid botanist, it meant an exploration of the natural world, the fauna and flora of this newly annexed region. Lewis and Clark were given very specific instructions as to what they would look for—they would explore the Missouri River, find a route over the Rockies to the Pacific, observe the weather, learn about the various tribes they might encounter, and study plant life. As previously mentioned, plant and flora samples were shipped back to President Jefferson by way of St. Louis after the first winter at Mandan, North Dakota. Before the journey would be complete the total would rise to 176 plants, seed, roots and cuttings. Many of them would be new to botanists back east although long known to Native Americans. Of the journey Jefferson wrote: "Lewis's journey across our continent has added a number of new plants to our former stock. Some of them are curious, some ornamental, some useful and some may by culture be made acceptable to our tables." Many of the plants the explorers collected still exist and may be seen in the Academy of Sciences in Philadelphia where Lewis had studied under Benjamin Smith Barton.

Medical science in the first decade of the nineteenth century, measured by the research and development of today's pharmacology, was in its infancy. Still the benefits of herbal medicine were known and practiced by many including the mother of Meriwether Lewis. The herbs used by Native Americans for medicinal purposes would be of particular interest to him. Echinacea grew in North Dakota and was commended for use by the native population to lessen the effects of colds and the flu and to fortify the immune system. Today it is widely distributed and can be found in the herbal section of your neighborhood drug store. The western tribes of North American knew that if you decocted willow bark the resulting tea relieved headache and fever and eased aches and pains. They also know that a tea made from wintergreen leaves broke a fever or made bearable sore muscles and rheumatism. The effectiveness of salicylic acid (salix, "willow") was known for years, but it was not until 1899 that Friedrich Bayer, a German chemist, brought the two out in pill form and called it aspirin. Overnight it became a household remedy found in every medicine chest in the western world. On second thought, make that the civilized world.

Looking over the list of 176 specimens collected in the course of the expedition I checked to see how many I had on my own rural Oregon plot or in near proximity: Oregon Grape (our state flower), fennel, hawthorn, Pacific blackberry, wild lupine, madrone, evergreen huckleberry, red flowering currant, the rhododendrons beyond counting (not the wild variety that the expeditions found near Fort Clatsop, which can be collected only with a permit). Today this same region that the Corps of Exploration passed through, from the mouth of the Willamette to the Port of Astoria on the Columbia, has become a horticultural cornucopia providing plants and shrubs for every climate zone in North America. Some of the delights of living in the area are the floral festivals that extend from the daffodil festival at Amity on the last weekend in March, to the Swan Island Dahlia show in Canby on the last weekend in August and the first weekend of September. Keizer, near the state capitol in Salem, has its Iris Festival in June. Portland's famed Rose Garden has given its name to the city's Rose Parade and to the coliseum where the professional basketball team plays its home games—the Rose Garden.

CHAPTER FIVE

Dr. Eliot's Five-Foot Shelf

THE PRESIDENT OF HARVARD University has always occupied a unique position in American higher education. Of all the persons who have occupied that position, none reached the influence of Charles Eliot, president for forty years. Retiring in 1909, Dr. Eliot was the best-known educator in America. The press frequently sought his views on various subjects. In his emeritus status Dr. Eliot launched a project popularly known as Dr. Eliot's Five-Foot Shelf. The publisher of this fifty-volume set of books, the Harvard Classics, was *Collier's*, a weekly magazine of general interest that rivaled the *Saturday Evening Post* in reader interest.

In all the Collier owned magazines, *Woman's Home Companion* included, ads appeared extolling the virtues of the classics well into the 1930s. Each ad offered a free guidebook to "the most famous books in the world" called *Fifteen Minutes a Day*. The claim was made that Dr. Eliot had chosen and arranged the 418 masterpieces so that, even in fifteen minutes a day the reader could obtain from the Harvard Classics, the culture, the knowledge, and the broad viewpoint that "can alone win for you an outstanding and solid success." Dr. Eliot, the publisher explained, had put into the classics "the essentials of a liberal education." Some 350,000 homes purchased the set of books. In the early part of the twentieth century and the last quarter of the nineteenth century buying a set of books that might appeal to all members of the family had great appeal, and the publishing world was ready to meet the need.

The self-improvement appeal the Collier's advertising writers used to promote the Harvard Classics seems common to other offerings. Encyclopedias were published by Thomas Nelson, Dodd & Mead (under the name of the New International) and the standby of generations, the Britannica. Dictionaries were widely represented in the advertising section of magazines. Funk & Wagnalls plugged their massive volume in their own magazine, the *Literary Digest, Time* and *Newsweek,* predecessor in the weekly news field.

When young Richard Dana shipped off his manuscript he got $250 and twenty-four free copies. And that was all he got until years later when the copyright reverted to him. Robert Lucid, editor of *The Journal of Richard Henry Dana, Jr.* published in 1968 estimates that Harper's made $50,000 on this book during their twenty-year proprietorship with the book selling at forty-five cents per copy. Overseas the British publisher Moxon, although not bound by international copyright, paid the author more for the book than Harper's had and in seafaring England the book proved more of a sensation than it had in America. Two thousand sailors are said to have bought copies of it in Liverpool in a single day. But oh, the exposure *Two Years Before the Mast* got here at home! First, it is published in Harper's Family Library series and well advertised in the pages of *Harper's Weekly*. On the occasion of the Civil War Centennial the author of this book subscribed to facsimile copies issued during the 1861–65 period. The coverage that Harper's field correspondents provided plus the illustrations—some drawn and some from photographs—brought what has been called "the defining event of American history" right into my living room week by week. *The Weekly* was started in 1857 and published its last issue in 1916. First, this neophyte twenty-five-year-old published by Dodd & Mead in their *Great Illustrated Classic Series,* and finally gets his book chosen by Dr. Eliot in *Collier's Harvard Classic* series as one of the great books of the ages.

Dana wrote one of the best sea travel books ever written. Compare it with any of the Hornblower or Aubrey-Maurin novels of more recent times and three observations emerge. First—the Hornblower and Aubrey-Maurin books are novels. Dana's book is based on real life experience. Second—the sea stories of the Napoleonic era are told from a Royal Navy officer's viewpoint while this book is a voice from the forecastle. Third—while the others are about a man-of-war, this is the tale of a peacetime merchant trader.

A scene from their first landfall at Juan Fernandez Island some 500 statute miles west of Valparaiso, Chile appeals to the author. "We were then nearly seventy miles from it; and so high and so blue did it appear, that I mistook it for a cloud, resting over the island. At length we could distinguish trees and rocks; and by afternoon, this beautiful island lay fairly before us and we directed our course to the only harbor. We had a boat ahead of us all the time we were working in, and those aboard were continually bracing the yards about every puff that struck us, until about 12 o'clock, when we came in 40 fathoms water, and our anchor struck bottom for the first time since we left Boston—one hundred and three days."[1]

It brings back memories of a landfall I made on the old flagship of the Matson line, the *Matsonia* that was converted to a troop carrier during World War II. We left San Diego bound for Noumea, New Caledonia, a staging point for Marine Corps landing at Guadalcanal. Our first landfall was Pago Pago, American

Samoa, and the harbor, an extinct volcano crater. I have long since forgotten how many days we were at sea. With the powerful engines of the ship, weather was never a concern. Enemy submarines were the problem. The landfall was just as Dana described it first, a deep blue speck rising from the sea, little by little becoming green.

California was raised by the *Pilgrim* 150 days out of Boston. It was January 14, 1835 when they finally came to Santa Barbara. "It was a beautiful day, and so warm that we had on straw hats, duck trousers, and all the summer gear; and as this was mid-winter, it spoke well for the climate." The landing was a bit tricky. But they had alongside a boat of Sandwich Islanders. They watched these experienced boatmen and followed their example. "We pulled strongly in, and as soon as we felt the sea had got a hold of us and was carrying us in with the speed of a race horse, we threw the oars as far from the boat as we could, and took hold of the gunwale, ready to spring out and seize her when she struck. We were shot up upon the beach like an arrow from a bow, and seizing the boat ran her up high and dry, and soon picked up our oars."[2]

Dana was a New England Yankee, born in Cambridge in 1815. His father was a distinguished man of letters and the Editor of the *North American Review*. His grandfather, Francis Dana, was appointed by President Washington to be the first American minister to Russia and was later the Chief Justice of the Supreme Court in Massachusetts. Young Richard entered Harvard in 1831 and all things being normal would have graduated in 1835. But all things proved not to be normal and after two academic years he contracted measles leaving his eyesight so impaired that further study was not advised. Chafing over his slow recovery, he decided on a sea voyage and signed on the brig Pilgrim as an ordinary seaman bound for California by way of the Horn. He left Boston August 15, 1834 and returned September 21, 1836. On his return Dana picked up his studies and graduated with the class of 1837.

He then entered Harvard Law School where he graduated in 1840. It was during his years in Law School that he was able to put the finishing touches on his book.

His grandson, H.W.L. Dana, in a preface to an edition published by Dodd, Mead in 1946, shares an interesting sidelight regarding the log that Dana kept. What he was able to keep was a brief log of only a dozen pages. One of his sea chests, which had contained the longer and more detailed account had become lost on his return to Boston. With the help of this salvaged small log he was able to reconstruct a fresh and vivid account of the journey. It is possible, the grandson observes, "that the loss of his original manuscript may really have proved to be a blessing in disguise and may have been part of the secret of the success of the book."[3]

When Dana was fifty-seven he wrote to his son, "My life has been a failure compared with what I might and ought to have done. My great success—my book—was a boy's work, done before I came to the bar."[4] Actually he made a very comfortable living from the law and it gave him the opportunity to further develop two of his greatest skills, oratory and quickness in debate. During his final year in law school he was offered (and accepted) the appointment as an instructor in elocution at Harvard, a position he greatly enjoyed.

In politics he was one of the founders of the Free Soil Party, which combined "Conscience" Whigs, the old anti-slavery Liberty Party and factions of the New York State Democrat Party. The party nominated Martin Van Buren for president and Charles Francis Adams for Vice President. The Free Soil Party eventually gave way to the formation of the Republican Party, but in the 1848 election it managed to elect only nine congressmen. The election turned into a last hurrah for the Whigs, who had the good fortune to nominate one of the heroes of the War with Mexico, General Zachary Taylor.

In 1861 President Lincoln appointed Dana to the office of U.S. District Attorney for the District of Massachusetts, a position he held for five years. When he stepped down from that position his legal career flourished and he twice was elected to the State legislature. He ran for a seat in the U. S. House of Representatives in 1868 and lost in a humiliating fashion receiving roughly ten percent of the votes cast. In 1876 President Grant nominated him as minister to England but the Senate rejected the nomination.

Both losses can be tied to a charge of plagiarism leveled against Dana in his role as the Editor of Wheaton's *International Law* by its previous editor, William Lawrence. When the Secretary of State, Hamilton Fish, sent his name to the Senate for confirmation he discovered that there were others more than willing to use this to beat the nominee. Ben Butler, of Civil

War fame, who resented the fact that Dana had contested his congressional seat and the Pennsylvania Republican power broker, Simon Cameron, who wished to see his son nominated to the post, combined forces to defeat the nominee. Fish knew that the charges against Dana had no real substance. But he had not foreseen that these unsubstantiated charges would be used so effectively by Dana's foes. The vote was 31 to 17 against confirmation.

To all intents and purposes his career hopes in the political realm were at an end. However, when Hayes was elected and appointed Dana's law school classmate and life long friend as Secretary of State, William M. Evarts, old hopes flickered. He received a post of U. S. Attorney at Halifax Fishery arbitration—not the sort of post that launches a political career! He tried his hand at further writing. One called *A Seaman's Friend* was a manual on seamanship and the rights and duties of mariners and masters. It had modest success. Another followed in 1859 *To Cuba and Back*. That same year he wrote an addendum to the book that had won him fame called *Twenty-Four Years Later*. It was based on a second trip to California, this one advised by his doctors. The first trip was by sail around the horn, the second was by way of the Isthmus of Panama and the steamboat Golden Gate. The objective of the first trip was to sell house wares, tools and trading goods and to buy and process hides for shipment for the New England leather trade.

So much had happened to change California since his first trip. Now it was a state. The War with Mexico had been fought and won. Gold had been discovered. But the greatest change of all was San Francisco, a change he could see before he ever set foot ashore.

"We bore round the point toward the old anchoring-ground of the hide ships, and there, covering the sand-hills and the valleys, stretching from the waters edge to the base of the great hills, and from the old Presidio to the Mission, flickering all over with the lamps of its streets and houses, lay a city of one hundred thousand inhabitants."[5] This time Dana came as a tourist with the purpose of comparing the past with the present. He visited all the old port cities where he had lived ashore in the old days. The title he gave his book, *Two Years Before the Mast* is something of a misnomer, for in point of fact he spent more time ashore processing hides than he did afloat! Here and there he would run into friends and companions from the first trip. And here we come to the reason Dana belongs in this book of western biographies. He ran into a man who had come across the country from Kentucky to Monterey and who had married into the Vallejo family. When Dana gave his name, 'he professed at once to remember me, and spoke of the book. I found that almost...every American in California had read it; for when California 'broke out'...in 1848, and so large a portion of the Anglo-Saxon race flocked to it, there was no book upon California but mine." Those who were praised in the book were delighted. There is a common saying that everyone is entitled to fifteen minutes of fame—or in the age of television let's make that fifteen seconds. For many of Dana's associates this was their moment. "Here I am, mentioned right here in this story of the wedding at Santa Barbara."

Not everyone was praised. The company agent in 1835–36, Alfred Robinson "received me, remembering what I had printed to the world about him at a time when I took little thought that the world was going to read it, but there was no sign of offense, only cordiality." Emerson, a towering figure of American literature, wrote a review for *The Dial*. "This is a voice from the forecastle. His book will have a wide circulation. It will do more than this. It will open the eyes of many to the condition of the sailor." Dana's book was *not* the only source of information. John C. Fremont's reports on his expeditions to the Rocky Mountains in 1842 and to Oregon and Northern California in 1843–44 were widely distributed and eagerly read. During Dana's second trip to California he visited the Pathfinder and his family at their Mariposa County home. Jessie Fremont, the daughter of Senator Thomas Hart Benton, is praised as a heroine at home in either the salons of Paris or the drawing rooms of New York or Washington or the roughest life of the remote and wild mining regions of Mariposa. In point of fact gold was discovered on the Fremont property turning the Colonel and his wife into instant millionaires.

Joel Palmer's practical book on the Oregon Trail taking the reader from point to point was another source published some five years after Dana's work. Some of the tracts and pamphlets on westward journeys were no more than real estate promotion pieces. Come to such and such a county, we have property to sell, or travel by this stage, this railroad. As for Dana he had nothing to sell but his book. So when he wrote that Monterey, the seat of government in Mexican days "is decidedly the pleasantest and most civilized looking place in California" the reader accepts it as fact. He also observed "if California becomes a prosperous country, this (San Francisco) bay will be the center of its prosperity. The abundance of wood and water, the extreme fertility of its shores, the excellence of its climate, which is as near to being perfect as any in the world, and its facilities for navigation, affording the best anchoring-grounds in the whole western coast of America, all fit it for a place of great importance."

During his first visit to California, Dana's Harvard education gave him a leg up on his shipmates as unofficial translator for the

Captain of the Pilgrim. Spanish was the lingua franca of the ports along the Pacific Coast. On the trip coming out Dana got a copy of Spanish grammar and with a background in French and Latin soon found it possible to converse in the language used by the bulk of the population ashore. He picked up the rudiments of a second language, Hawaiian, for many of the workers in the hide drying enterprise were from the Sandwich Islands. During his second trip he interrupted his visit for several months and sailed to the island kingdom in the Boston clipper ship Mastiff, which was burned at sea. Crew and passengers escaped in boats and were carried by a British vessel to Honolulu. Never a dull moment with this man at sea! After this he returned to the mainland where on January 11, 1860 he continued to the Orient and traversed the world.

"As the shores of California faded in the distance, and the summits of the Coast Range sank under the blue horizon, I bade farewell—yes, I do not doubt, forever—to those scenes which, however changed or unchanged, must always possess an ineffable interest to me." He returned by way of China, Japan, Singapore, Ceylon, Bombay, Suez, having set foot on all the continents, save Australia.

One of Dana's lesser achievements was his lifelong correspondence with his law school classmate and confidant, William M. Evarts. Evarts, normally very reticent to divulge any personal feelings, found he could count on his friend Dana to be discreet. Dana says of his classmate "the most successful speech made at the school during the whole time I was there, was made before a jury of undergraduates, Judge Story on the bench, by William M. Evarts." Twice he tried to get his friend named as Supreme Court Chief Justice.

Dana was widely recognized as one of the United States leading figures in the field of international law. The final action of his life was to go to Rome to rest and to continue his research in this field. There he died in 1882 and was buried in the Protestant Cemetery where lie the ashes of Keats and Shelley.

CHAPTER SIX

Meadville and a Citizen Soldier

Meadville—a Rail Center

General George B. McClellan, one time commander of the Army of the Potomac, was a man of many talents. As a graduate of the U. S. Military Academy Class of 1846 he was both an engineer and an officer schooled in the military arts. In McClellan's time West Point was one of the ranking engineering schools in the country. To this day the works and projects of the Army Corps of Engineers carry on this tradition. The newly emerging railway systems frequently turned to graduates of the Academy to fill important posts. In McClellan's case, having attained the rank of Captain in just nine years (rapid advancement for that time) he resigned his commission to accept a position of Chief Engineer of the Illinois Central Railroad. The Illinois Central was one of the first land grant railroads, stretching some 704 miles from north to south, connecting Chicago with Cairo, where the Ohio enters the Mississippi. His salary was $3,000 a year, more than double what he was getting in service. He went to work for the railroad in 1856 and within a year was promoted to Vice-President. One of his early achievements was to double the reach of the IC by contracting with a group of steamship owners to carry freight and passengers on a regular schedule based on Cairo to Memphis, Vicksburg, and New Orleans. He foresaw the eventual rail link with these same cities that would follow after the war.

In 1860 McClellan was offered, and accepted, the Superintendency of the Ohio & Mississippi Railway, a 340-mile line between Cincinnati and St. Louis. By this time his salary had reached dizzying heights—$15,000. Had there been no war, McClellan's march up the railroad hierarchy would have been swift. But there was a war and he heeded the call to return to the service having been offered the post of Major General of Volunteers by the governor of Ohio. The Federal Government, desperately short of well-qualified officers, shortly matched Ohio's offer and made him a Major General in the regular army and placed him in command of the Department of the Ohio which consisted of three states—Ohio, Indiana, and Illinois with headquarters at Cincinnati.

Within a month of his appointment, his experience in railroading was put to good use. At the suggestion of the General-in-Chief, Gen. Winfield Scott, McClellan entrained several regiments and moved them to Grafton, Virginia, a key junction point on the Baltimore and Ohio. Grafton was occupied and the bridges the Confederate forces had burned were rebuilt. McClellan then sent his reinforcements—largely from Indiana and Ohio—under a fellow West Pointer, Thomas Morris to pursue the Confederate force. On June 3, after marching all night in a drenching rain, the columns converged on the unsuspecting southerners camped at Philippi and routed them. The battle was dubbed by the northern press as the "Philippi Races." It was the very first victory of the Union forces and was played up as a major event in the press. One of the young officers on the Union side was Captain Fielder Jones of the 6th Indiana. We shall learn more about him when we discuss the role of citizen soldiers in the Civil War. The victory definitely played a part in McClellan's military career.

When President Lincoln was looking around for a commander of the Army of the Potomac who would fight, he chose McClellan. It also played a part in the decision of the western counties of Virginia where secession had been opposed in a recent referendum and encouraged the leaders of the pro-Union majority to break away and form their own provisional government at Wheeling. From henceforth this new state would be known as West Virginia.

Long after the war, and after General McClellan had been the standard bearer for the Democratic Party in the national election of 1864, he became the President of the Atlantic and Great Western Railroad.[1] The problem with this mid-western railroad, to be candid, was that it was not great but rather small. It was not western but regional, and the only way it would ever reach the Atlantic would be over some other railroad track bed. But it had a grandiloquent title that puts one in mind of the great grocery chain known as the A&P—long title—The Great Atlantic and Pacific Tea Company—which at one time really did stretch from coast to coast.

By the time McClellan took the job with the Atlantic and Great Western he was an acknowledged transportation engineer who was asked to serve on corporate boards. At the time he took the job he was a director of this railroad and the Chief Engineer of New York City's Department of Docks with a home across the river in New Jersey.[2]

The Atlantic and Great Western began life as three separate railroads centering on Jamestown, N.Y., Meadville, Pa., and Franklin, Ohio in the early 1850s with Meadville as the headquarters. By 1864 the road reached from Salamanca, N. Y. in the east to Dayton, Ohio, 369 miles distant. From Dayton south to the Ohio River, the Atlantic and Great Northern went over the tracks of another regional line where contact was made with the Ohio and Mississippi (General McClellan's old connection) and on to St. Louis. All of this growth was made possible by English capital and much of the mileage was built during the wartime period. One of the reasons the road was riding high was the swift development of the oil industry in northwestern Pennsylvania. During a five-month period in 1861, with its spur line into Oil City, this road shipped 50,000 barrels of oil. There was even talk of extending the line eastward to the Atlantic. By the time McClellan accepted the presidency in 1872, the bloom was off the bush, and the talk on Wall Street was that the Erie would soon take over the assets of the line, whose rail bed the Erie had leased over many years.

Here is an excerpt of a letter McClellan received from Sobieski Ross of the Jersey Shore, Pine Creek, and Buffalo Railway Company explaining why the Pine Creek route through Pennsylvania presented an ideal connection with the east coast:[3] "There is no need of calling to your attention to the great importance of this fact, in connection with traffic, as you are perfectly familiar with the subject, or to the absolute necessity, in a financial point of view, for the Atlantic and Great Western Railroad Company to secure a line independent of the Erie Company, whose gross mismanagement is but too notorious."

There was also the small matter of some several millions of dollars to create a tunnel and a roadbed. There is no record of McClellan's reply. But the long and the short of it was that the coffers were dry. One of his first acts as president of the railroad was to wire the English capitalists to send two hundred thousand pounds "or I shall be compelled to take off passenger trains."[4] It took another twenty years or so for the Wall Street rumors to come to pass. It was reorganized as the New York, Pennsylvania and Ohio Railroad with headquarters moved to Cleveland. Later it was leased to the Erie, which finally acquired the entire capital stock in 1896.

The Erie Railroad

The original charter of the Erie Railroad was issued by the legislature of New York on April 24, 1832. Pressure for its passage came from the Southern Tier of counties with their New York City allies. Towns and villages along the canal had prospered. People had moved in to the lands immediately adjacent to the canal with business and industry soon to follow. All of this made the canal counties pleased and made the counties along the Pennsylvania line angry—angry enough to push for a Hudson to the Great Lakes railway. That it was passed at all bordered on the miraculous, for formidable opponents felt it would seriously jeopardize the financial well being of the state-financed Erie Canal. Foremost among the opponents was none other than the Little Magician himself, Martin Van Buren. Although as a state legislator he had backed the canal, he had opposed the policies of DeWitt Clinton for years, a struggle for power that was to last until Clinton's death in 1828. In that same year Van Buren resigned his seat in the U.S. Senate, and ran successfully for governor. He served for two and a half months and was appointed by President Andrew Jackson as Secretary of State. Van Buren served for four years as Jackson's Vice President and four more years as his successor. The backers of the southern tier railroad, looking around for the means to pay for the survey of the line were told that Jackson was a keen supporter of internal improvements. For a time it seemed such was the case. Plans were made to begin the survey and then there was an abrupt cancellation by orders of the War Department.

How to account for this sudden change? Supporters of the plan saw the fine hand of Van Buren and the "canal gang" in Albany as the chief culprits. The railroad managed to raise enough money from private sources to pay for the beginning of the survey. It took the Erie eighteen years to move from legislative approval to completion of the line. There would be many times when the officers of the railroad would be forced to return to Albany for modification of that charter and for added funds. What mellowed the opposition in Albany was the gut feeling that the age of railroads had dawned. Railroads were springing up all over. Two roads practically ran right along side of the canal, one from Albany to Schenectady and the other from Rochester to Batavia. By 1853 both of these roads, with others to come, would be melded in to what would be an Albany to Buffalo line.

Thus the Erie was the first to make the Hudson to the Great Lakes connection. When the line was first conceived in the 1830s there wasn't a town along the projected line with a population that exceeded 3,000! Consult a topographical map of the region and you will see the problems the surveyors faced. Begin at the Eastern end with the Catskills. Add the already existing Delaware-Hudson Canal, whose line must be traversed. The Susquehanna River Valley must be dealt with along with all of those defiles and moraines scattered along the route from Binghamton to Elmira. Finally there was the escarpment where the line approached Lake Erie. Limitations of the equipment must be considered. Ascending slopes of the roadbed must not exceed 100 feet per mile. The line must be laid out so that one locomotive may pull the train. These are just a few of the problems to be faced. The Erie was fortunate in the selection of its chief engineer, the widely respected Benjamin Wright.

He had the same position with the Erie Canal and his proven record in the position served to soften the opposition in the legislature, which agreed to pay for the survey. Wright had instructions he must observe. The railroad must be laid out within the confines of New York State. It must not invade the counties being served by the canal. In the interest of sound engineering principles and cost considerations, surveyors recommended a "dip" into adjoining states. Each exception was approved, not just by one state but by two! Pennsylvania gave its grudging approval to the "dip" into its territory where the road followed the Susquehanna River valley as it made its approach to Binghamton.

MEADVILLE and a CITIZEN SOLDIER

Wright's survey report was in the main followed, but deviations were often dictated by political considerations. What town or city has aided our task? Which towns can guarantee us a market? Which communities have aided our efforts with grants of land and rights of way? Edward Hungerford, the primary historian of the Erie, tells how Dunkirk and not Portland became the terminus of the line. Dunkirk gave the new railroad 425 acres on which to base their operations.

To celebrate the completion of what was for a time the longest railroad under one ownership in the United States, invitations were sent out to the high and the mighty of the day, and most were accepted. On the inaugural trip over the 446 mile road, President Millard Fillmore came with his Secretary of State, Daniel Webster and three other cabinet members. The governor of New York and three former governors were in attendance, along with both U.S. Senators and a large delegation of legislators from Albany. All along the line there were speeches and celebrations and finally the celebration at Dunkirk where the *U.S.S. Michigan* laid offshore ready to render the presidential salute. The menu of the banquet served on that occasion included chowder, a yoke of oxen, ten roasted sheep, beef, boiled ham, corned beef, buffalo tongue, bologna sausage, smoked and pickled beef tongue, one hundred roast fowls, coffee, barrels of cider, and loaves of bread ten feet long.

After the railroad was completed it managed to attract some legendary financial predators—Daniel Drew, Jay Gould and Jim Fiske among them. As a result of their machinations it became necessary for the road to operate on a lean budget. If there were a way to control expenses, the Erie would find it. It went through the throes of bankruptcy and name change four times in the course of its existence. Yet during those same years it managed to compete in an environment dominated by the New York Central, the Pennsylvania, and the Baltimore and Ohio. As the years progressed, the twenty-four mile boat trip up the Hudson from the City to Piermont proved an obstacle. Once again the Erie dipped over a state line, bought a feeder line that led directly to the docks of Jersey City and Weehawken, New Jersey. The Erie turned a liability to an advantage with its very own New York harbor based "Navy." Trains arriving from the west were met by the Erie Ferry and whisked to terminals in Manhattan. Freight cars were loaded on to barges where tugs delivered them to piers along the East River.

The most important "dip" of all was the eventual tie-in with the Atlantic and Great Western, already mentioned. This was means by which Jamestown and Salamanca were tied into the Erie. The acquisition of this railroad was the means by which the Erie changed its role from that of a regional railroad to a New York to Chicago railroad. Chicago gave the Erie connections with the western roads and by the end of the nineteenth century was carrying perishable goods to eastern markets on its famed fast freight, known to the trade as the Erie 98.

So what killed the Erie? Nebraska born Edith Warton, Pulitzer Prize winner for her *The Age of Innocence* was once asked why she preferred the car to public transportation. "Because you can go when you want to," was her answer. At least that is what killed the passenger segment of the business. In 1973 the Erie and dozens of other eastern roads became a part of the federally funded Conrail.

Allegheny College and Seymour, Indiana Produce a Citizen Soldier

For now a discursive return to Meadville, Pennsylvania, just prior to the Civil War. Besides being the headquarters of the Atlantic and Great Western, the town was also the site of Allegheny College, a small liberal arts college affiliated with the Methodist Church. Here we will pick up on the life of the man who was destined to become a Brigadier General of Volunteers and a citizen soldier who served in almost continuous action for the four long years of conflict. His name was Fielder Jones and his home was in Sharon Center, Potter County, Pennsylvania where he was born February 27, 1833. His father had come to this lumbering region just south of the New York state line a few years before the birth of his oldest son. Lumbering and the clearing of land were the two occupations the father indulged in. He married a local schoolteacher and to them three children were born to them—Fielder, Benjamin, and Roxanna. In 1837 a falling tree killed the father and the mother was a widow with three children. She did what most widows in the nineteenth century did—she married again. Five years and two infant daughters later she was widowed a second time. By this time the eldest son, Fielder, was twelve. He helped his mother support the family by hauling pine logs with an ox team for five dollars a month. He spent his leisure time studying until at age fifteen he enrolled in a local academy where he paid special attention to music. By 1852 he was a teacher of music at the Waterford Academy in Erie County.

In 1855 he entered Allegheny College in Meadville as a sophomore where once again he managed to combine the roles of student and teacher. After graduation he found time to study law in the office of Hiram L. Richmond of Meadville and was admitted to the bar in 1859. Richmond, a graduate and later a trustee of the local college, was a staunch Whig during the early part of his life. He cast his lot with the Republican Party after its organization in Pennsylvania and was elected as a Representative in the 43rd Congress, 1873–75. Jones devoted some of this time while at Allegheny to the affairs of the heart. In the same year that he passed the bar exam he married Kate Saeger of nearby Saegerstown. Then he was off to Indiana, where apparently he was torn between two professions—the law and teaching. He opted for teaching and became the principal of a school in Seymour. He held this position for two years before the outbreak of the war in 1861. President Lincoln made his first call of 75,000 volunteers to serve in the armed forces for three months. It was a time frame conceived in optimism that would come back to haunt the Union. Jones was among the first to volunteer from Seymour. When the 6th Indiana Infantry Regiment was formed, Jones was elected as a Captain.

The way in which officers were chosen for the Union Army will come as a surprise to the veterans of more recent wars. To begin with there were few trained officers available. The officer needs of the Civil War would far outstrip the pool of graduates of West Point and the various military academies. The veterans of the last war the nation fought in 1846–48 would be well past middle age. Add to this better than half of the officer personnel of the Regular Army were from the southern states and it soon becomes clear that although the north was rich in manpower, it faced a dearth of trained experienced officers. This is the way the Stephen Towne of the Indiana State Archives describes the situation: "Officers were chosen primarily for their popularity in the community where the men were recruited. Elections were held to choose the commissioned officers of companies (however, the governor was not bound by these elections, and often chose whom he liked for the appointments). Local political leaders were the likeliest sorts to obtain commissions. These men were able to recruit men for their units based on their name recognition and the winning ways of the politician. Once in the army, they studied army regulations and Hardee's Tactics to learn the job of soldiering."[5]

In the case of the 6th Indiana the subsequent facts suggest they chose wisely. They probably chose him because many had known him in school. A few might know that this man knew what hard physical labor was like. This was a man who knew how to handle oxen, horses and men. And, in common with most young men from the rural areas, he would know how to use firearms.

This newly minted captain hit the books and in a month's time his company was on one of those trains General McClellan had commandeered to carry raw volunteers into the battle zone near Grafton. Jones was wounded July 16, 1861 at Cheat River in western Virginia while bring up the rear of General Morris's Brigade. He received three gunshot wounds, one in the thigh, one in the body and one in the arm. A later pension application filed after the war reveals the shot to the body entered the liver causing chronic diarrhea and ultimately was the cause of his death. At the time Jones seems to have made light of it. If he spent any time in a field hospital the record doesn't disclose it. He was mustered out of his three-month enlistment obligation on August 2, 1861. On August 29 he was back in service, this time elected the Lieutenant Colonel of the newly formed 39th Regiment of Sharpshooters (later called the 8th Indiana Mounted Infantry and finally in 1863 as the 8th Indiana Cavalry) with Col. Thomas J. Harrison commanding. The regiment saw continuous action for four long years attached to the Army of the Ohio and then to the Army of the Cumberland.

Fielder Jones's action at Murfreesboro and Stone River, December 26, 1862 through January 2, 1863 is an action the author can identify with, having personally walked over the battle grounds. General Rosencrans was in overall command of the Union forces and his mission was to stop the Confederate forces under General Bragg from reentering Kentucky. The two forces engaged in a three-battle day, judged by many as one of the bloodiest contests of the war. Of the approximately 44,000 Federals and 34,000 Confederates engaged in the action each side lost 13,000 killed and wounded.[6] The 8th Indiana, a part of the weak right wing of Rosencrans's forces suffered severely with thirty-one killed, 118 wounded and 231 missing in action.

It was in this action Jones picked up his nickname of "No Surrender Jones" when a company of Brigadier General Joseph Wheeler's cavalry surrounded him. He was mounted and alone when he refused to surrender and made a dash through their lines and made good his escape. For his action at Stone's River his Brigade Commander, Col. H. W. Gibson wrote: "Lt. Col. Jones discharged his duties in the most gallant manner, ever active and brave, he rallied his men at every point and yielded only before overwhelming numbers. He met the foe in hand to hand conflict and owes his escape to the skillful use of side arms."

After the battle the regiment remained in camp near Murfreesboro for several months recuperating awaiting supplies and replacements from Indianapolis. By April they were in action again, had a second fight with Joe Wheeler's cavalry. Reading of Jones's various skirmishes, it seems that he was forever running into the diminutive Georgian, Joe Wheeler, whose principal assignment seems to have been to disrupt Sherman's supply lines. Between Wheeler and John Hood, West Pointers both, bridges were destroyed, rails were torn up, and the Union's Railroad Construction Battalions were constantly harassed. But the road gangs repaired the damage as fast as it was inflected. At battle's end the Union forces were still in control of the Nashville to Chattanooga railroad supply line. Forced to move rapidly from an

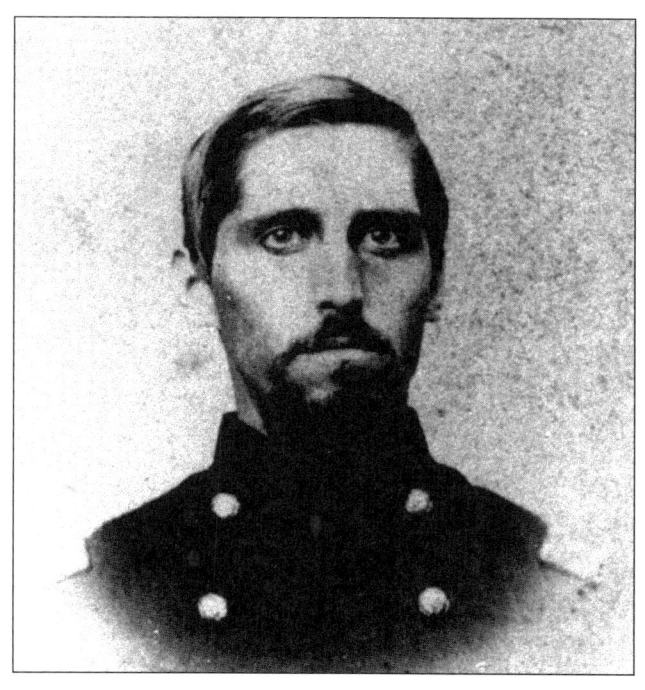

BRIG. GENERAL FIELDER A. JONES

MEADVILLE and a CITIZEN SOLDIER

offensive to a defensive posture, Rosencrans troops dug in, and with deadly accurate rifle and artillery fire forced Bragg to withdraw.

The next major battle the 8th Indiana was involved in was at Chickamauga, September 19-20, 1863. General Rosencrans was still in charge of the Army of the Cumberland, and General Braxton Bragg was still in command of the Confederate's Army of the Tennessee. Call it Rosencrans versus Bragg, round two. Four Union brigades execute a masterly deception crossing the Tennessee River upstream from Chattanooga. Bragg abandoned Chattanooga without a battle and prepared a counter strike. The Confederate forces and the Federals were at roughly even strength when the battle commenced near LaFayette, Georgia. The battle may have turned on one of the rare Confederate uses of transferring major forces from the eastern sector to the west. Confederate President Jefferson Davis had been Secretary of War in the Pierce administration. He knew the importance of holding the railroad junction point at Chattanooga. He stripped one chief component part of the Army of the Virginia and shipped General Longstreet forces by rail to prevent this entry into the south's heartland. Rosencrans's line was split by a corps led by General Hood who happened to hit a portion of the Federal line where troops had been moved to strengthen defense elsewhere. They moved as ordered. The replacement unit did not show up in time to oppose the forces of Longstreet who poured through the gap. This created chaos for the Army of the Cumberland. Forces were on both sides of the gap. The Union line crumbled, and Rosencrans effectively lost control. General Thomas became the Federal hero of the day. He successfully gathered up the remnants of the Army and made a stand at Chattanooga. General Rosencrans found his reputation in tatters and was ultimately relieved.[7]

Once again the casualties were high. Bragg lost 18,000 troops the south could ill afford to lose. The Federal forces lost close to 16,000. By the time the Battle of Chickamauga ended it appeared the winner of round two of the Rosecrans-Bragg fight was Bragg.

The battle of Chickamauga was quickly followed by round three. The besieged Union forces, now under the overall command of General U. S. Grant, placed General Thomas in charge of the Army of the Cumberland and requested the transfer of General William T. Sherman and 20,000 troops from Mississippi. On the Confederate side Bragg did not follow up his victory with an assault on Chattanooga and found his subordinates had lost faith in his leadership. Soon President Davis had no choice. He replaced him with one of the best Generals the South possessed, General Joseph E. Johnston. Now it would be Sherman versus Johnston, Grant having been transferred to the eastern sector to command the Army of the Potomac.

By mid-June 1863 the 8th Indiana, carried on the books as an unattached Cavalry Corps, participated in actions at Liberty Gap and Tullahoma in support of Alexander McCook's division. At the battles of Chickamauga and Chattanooga, Generals McCook and Johnson complemented Jones for his actions in battle. He received a gold-headed cane from his regiment as a mark of their appreciation and from the officers a magnificent gold watch. It is clear from reading the letters from Jones to the Governor of Indiana that Jones was anxious to be promoted to full colonel. Not only did he personally raise the issue with Governor Morton, but he encouraged officers he had served with to do the same. One of his constant refrains is "I am the oldest Lieutenant Colonel in the Army." His commanding officer wrote on his behalf, trying to get a colonelcy in the Indiana 4th Cavalry. Harrison makes bold to bring up a sore point with the volunteers. A regular officer, a Captain Gay apparently is favored over Jones because he is a regular. Harrison drives home his own testimonial: "Col. Jones is his superior in every requisite for a military man, and as he is a citizen of Indiana, has an interest in common with other Indianans in promoting its reputation, and while our citizens have the talent, capacity and reputation they alone should be the ones to lead her armies in battle."[8] One can sense

MEADVILLE and a CITIZEN SOLDIER

that Harrison has warmed up to his task, citizen soldiers versus outsiders, for he goes on to tell the State Adjutant General that Captain Gay "has been with the regiment for some time with no command and is an army loafer." In spite of this "call a spade a spade" letter we do know Jones wasn't assigned to the Indiana 4th. Jones shared his disappointment with a fellow volunteer officer. "Has it come to this, that we must do the work and the regulars only be rewarded?" Both these letters are dated right after the Battle of Stones River.

After the Battle of Chattanooga the regiment was placed on courier duty between Chattanooga and Ringold, Georgia. This was humdrum defensive duty, the protection of General Sherman's flanks and insuring that supplies move over the rail line as the Federal forces move ever closer to their objective—Atlanta. In April of 1864 the 8th Indiana was given a veteran's furlough. What a tonic that must have been for this unit that had played such an important role in the war in the west. By the time they had completed their R & R duty (rest and rehabilitation) they were back in the line as a part of General Rosseau's raid 500 miles into Alabama. The Battle of Atlanta lasted from July 17 to September 2, 1864 when Sherman's message to Washington was sent. "Atlanta is ours, and fairly won." This victory is said to have tipped the scales in favor of President Lincoln's reelection. The northern Democrats felt that the country was tiring of the war. A loss at Atlanta would have ensured a military stalemate.

The commanding officer of the 8th Indiana, Col. Harrison had been captured and wounded in an action just prior to the fall of Atlanta and for the last year of the war Lieut. Col. Jones was in command of the 8th. Col. Jones's action in the field pleased his superiors whatever his rank might be. He was placed in command of a cavalry brigade consisting of the 8th Indiana, the 5th Iowa and the 4th Tennessee. Let Jones tell the story: "Charged the enemy about 5 p.m., broke his lines and brought off nearly 1200 men. Arrived at Marietta, Georgia, August 4th, thoroughly exhausted. For five days and nights the command got neither rest nor sleep, except such as could be obtained in the saddle or while the horses were feeding." From Atlanta Sherman had devised a strategy that would free him from dependence on the railway supply lines now stretching from Cairo to Atlanta. His forces would make a dash for Savannah and live off the land. During the march to the sea the 8th Indiana Cavalry was actively engaged in action in long forgotten battles at Lovejoy Station, Reynolds Plantation and the siege of Savannah December 10-21, 1864. In January of 1865 the campaign of the Carolinas got underway with Goldsboro as the first major objective. By this time the Jones Brigade was a part of Kilpatrick's, Third Division Cavalry Corps. In this, the last campaign of the war, Sherman divided his force of 60,000 men into two parts, each following a different line of advance. General Howard commanded the right wing, General Slocum commanded the left, with Brigadier General H. J. Kilpatrick in charge of the cavalry. In five days time Sherman had moved his army from Savannah to Fayetteville, North Carolina.

The major battle between the two forces took place at Bentonville. The Confederate commander, Joseph E. Johnston, was out numbered by Sherman's forces three to one. But what he lacked in numbers he made up for in skill. Arrayed against Sherman were such experienced southern generals as Hardee, Buell, Hampton and Jones's old nemesis, Cavalryman Joe Wheeler. Wade Hampton's command discovered that Sherman was marching on Goldsboro, not Raleigh as originally suspected, and that the right wing (Howard's) was approximately half a day's march in advance of the left wing (Slocum's). Johnston saw his opportunity to crush one of the wings as it separated from the other. Bentonville, North Carolina, twenty miles west of Goldsboro, March 9-21, 1865 was the scene of this last chance effort by the Confederates.

In the end it wasn't lack of will, it was the lack of manpower. As one observer described it, the southern regiments were scarcely the size of a company and divisions not much larger than regiments. In some of these final actions the Union veterans found themselves facing regiments made up of North Carolina Junior Reserves—none over eighteen and many as young as sixteen. The ability of Slocum's unit to switch swiftly from offense to defense saved the day at Bentonville. Log breast works thrown up in great haste contributed to the Union's ability to dig in and await the return of Howard's right wing. The action at Averysboro, Jones's unit ran into Rhett's South Carolina brigade of Infantry, another demonstration that the Confederates had plenty of fight left in them. Jones fought these last two battles as a full Colonel. It must have been a source of great satisfaction to him. He had fought hard in continuous operations. Just before the negotiations were opened between Johnston and Sherman, the 8th Cavalry whipped Wade Hampton's entire force at Morrisville, and thus had the honor of fighting the last battle to be fought in North Carolina.

The 8th remained on duty in North Carolina until July 20, 1865 on which date Colonel Jones was mustered out as a brevet Brigadier General of Volunteers backdated to March 13, 1865. While the title, Brigadier General, has a nice ring to it, do not be overly impressed! E. J. Warner, the author of *Generals in Blue* writes, "brevet promotions had become almost as common as Good Conduct medals did later." During the Civil War the conferring of brevets in all grades was overdone. The brevets were highly valued especially among the volunteer officers just as Legion of Merit or the Silver Star is today. It is an acknowledgment by the military authority of the recipient's services. From a personal point of view, the ceremonial sword presented by the men he served with and the gold watch presented by his officers probably meant more to him than brevet rank he received shortly before discharge.

The unit was shipped home, reaching Indianapolis for a public reception on July 31 and a few days later the regiment was finally discharged. He did not return to Seymour, instead opting to move to Macon, Missouri, where he resumed his law practice. His wife, who had never moved to Seymour, did move to Macon but died in July 1866. He was twice elected prosecuting attorney in his judicial district and in 1870 took on the additional duty as editor of the Macon Republican. In politics he made an attempt to run for the State Senate but was defeated. In 1870 he married Sallie Clayton. As early as 1866 Jones realized that the wounds he received back in Tucker County, Virginia, were debilitating. He was granted a pension of $50 a month. A liver and a lung were injured in that action and eventually caused his death. He died shortly before his 49th birthday enroute to the scenes of his childhood, in Potter County, Pennsylvania, where his mother still resided.

Jones is an example of the citizen soldier our country has depended on from the very first days of the republic. The nation has the resources to keep a modest standing army and navy in peacetime. But in time of emergencies it must turn to its citizens to flesh out the divisions, the ships personnel, the flight crews and the maintenance shops. Thus it was in the Great War (1917–18) and World War II (1941–45). Whether by volunteers or by draft the citizen puts aside civilian duties and becomes after a time as skilled as the regular officer serving along side.

This was Fielder Jones, who began his preparation for military service back on the farm felling trees and hitching beasts of burden to haul them to a mill, who learned to fire a gun to kill game for the family table, who learned music to put himself through high school and college, who studied the military manual written by Confederate General Hardee and who lived to see action against that worthy foe in the final battles in North Carolina, and who attained a high rank in the service of his country.

What a price he paid—what a price his family paid. Fielder Jones and his brother both eventually died from war wounds, he from a gun fired from ambush at close range, his brother, Lt. Benjamin F. Jones, died from the ill treatment he had received as a prisoner of war in a Georgia camp. Before his death Benjamin fathered two sons, the eldest he named Willard, the younger was named after his famous uncle, Fielder A. Jones.[9]

CHAPTER SEVEN

McCallum and Military Railroads

THE CIVIL WAR MIGHT WELL be called a railroad war. In a previous chapter, mention was made of how Captain Fielder Jones and his 39th Indiana Regiment were carted off to battle to protect the Baltimore and Ohio, one of the important east to west rail connections of the period. In the first hostile act against the Federal Government, Stonewall Jackson set fire to the arsenal at Harper's Ferry, severed the main line of the railroad destroying seventeen bridges and then took possession of locomotives and rolling stock needed by the South. The haul was fifty-six locomotives and 350 cars and constituted the largest capture of railroad equipment that would be taken by either side during the entire war. As if this wasn't damage enough, Jackson's troops derailed a train of fifty coal cars into a chasm of the Potomac River and then torched it producing a fire that lasted for days!

Thus from the very first railroads became an attractive target. For an extended period of time the Baltimore and Ohio was useless.

Looking around for the original train snatcher? Look no further—Stonewall Jackson is your man! On the other side an experienced railroad veteran, George B. McClellan, moved his troops rapidly from Indiana and Ohio by rail to western Virginia, disembarked them at Grafton where they hit the unsuspecting Confederates a hard blow, and gave the Union its first taste of victory.

The North began the war with an enormous advantage. It had more than twice the mileage of all the Southern railroads combined. It had the rail beds where it counted—east to west. By the time the war began the North had four roads that could carry freight from the eastern seaboard to the midwest—the New York Central, the Erie, the Pennsylvania and the Baltimore and Ohio. The South had just two—one that led down through the Appalachian gap connecting Lynchburg with Knoxville and Chattanooga, and a second that connected the eastern seaboard with Atlanta, Montgomery, Jackson and Vicksburg on the Mississippi.

Jefferson Davis, who had been President Pierce's Secretary of War and should have been well tutored in the importance of quartermaster supply, must have overlooked the significance of rail transportation. President Lincoln, through his Secretary of War, Edwin Stanton, assumed the authority to take over all railroads. The South left the control of railroads in the hands of their civilian directors who gave the advantage to their own commercial car loadings rather than the needs of the military forces. Two bright experienced railroad men, Daniel McCallum and Herman Haupt, were appointed as directors of operations by the Union. In this McCallum's role will be highlighted. Haupt's service to the North was mainly in the eastern sector where he can be credited with bringing order out of the chaos following the two defeats the Army faced at 1st and 2nd Manassas. He left the service in mid-war to take care of one of his railroad properties. McCallum stayed the course, served the entire war with various titles. The one that suits him best was "military director and superintendent of railroads in the United States." In December 1863 he transferred his seat to the

MCCALLUM & MILITARY RAILROADS 95

Military Division of the Mississippi where he operated as General Grant's rail guru.

By the time McCallum had made the transfer from Washington to Nashville both sides had come to discover the nature, capacity and value of railroad lines. McCallum reorganized the Division of the Mississippi to counter the raids made by the South to disrupt supply lines. The military railroads of the west came under the direction of McCallum by General Grant's order of February 4, 1864, which gave him the position of General Manager of Military Railways in the West. Already on the books was special order No. 337 of the War Department which stated: "Commanding officers of troops along the United States military railroads will give all facilities to the officer of the roads for unloading cars so as to prevent any delay. On arrival at depots, whether in the day or night, the cars will be instantly unloaded, and working parties will always be in readiness for that duty. Any military officer who shall neglect his duty in this respect will be reported by the quartermasters and the officers of the railroad, and his name will be stricken from the rolls of the army. No officer, whatever may be his rank, will interfere with the running of the cars as directed by the superintendent of the road. Anyone who so interferes will be dismissed from the service for disobedience of orders."

Of this order McCallum wrote at the war's end: "The above order was given in consequence of several attempts having been made to operate railroads by army or department commanders, which had, without exception, proved signal failures, disorganizing in tendency, and destructive of all discipline. The great benefit resulting from this order was more especially exhibited during General Sherman's campaign from Chattanooga to Atlanta. Having had a somewhat extensive experience,[1] both before and after the rebellion, I consider this order of the Secretary of War to have been the very foundation of success; without it the whole railroad system, which has proved an important element in conducting military movements, would have been not only a costly, but a ludicrous failure."

Confederate raids forced the Construction Corps to do a good deal of repair work. One bridge had to be replaced five times, another four. Such tasks help to explain that the material and labor costs along the main line in 1864–65 was over $4,000,000. Altogether 130 miles of track were rebuilt and thirty-five water towers reconstructed. During the period just before Sherman's move from Chattanooga to Atlanta, 139 ten-ton cars loaded with food, ammunition, army supplies arrived at the base city each day. The northbound return trip featured empty cars, prisoners, and hospital cars.

One of the great difficulties facing the military railroads was recruiting experienced personnel. Due to the rapid growth of the railroads just prior to the war, there was a demand for skilled labor far in advance of the supply. Add to this the number that had seen fit to volunteer their service in the armed services, the modest pay being offered by the military railroads, it was difficult to attract skilled labor. Not only were the wages greater in the civilian sector, there was also the fact that the construction corps was subject to hardship, exposure and perils beyond any other non-combatant employee of the government—in many cases only equaled by the front line soldier. It was by no means unusual for a train crew to be out with their trains for five to ten days at a time, with little sleep and only such food as they had the foresight to pack along.

I became interested in this often overlooked branch of the military service because my grandfather, William Barton, who was working in Michigan at the time, signed up for a three and a half month service with Sub-Division 1, 4th Division Construction Corps of the U. S. Military Railroads, Division of the Mississippi. He served from mid-September to December 27, 1864. Although he served for a short period, he picked a time when memorable events were transpiring. On September 3rd Atlanta had fallen. Shortly Sherman would break away from the supply lines that had supplied 100,000 troops and 60,000 animals and, with 60,000, march to the sea. Conventional wisdom would suggest that this was great timing on Barton's part. He was twenty-nine at the time, recently widowed and already employed in his lifetime occupation of carpentry and masonry. The Construction Corps, that built bridges, laid track and siding and kept the supply lines running in spite of the vigorous efforts of Confederate forces to hinder them, could look forward to some less hazardous duty for a change now that Atlanta had been taken. In spite of his recent loss of that important city, General John Bell Hood was no conventional tactician. He had at his disposal an intact force of some 35,000. If his opponent would move east to Savannah, he would move west, destroy the Union supply lines and move north to the Ohio forcing Sherman to return and deal with him. No doubt these plans were aided and abetted by the success that Confederate cavalry commander Nathan Bedford Forrest had recently achieved in his Middle Tennessee campaign with a modest force of some 4,500 troopers. In two weeks time, September 22 to October 6, 1864, Forrest had captured 2400 blue coats, had destroyed eleven blockhouses, together with trestles and bridges they were meant to guard. He captured 600 horses, 2000 rifles, 100 wagons and ammunition beyond their ability to haul away. He also sent a fifty-man detachment to disrupt the main Nashville-Chattanooga line—which was quickly repaired by the Construction Corps. Later in October Forrest pulled off his most successful raid on the military supply depot at Johnsonville on the Tennessee River. On November 4th he destroyed three gunboats, eleven troop transports, eighteen barges and two warehouses. His raid caused millions of dollars in losses. Forrest estimated the damage he had caused at over six million dollars. Far more important was the moral factor. The message sent to friend and foe was simple—the South still packs a mighty punch!

Forrest returned to Tuscombia where he joined General Hood for the march north to confront the Union force under General Thomas, the "Rock of Chickamauga." Actually the march north was decided at Franklin—a battle the South could claim that it won. But in winning they took 6,000 casualties they could ill afford. When they finally faced the Union forces at Nashville, the attackers were outnumbered two to one, perhaps even three to one. The battle took place in November and ice cold December. By the time Barton's enlistment was up, Nashville had been defended and Hood was in retreat. The battle had lasted forty days. And during the siege, word had come that Savannah had fallen. The purpose of this move north to the Ohio was to make Sherman turn back from his eastward march forcing him to defend his supply line.

Uncle Billy, that's what his troops called the red-headed Ohioan, never flinched from his purpose, trusting that Thomas would deal with Hood. He did, although from reading dispatches it is clear that his superiors felt he should have done it in a shorter period of time. After the Battle of Nashville there were minor military actions in the west but none compared in size or importance.

After his service in the Construction Corps war my grandfather returned to civilian life, settling in Mansfield, Pennsylvania, where he worked as a foreman in building the Old Main building (since replaced) at the Normal School. He married an 1876 graduate of the Normal School, Kate Augusta Slingerland. With the recent interest in women's rights, has anyone given thought to the importance these two year colleges have had in achieving equality for women? They had three daughters, all three graduates of the Normal School. Rail service was such during Barton's life that he could commute from his home in Tioga County to any city, large or small, in his new home state. Apparently he never talked much about his war-related service. The only reference to his war service my mother could ever remember was his comment. "That's where I learned how to build bridges."

We do know that during the year 1864 there was feverish activity along the main supply line—Louisville to Nashville to Chattanooga in order to provide provisions for Sherman's advance on Atlanta. The single-track 185-mile supply line from Louisville to Nashville was augmented by the construction of a 78-mile rail bed between Nashville to Reynoldsburg on the Tennessee River to which supplies had been carried by water. In time this new rail connection used Johnsonville as the terminus on the Tennessee in place of Reynoldsburg. To complete this work, chief engineer, Col. W. W. Wright brought in 2000 laborers and mechanics from the north supplemented by the 1st Missouri Engineers, the 1st Michigan Engineers and the 12th & 13th Regiment of Colored Infantry. At Johnsonville (named for the military governor of the state, and shortly to become Vice-President) two large freight houses were built. Just as the work was completed Nathan Bedford Forrest's mounted troops appeared effectively negating this attempt to improve the Union supply lines. It is worth noting that when Hood and Forrest moved north for the confrontation at Nashville in late 1864, they destroyed 35 miles of track, 455 lineal feet of bridges but in less than two weeks the line was repaired and the trains were moving over its entire length.

A typical sub-division of the construction corps would look something like this:[2]

> Headquarters consisting of a division engineer and assistant, a rodman, a clerk, & two messengers: 6
> Train crew; conductors, fireman, engineers & brakemen: 11
> Bridge builders, mechanics and laborers: 300
> Track layers: 300
> Support staff—commissary, quartermaster, surgeon, blacksmith, cooks, masonry, ox brigade, maintenance of water stations: 65
> Total: 682

These sub-divisions could be expanded or contracted as the local situation might dictate. In all, 12,000 men served in the Military Railroads of the West during McCallum's superintendency. One of his principal jobs was the procurement of rolling stock, which required the active participation of the Secretary of War, Edwin Stanton, who addressed an appeal to the country's locomotive manufacturers on March 23, 1864 labeling it as "a military necessity paramount to all other considerations." The response of the manufacturers was immediate and they completed and delivered engines as fast as they were able. By the end of 1864 one hundred and forty new locomotives were delivered. Car deliveries were also high on the want list with some 200 deliveries per month. Beside all this new rolling stock, McCallum also leased equipment from railroads that had served the western theater prior to the war—such railroads as the Louisville and Nashville that provided 120 cars and fourteen engines. By the end of 1864 McCallum could show that his original estimate of 202 locomotives and 3000 cars in service had been met. To care for all of this equipment it was necessary to expand machine shops, car shops, and other repair facilities at both Nashville and Chattanooga. Every effort was made to center maintenance activity at these two centers. At the latter city the Union Forces had captured a rolling mill that gave the pennywise chief superintendent an idea. He communicated to Grant on February 17, 1864, still in command of the Military Command of the Mississippi, as follows:

"General: When the track of the Nashville and Chattanooga railroad is relaid, we will have on hand three hundred and two miles of old rails, weighing eleven thousand eight hundred and sixty-four gross tons. At present rate new rails delivered at Chattanooga will cost one hundred and forty-five dollars per ton.

"There is at Chattanooga a rolling mill partially built by the rebels, which if completed—say at a cost of thirty thousand dollars—these old rails can be rerolled at a cost of about fifty dollars per ton, coal being contiguous and abundant. This would not only be a large saving to the government, but what, in my opinion, is of greater importance, the rails would be on hand ready for use when and where required."[3] General Grant telegraphed his approval the same day.

But after an examination of the mill it was discovered that many of the essential parts of the mill were missing, the strong probability being that the former rebel operators removed them. The decision was made to build with entirely new machinery and before long it was decided that the mill should be located within the Union's defensive perimeter. When the mill was finished it was not a rebuilt version of the Confederate mill, but an entirely new mill with entirely new machinery. The cost was just over $290,000 and it didn't open until April 1, 1865 when the war was pretty much over.

The mill with its out buildings and rail lines was entirely built by the Construction Corps and stands out as one of its major achievements. It was employed for the manufacture of rails for six months and five days and turned out just over 3818 tons of new rails at an average cost per ton of $34.42—far less than the $50 per ton estimate he had early made to Grant. One gets the impression that this man McCallum knew where every dollar was spent during his period as superintendent. Of course he had good bookkeepers who kept the boss informed. The other impression the reader gets is that he was proud of what these civilian employees were able to accomplish.

He writes in his report to the Secretary of War: "Since the end of the rebellion, I have been informed by railroad officers who were in the service of the enemy during the war, that they were less surprised at the success of General Sherman, in a military point of view, than they were at the rapidity with which railroad breaks were repaired, and the regularity with which trains were moved to the front."

General Sherman is fulsome in his praise of the military railroads in his Memoirs. "The Atlanta Campaign would simply have been impossible without the use of railroads. That single stem of a railroad supplied an army of 100,000 men and 35,000 horses for the period of 196 days. To have delivered that amount of forage and food by ordinary wagons would have required 38,800 wagons of six mules each, a simple impossibility in such roads as existed in that region."

Perhaps the greatest compliment the construction corps ever had, didn't come from any high ranking Blue or Gray officer, but from Confederate enlisted men serving in Johnston's army as they slowly and reluctantly fell back towards Atlanta under constant pressure from Sherman's force. They were convinced the General had spare bridges stashed just waiting to be used as replacements.

Too often they had seen someone like cavalryman Joe Wheeler rip up tracks and before nightfall see in the distance Union trains chugging down the supposedly damaged rail bed.

General O. O. Howard, one of the corps commanders, said that the thing that impressed him the most was "the rapidity with which the badly broken bridge was repaired. We had hardly left Dalton before trains with ammunition and other supplies arrived. While our skirmishing was going on at Calhoun, the locomotive whistle sounded at Resaca. The telegraphers were nearly as rapid: the lines were in order to Adairsville on the morning of the 18th."[4] (These Georgia place names are important way stations along the path from Chattanooga to Atlanta where highly contested battles were fought.)

The Construction Corps was at all times prepared for any emergency, either bridge building of some formidable size, or laying miles of track. Attacks on the main supply lines were so frequent that to insure speedy repairs, detachments were scattered along the line together with the basic tools and materials necessary for the job hid in places well out of sight.

One last story about Daniel McCallum and his resourcefulness. As the war progressed, his superintendency, initially limited to the west, was extended to the entire military rail system. It is not surprising to learn that when Sherman reached Savannah, a portion of the Construction Corps was ordered in December of 1864 to proceed to Baltimore by rail and embark for Savannah. "Upon reaching Hilton Head, information was received that General Sherman would not use the railroads near Savannah, and orders were given to proceed to New Bern. North Carolina, and open the railroad to Goldsboro. On February 6th the construction corps from the Division of the Mississippi landed at Morehead City and relieved a corps from Virginia that had just finished rebuilding a bridge over one of the streams to be found in the eastern part of the state. The roadbed was repaired as fast as the army advanced and was opened to Goldsboro, March 25, 1865, the day following the arrival of

General Sherman and his army. To provide another source of supplies, a line 85 miles long, between Goldsboro and Wilmington was repaired and opened April 4th. When military operations resumed on April 10 the rail line was extended to Raleigh and Hillsboro. During this eastern excursion by the division, 293 miles of usable rail were added. The division added some 3,263 lineal feet of bridges and a new wharf at Morehead City covering an area of 53,682 square feet, and consuming 700,000 feet of timber. Can't you imagine the glee of the civilian owners of this railroad when the rail bed was returned to them at the close of the war? Everything in ship shape order. No doubt the attitude of the superintendent was—we've got the skilled labor—let's keep them at important tasks and keep them happy.

This brief account of military railroads during the war must not leave the impression that the destruction of rail beds, cars and bridges was something that only the South engaged in. That they were masters of this military practice cannot be denied. But when the occasion demanded, the Union could match them. When Sherman's troops gradually surrounded Atlanta they cut the rail lines out of the city, one by one, until Hood was forced to abandon the city. When Sherman marched east to the sea he broke up the West Point Railroad, one of the principal supply lines, lest Hood try to put it back in commission. His troops became highly skilled in operations of this sort. "The track was heaved up in sections the length of a regiment, then separated rail by rail; bonfires were made of the ties and of fence rails on which the rails were heated, carried to trees or telegraph poles, wrapped around and left to cool." These twisted loops were called Sherman ties. And then they added a new wrinkle. They filled up deep cuts with trees, brush, and earth and commingled with loaded shells arranged so that any repair party would have a difficult time.[5] The war was over and all property returned to its owners. The Construction Corps threw on the labor market close to 24,000 workers experienced in some phase of the railroading enterprise. The actual number of persons employed by the two divisions, east and west is hard to come by, because of the constantly changing needs of the service. It is fair to say that in the great growth of the railroads following the war, many of the engineers, conductors, laborers, bridge men and masons honed their skills in the United States Military Railroads.[6]

CHAPTER EIGHT

Sheridan in the West

THE THREE GREAT GENERALS OF the Union were Grant, Sherman and Sheridan. The three had several things in common. All were West Point graduates. All were born in Ohio. All spent time in the prewar west. Grant served as a Captain at Columbia Barracks, Fort Vancouver, Washington Territory, 1852–54 before resigning his commission. Sherman left the service and became a banker in San Francisco. Sheridan, youngest of the three, served in Oregon and Washington Territory from 1854 to the beginning of the Civil War in 1861.

Grant has some nice things to say about the Northwest. His wife, Julia Dent Grant, did not wish to live on the frontier, and the future president of the United States perforce lived the life of a single man during his stint at the barracks. One consequence of this situation was that he wrote his wife with circumspect regularity. The letters were saved and eventually printed in his *Memoirs*. This he had to say in his December 19,

1852 letter, "So far as I have seen it opens the richest chances for poor persons who are willing and able, to work, either in cutting wood, saw logs, raising vegetables, poultry or stock of any kind, of any place I have seen. Timber stands close to the banks of the river free for all. The soil produces almost double it does any place I have been."[1] All this praise in spite of a severe winter with snow at least ten inches deep, an almost unheard of condition at this low elevation. For anybody born and raised in the mid-west a mere ten inches must have seemed like child's play. One other comment in the *Memoirs* that is revealing, in view of our interest in railroad transportation, is an entry dated October 25, 1853 written to Major Osborn Cross complaining about the workload. "The constant, and unremitting, calls upon the time, both of myself and clerk, consequent upon the fitting out of the expeditions connected with Northern Pacific railroad survey, in addition to the current duties of the office..."[2]

The Northern Pacific wasn't chartered until 1864. Interest in a rail route from the Great Lakes to the Pacific goes back to a period well before the war years. The governor of the Washington Territory, Isaac I. Stevens, was in charge of the party that was to explore the line from the Twin Cities in Minnesota, to the Rocky Mountains, while Captain George McClellan was in charge of the western section. Since both Stevens and McClellan were Army men and trained engineers, it is not surprising that officers assigned to barracks in the northwest were used in the survey. Grant would soon be on his way to Galena, Illinois to join his father in the tannery business.

Sheridan is singled out in these pages because of the years he spent in the Northwest and for his extensive remarks that deal with the region. A section of his *Memoirs*, "Indian Fighting in the Fifties" has at times been published as a separate book. It is a revealing picture of what it must have been like to be an officer in the pre-Civil War army in the West. He had a rocky time at West Point. He should have graduated with the class of 1852, but a little matter of a fistfight between Sheridan and the cadet officer of the day caused the fiery Ohioan to be expelled for a year. During the period of expulsion he went back to his hometown in Somerset, Ohio, where his father had once worked on the National Road. There he served as the bookkeeper of the town's general store. Actually those nine months with Finch & Ditoes, where he ordered merchandise and paid the bills, were like a post-graduate course. When he did graduate a year later he was assigned first to a unit in Texas and then to the Department of the West in San Francisco, under the command of Major General John B. Wool.

Sheridan and other young officers languished for years in the same frozen rank. In Sheridan's case he served for eight years before being promoted to First Lieutenant in March 1861 and then given his Captain's bars two months later. Like many a lonely young officer at isolated posts Sheridan found a female companion in Frances Sednayoh, the daughter of Indian Chief Quately of the Willamette Valley Klikitats. She began living with the young Lieutenant at Fort Hoskins. Sheridan makes no mention of this in his *Memoirs*. He met her in Washington, D.C. many years later. She was in the capitol on behalf of Indian rights.[3] Sheridan was proud of the fact that he could speak in Chinook, which he described as the "court language" for the coastal tribes, almost as well as the Indians themselves.

When Sheridan was first ordered to the Northwest he relieved Lieutenant John Bell Hood (who would leave the Army and become a general in the Confederate cause). When he relieved Hood the troops did not like the change. They expressed this in various ways that enlisted men have of testing a new officer. "With appreciative and unremitting care, together with firm and just discipline, soon quieted all symptoms of dissatisfaction and overcame all prejudice." In time he was able to make of them a cohesive and obedient detachment. "In the past year they had made long and tiresome marches, forded swift mountain streams, constructed rafts of logs or bundles of dry reeds to ferry our baggage, swum deep rivers, marched on foot to save their worn-out and exhausted animals, climbed mountains, fought Indians and in all and everything had done the best they could for the service and their commander. The disaffected feeling they entertained when I first assumed command soon wore away, and it its place came a confidence and respect which gives me the greatest pleasure to remember, for small though it was, this was my first cavalry command."[4]

Much of Sheridan's time was spent at two forts, Siletz and Hoskins. He was sent to the Indian Agency at Siletz in the summer of 1856 to protect the agent from unhappy and hungry Indians. He brought along with him several heads of cattle to feed the Indians. Sheridan posted four guards to protect the distribution of meat. The Indians, too, formed a circle around the guards and were bent on taking care of the distribution on the spot. Sheridan was joined in the middle of the circle by Chief Tetooney John and two other Indians. The Chief's conciliatory words calmed the famished Indians. Soon the rest of Sheridan's detachment arrived to supervise the fair and equal distribution of the meat. Fearing that the Indians might break out of the reservation provided for them along the coast, the remainder of Sheridan's company was rushed out from Fort Yamhill, some thirty miles away. Their three forts, Siletz, Hoskins and Yamhill, were all scattered along the coastal range in what is today Yamhill, Polk and Benton counties. These forts were occupied all during the Civil War period and abandoned shortly thereafter.

Corporal Royal A. Bensell kept a diary of the time spent at these posts. Bensell, the son of a miner, came north with a contingent of sixty-six men from Volcano, California. Company D, Fourth Infantry, passed through the Golden Gate on the Steamer *Cortez* and arrived at Fort Vancouver on November 1, 1861. On the following day the company was assigned to garrison Fort Yamhill. In keeping with the policy of replacing regulars with hastily trained volunteers, Bensell's company relieved I Company, Ninth Infantry that had been ordered east. The precise location of Fort Yamhill was a source of some controversy for a number of years. When it was closed down and all useful accoutrements disposed of at auction for $1,260.00, the blockhouse was moved from Polk County north to the Indian Agency at Grand Ronde, Yamhill County. Then, because of his illustrious military career, the name of General Sheridan was given credit for things he never claimed in life— among them the building of the block house. William B. Hazen, another future Union general, who served as commanding officer of the Fort in the mid-50s clearly is the builder. "I shall proceed at once to build a Block House," Hazen informed the Adjutant general in Washington on March 31, 1856, six days after establishing his camp near Grand Ronde. Sheridan has a city in the western portion of Yamhill County named for him. In 1910 the blockhouse, often repaired, was moved to the city park in Dayton, a port city on the Yamhill River, where it can still be viewed.

Bensell began every entry in his diary with a brief weather report.[5] Take his last entry on July 6, 1965: "Clear. Start early in the morning for home. Bid all hands good Bye. Stop at several neighbors [sic] houses and do the same. As I crossed the Yamhill I turned in my saddle and gazed perhaps for the last time on the place where I saw so much of human nature, some good and some bad. Altho' I regret to part with so many friends I feel proud to know I earned their friendship by respecting myself, and I am happy to feel that if ever I am tossed to this part of the world again it will be to find true friends."

Although Bensell speaks of leaving for home, it was not Volcano he had in mind. He filed a claim on land near Yaquina Bay where he and a partner built a sawmill. The 1870 census lists him as a lumberman. Newport became the center of his activities. He was one of the first to urge the completion of a railroad that would connect the coast with the Willamette Valley. In 1876 he served a full term in the Oregon State House representing Benton County. He was justice of the peace at Newport and collector of customs for the Yaquina Bay District during the Hayes and Harrison administrations. He was elected mayor of Newport four times. Bensell had married three years after his discharge. He died in 1921. The paper that carried his obituary still carried his old familiar ad: R. A. Bensell, Notary Public, a resident of the Bay since 1866. Deeds, Mortgages, etc., carefully prepared.[6]

When Sumter was fired upon by the Confederates in April of 1861, Sheridan was on duty at Yamhill. In short order, the regulars, officer and enlisted, were shipped off to the East. Sheridan was to be relieved by a Captain James J. Archer of the Ninth Infantry. It was rumored that Archer intended "to go south," a euphemism employed by Sheridan, meaning to desert. So Sheridan refused to hand over the command to him. Finally the news came that he had been granted a leave of two months. By September first relief finally came and Sheridan was free to go. During the four-month wait, news came of the Union loss at Bull Run. The accounts of the battle were greatly distorted. It was stated that each side had lost 40,000 men killed and wounded. Forty thousand! That was more men than were in the whole peacetime army. Week by week the losses were toned down, until finally they had shrunk to a few hundred.

"We received our mail at Yamhill once a week, and then had to bring it from Portland, Oregon, by express. On the day of the week that our courier, or messenger, was expected back from Portland, I would go out early in the morning to a commanding point above the post, from which I could see a long distance down the road as it ran through the valley of Yamhill, and there I would watch with anxiety for his coming, longing for good news: for, isolated as I had been through years spent in the wilderness, my patriotism was untainted by politics, nor had it ever been disturbed by any discussion of the questions out of which the war grew, and I hoped for the success of the government above all other considerations. I was ready to do my duty to the best of my ability wherever I might be called, and I was young, healthy, insensible to fatigue."[7]

A two-day ride took him to Portland where he boarded a ship bound for San Francisco. There he transferred to another ship and took the usual route, San Francisco to the Isthmus of Panama, transferring to still a third ship which took him to New York. From New York he traveled half way across the continent to his new assignment as quartermaster of the Army of Southwest Missouri. With Sheridan as quartermaster, the Army soon learned that there were no supply problems. From Missouri he was transferred to join Major General Halleck in Tennessee where he was in charge of the commissary, and in short order the general's camp was run efficiently. With time on his hands Sheridan began to look around for a command that would give him a chance to improve his fighting skill. The Governor of Michigan, Austin Blair, was in need of a regular Army colonel to head up the Second Michigan Cavalry, and Sheridan got the job. By June 24, 1963 Sheridan found himself in command of the Third Division, 20th Corps, of the Army of the Cumberland with the rank of Major General.[8] After all those years stuck at the bottom of the promotion ladder, the little Ohioan had suddenly discovered pay dirt. In his *Memoirs* the composition of the Division is outlined, unit-by-unit. It was here that I "discovered" Lieutenant Colonel Fielder A. Jones, of the 39th Indiana Mounted Infantry, the citizen soldier we have already met. Sheridan's unit fought in some memorable battles—Stone's River, Chickamauga and Missionary Ridge where he had the good fortune to be under the watchful eye of General Grant. In the future where Grant would go, Sheridan would be sure to follow.

When Grant went east to command the Army of the Potomac, he went with one idea—to end the war, now in its fourth spring. The North now had roughly a two-to-one advantage in men at arms. Grant proposed to improve these odds by seeing that there was no rest in any quarter. He would send his troops on the attack on every front until something broke. He would keep his foes off balance by this unremitting pressure and never again would they be able to move troops from one sector to another without paying a stiff price. Finally he would subtract the Confederate strength in the field by a one-by-one dwindling of defenders. Grant and Sherman were among the disciples of Dennis Hart Mahon, who had taught the concentration of massed forces on the enemies' weakest point and the need to harry a foe without rest and then the revolutionary proposition that the defeat of an enemy army, not a strategic position on the map, was the great object of the campaign.

Sheridan's command, called the Army of the Shenandoah had 35,000 men at arms. Moreover he could call on additional support from the Army of West Virginia, commanded by his oldest and dearest friend, Major General George Crook. Sheridan's *Memoirs*[9] is the book to pull out of the library shelf for a full description of the Cavalry raid of May-June 1864 and the decisive battles fought in the Shenandoah Valley. Actually the Confederate General Early had made the Union forces pay dearly for their victory in the valley. The Union had roughly a thousand more casualties than the Southern force. But it was a vindication of the Mahon doctrine. Early lost a fourth of his outnumbered command, Sheridan less than an eighth.

What captures the imagination of the North was not so much Sheridan's victorious ride through the Shenandoah, as his horse, Rienzi. The horse was a gift from one of the young officers on the staff. Rienzi was a three year old of Morgan stock. He was jet black, excepting three white feet, strongly built, with great powers of endurance. This was the horse that Sheridan rode from

BOOK COVER USED ON *MEMOIRS*

Winchester to Cedar Creek and in every campaign he was involved in to the war's end.

At the urging of retired actor James E. Murdoch (no relation) who had visited Sheridan's camp a year earlier at Chattanooga to claim the body of his son, a poet, Thomas Buchanan Read unburdened himself of a sixty-three line poem called "Sheridan's Ride."

It was no masterpiece, the best lines going to the horse. Debuted by Murdoch in Cincinnati's Pike Opera House, March 1, 1864, the poem took the North by storm. When Lincoln swamped his Democratic rival, McClellan, a week later, many credited the poem with swelling the rout. Generations of children yet unborn would stand at the head of the class, reciting the epic, as once again the great horse Rienzi completed his twenty-mile ride and announces:

With foam and with dust the black charger was grey;
By the flash of his eye, and his nostril's play,

He seemed to the whole great army to say,
I have brought you Sheridan all the way
From Winchester down, to save the day.

There is no doubt about it, in Sheridan the North had at last found a Cavalry commander every bit as daring as Jeb Stuart, Lee's chief of reconnaissance. In an acrimonious confrontation with General Meade, Grant's choice to lead the Army of the Potomac, Sheridan said that he could whip Stuart if Meade would let him, but since he insisted giving his cavalry directions without consulting its commander, he could jolly well command the cavalry. And one very angry Sheridan stamped out. Meade repeated the conversation to Grant mentioning that Sheridan could whip Stuart. "Did he say so? Then let him go out and do it." Three divisions of mounted troops left Fredericksburg on May 8, 1864. They took three day's rations for the 12,000 men, and half rations of grain for the horses. Riding four abreast and moving at a walk the column was thirteen miles in length. Not concerned much with deception nor speed, Sheridan's command depended on power, the ability of this force to destroy anything that got in its way. Each trooper was armed with rapid-fire carbines. Southward, the line of march stretched out across the tributaries of the Mattaponi rivers and reached Chilesburg on May 9, with Stuart's brigades in full pursuit.

The crash between these two forces took place at Yellow Tavern just miles away from the Confederate capitol. Sheridan's troopers were not headed from Richmond, though it loomed up large and inviting on their right flank. They were headed for Haxall's Landing where they hooked up with Butler's Union force trying to assail Richmond from Petersburg. The mounted force reached the Union lines by May 14 bringing with them 400 freed Union prisoners plus some 300 captured Confederate defenders. How many of the enemy had been killed or wounded could not be determined, but Sheridan was aware that in the fight at Yellow Tavern, Stuart had been mortally wounded. After three days rest with General Butler, Sheridan's raiders were off for their northward march to rejoin Meade and Grant. In two weeks and a day these three divisions had approached the very gates of the enemy capitol. The need for rations and provisions deterred them from the temptation to harass the defenders of that city. Lee was bereft of an able commander, but he managed to keep the Blue forces of Meade and Butler at bay for close to a year. As for Sheridan, his famous ride down the Shenandoah was still before him.

After the war Sheridan was dispatched by Grant to proceed to take charge of the West of the Mississippi command. His duty was "to restore Texas and that part of Louisiana held by the enemy, to the Union in the shortest practicable time, in a way most effectual for securing permanent peace." Of great concern to the government in Washington, now under Andrew Johnson, was the existence of a Confederate Army under Major General Kirby Smith, which had not surrendered at the time this order was issued on May 17, 1865. To do this Sheridan would have placed under his command all the troops that could be spared by Major General Canby, the Union commander of the force then west of the Mississippi, some twenty-five thousand men at arms. Before Sheridan arrived at his new command he received word from Canby that Smith had surrendered under the same terms accorded to Lee and Johnston.

Smith may have surrendered but some of his Texas troops marched off to the center of the state taking with them arms, munitions, camp equipage, intending (so the rumor mill had it) to join forces with the Emperor Maxmillian's French-Austrian puppet state. Sheridan was strongly tempted to take up the cause of Benito Juarez and the Republic of Mexico's side and ride across the border to rid the continent of a French presence once and for all. But the patient hand of William H. Seward, Secretary of State, intervened. No act was to be taken which would involve the country in war. This would not be the only clash Sheridan would have with the new Johnson Administration. After a stormy period as Military Commander of the Fifth District, Texas and Louisiana, Sheridan found himself right in the center of two conflicting views of the reconstruction period. One view, attributed to President Johnson, would rehabilitate the seceded states under conditions that existed before the rebellion, without the slightest regard to the status of the emancipated freedmen. In the other view, representing the majority in both the Senate and the House the states that had seceded would be divided into military districts and returned to their former status only after rehabilitation.

Amid all of its numerous provisions of the reconstruction Laws, the one that became an obstacle for those supporting the President's view, was the loyalty oath "that I will faithfully support the Constitution and obey the laws of the United States." The first of these laws was passes March 2, 1867, vetoed by President Johnson, passes by both Houses over his veto and became the law of the land on March 11th. Great powers resided in the hands of the several Military District commanders. Before he was through, Sheridan had to remove from office the Mayor of New Orleans, the Chief of Police of the same city, a judge from a district court, the Attorney General of Louisiana, and eventually the governor of the state.

In his report to secretary of War, Edwin Stanton, Sheridan writes: "Governor Wells is a political trickster and a dishonest man. I have seen him myself, when I first came to this command, turn out all the Union men who had supported the Government and put in their stead rebel soldiers who had not yet doffed their gray uniforms...His conduct has been as sinuous as the mark left in the dust by the movement of a snake." Do you get the impressions that Little Phil didn't like this guy? It turns out that General Steadman, who can best be described as president Johnson's personal contact in the Fifth District, wrote to President: "My conviction is that on account of the bad character of Wells and Monroe (the mayor of New Orleans), you ought not to reinstate any who have been removed."

Sheridan's next assignment placed him at Fort Leavenworth, Kansas, where he was placed in command of two states and two territories—Missouri, Kansas, Indian Territory and New Mexico. He would first serve under General Sherman, and eventually take over command of the whole of the western frontier. This duty on the plains was the common lot of those who elected to continue their service in the army. Sherman and Sheridan were among the lucky ones who had been promoted on the regular list. Some of the prominent generals of the war years, who received brevet promotions, after the war reverted to their permanent rank. It must have been a humbling experience for those who went from Brigadier General back to a permanent rank of Captain. For most officers and men of the regular army, the west was where the action was. A growing number of the enlisted personnel were often recent arrivals from Europe, seeking to secure a foothold in this new land. This was not the kind of duty that gave those involved a feeling of accomplishment. Little by little the strength of the Army was whittled away until it seemed to each field commander that it was impossible to provide all the services demanded.

When Grant came to the Presidency in March 1869 one of his first acts was to appoint Sherman to command the Army. Sheridan was promoted to Lieutenant General and assigned to head the Division of the Missouri with headquarters at Fort Leavenworth. This was where the action was and President Grant wanted one of his most competent subordinates to head the operation. Sheridan's participation in the Plains War of 1868 and what followed is typical of the post Civil War life of senior military officers. They were asked to do much with little in the way of manpower resources. We will save the details for a later chapter on one of the connector railroad lines, the Kansas Pacific.

In 1883, when Sherman retired, Sheridan was appointed as his successor and became a four-star General. One assignment in these last years of active service that he enjoyed was a trip to Europe to observe the Franco-Prussian War. The Kaiser and Count Bismarck received him and his party. In all, Sheridan spent almost a year overseas. By his own account, at age thirty-three when in command of the Army of the Shenandoah, he was five foot five and weighed one hundred fifteen pounds. The advancing years were not kind to the general. As a hero of the war he was wined and dined a bit too often. Gradually with the passing years he became a rotund figure—as one can tell from photographs of the general as he approached his fifty-seventh and last year. He lived long enough to finish his memoirs. His writing "penned by my own hand" speaks well of the education he received at West Point.

He became, during the Reconstruction period, the idol of the Radicals, although it is fair to add that he had no overt political motivation nor aspired to political office. The Indian wars he and his troops fought may have been a popular theme for the old cowboy and Indian movies of my youth. Today they are looked upon as an embarrassment. Still they are part of the story of our great struggle for national existence, and as Corporal Bensell observed, some of it good, and some bad. Little Phil was that kind of a mix. When he put the Shenandoah Valley to the torch to deny the Confederacy its breadbasket, he injured countless numbers of Mennonite farmers, a peace loving denomination that took no stand on the moral merits of the war. Was that a bad act? Or did it shorten the war, and did that make it a good act? That is a sample of the kind of decisions a field commander must make. At the very least give Little Phil his due—like the fighter he was at West Point, he never avoided the tough decision.

The first that the General saw were the groups
Of stragglers, and then the retreating troops;
What was done,—what to do,—
A glance told him both,
And, striking his spurs with a terrible oath,
He dashed down the line mid a storm of huzzahs,
And the wave of retreat checked its course there, because
The sight of the master compelled it to pause.
And when their statues are placed on high,
Under the dome of the Union sky
The American soldier's Temple of Fame,
There with the glorious General's name
Be it said in letters both bold and bright:
Here is the steed that saved the day
By carrying Sheridan into the fight,
From Winchester, twenty miles away![10]

CHAPTER NINE

Wright, Protector of the West

GEORGE WRIGHT WAS BORN IN Norwich, Vermont, Oct. 21, 1803, into a family that had strong military ties. A cousin on his mother's side, Alden Partridge, had recently been the Superintendent of the Military Academy at West Point. Young George arrived at the academy after a year at the Partridge Military Academy eventually known as the Norwich Military Academy.[1] Sylvanus Thayer, often referred to as "the father of West Point" was the superintendent. Wright graduated in 1822 and received a commission as Second Lieutenant at the age of 18. The Army that Wright was to serve in for forty-three years had been limited to seven regiments of infantry and four of artillery—which adds up to roughly 5,200 men. His first assignment was at Fort Howard that guarded the east end of the Fox-Wisconsin waterway between Lake Michigan and the Mississippi River. Here he had his first taste of frontier duty in which he would spend more than half of his military service. He later served at

Jefferson Barracks, St. Louis, and Fort Leavenworth in Kansas. His first touch of actual warfare came in the Seminole War and then in the War with Mexico 1846–48.

He was wounded at the Battle of Molino del Rey while serving with General William J. Worth's 8th Infantry. "To Brevet Major Wright I am greatly indebted for the assistance he rendered on all occasions and particularly in forming the troops and moving them on to the assault." Worth reported to the War Department. He was promoted to Lieutenant Colonel and later to full Colonel. After the war he was assigned to the 4th Infantry that was ordered to the west arriving at Benicia, California in late August 1852. Of the five hundred recruits which had preceded the main body earlier in the year, one hundred had gone AWOL and headed to the gold fields, not so surprising when you discover that privates were paid sixteen dollars per month. Wright was placed in command of the northern district based at Redding, California.

In 1855 Wright was given command of the 9th Regiment of Infantry. Yes, the peacetime Army was growing, now there were nine regiments of infantry! The regiment embarked on the steamer *St. Louis* arriving at Aspinwall, Panama, in ten days. The crossing of the isthmus by rail was expeditious. Staff and troops boarded the steamer *Oregon* on the afternoon of the same day of arrival. The destination was Oregon. On his way to the northwest the ship encountered General Wool, Commander of the Department of the Pacific on his way back to San Francisco after a visitation of the Columbia River District. He ordered Wright to take over command of that district and to move his headquarters from Ft. Vancouver to Ft. Dallas to be nearer the scene of action developing in the Washington Territory and Idaho where over 7,000 emigrants passed over the Oregon Trail in to the Pacific Northwest.

The strength of the Ninth Regiment was given by the then Lieutenant Philip H. Sheridan, who had recently been assigned to this command: twenty-seven officers, two surgeons, and 736 enlisted bring the total of regular army troops serving in the northwest to 2,000. Congress, due to the passage of the Donation Land Law, passed the movement of this large number of emigrants in 1850 to encourage settlement in this area. The protection of these settlers and miners was from the first of paramount importance to the Department of the Pacific commander down in San Francisco, whoever he might be. We might note in passing that some of the future general officers who were to win fame in the Civil War served in this Department. Grant served at the Columbia Barracks Fort Vancouver as a Regimental Quartermaster in the 1850s.

It was from his post in the Northwest that Grant decided to call his military career quits. Accordingly he resigned his commission in 1854 and was in private employment back home in the mid-west before returning to the service in 1861.

Sherman served in California during the Mexican War, and in 1853 he returned to set up a branch bank of a St. Louis firm. He was eminently successful in this venture and in 1857 moved to New York and eventually practiced law in Leavenworth, Kansas before his return to active duty in 1861. So of the three Union General officers who achieved lasting fame in the War, Grant, Sherman and Sheridan, it is fair to point out that all three received some of their pre-war training in the Department of the Pacific.

Sheridan is a special case. He didn't resign his commission. He spent most of his pre-war service in the West, much of it in Yamhill County, Oregon, where a town is named for him. Sheridan graduated from West Point in 1853 years after the Mexican War and at the time of his graduation the Army had reverted to its pre-Mexican War strength of 13,821. Lieutenants at this time received twenty-five dollars a month and promotions were glacially slow. It was not unusual for qualified officers to need at least thirty years of service to qualify for major. Alone among the Union "big three" Sheridan, in his *Memoirs*, gives his readers vivid details of what it was like to serve on the frontier and for that reason he rates a special section in this book. It is worth reflecting that when Second Lieutenant Philip H. Sheridan reported for duty in the Department of the Pacific, George Wright was a full Colonel, his senior by some thirty-one years.

Wright's commands in the West began at Redding in Northern California, then with the Columbia River District, the Oregon District, the Southern California District and on October 26, 1861 he assumed command of the Department of the Pacific, a position he would hold until July 1, 1864.

In his first report to the Adjutant General Wright reveals that his primary concern was to discern what action to take against the large pro-secessionist group that existed throughout the West on the eve of that war. Many of the early emigrants had come overland from the mid-west and in particular from the states of Iowa and Missouri. That pattern continued during the war years with pro-union and pro-secessionist often in the same wagon train. The presidential election of 1860 provides a good indicator of just how strong the support for the South was. The majority party of the recent past was the Democratic Party, and now that party held two conventions, one nominating Stephen Douglas and the other nominating Breckinridge and Lane. The new Republican Party combining Free Soilers, Conscience Whigs and anti-slave sections of the Democratic Party in the northeast was represented by Abraham Lincoln and a fourth party, the Constitutional Union Party nominated John Bell of Tennessee. Lincoln gained the electoral vote of Oregon by the slim margin of 217 votes. Breckinridge, whose running mate was Oregon's Senator, Joseph Lane, carried eight counties, Lincoln seven, Douglas four. John Bell was a factor on the national level, gaining more electoral votes than the better-known Douglas. But in the west he gained little support. At least two western governors gave open indications of their sympathy for the South.

For the two Department of the Pacific commanders, first Sumner and then Wright, to express concern over these disloyal elements isn't something they dreamed up. It was an ever-present matter that required constant surveillance. "For several weeks past small parties have been organizing in the Southern District of this State, with the avowed purpose of proceeding to Texas to aid the rebels. To enable me to frustrate their designs I have seized all the boats and ferries on the Colorado River, and have them strongly guarded. I have reinforced Ft. Yuma with two more companies, one of infantry and one of cavalry. Major Rigg, First California Volunteers Infantry...has arrested a man by the name of Showalter, a notorious secessionist, and his party of seventeen men. I have ordered the whole party to be taken to Ft. Yuma and securely guarded until further orders."[2]

A statement was taken from each of the alleged secessionists of which the following from F. N. Chum is typical. "I am from Texas; was born in Choctaw County, Miss.; left Mississippi when quite young; am thirty years of age; came to California in 1856 from Arkansas; considered Texas my home; am a laborer by occupation; lived in Tuolumne County mostly; my last residence was in Los Angeles...my object in going to Texas was to see my aged mother, whom I am anxious to see once more; had no intention of taking up arms against the Government of the United States; consider myself a good and loyal citizen of the United States; am perfectly willing to take the oath of allegiance."[3] Major Rigg observes that all of the men in the party were armed with a rifle and a pair of revolvers.

The Showalter Party gave Riggs men a hard chase and finally chose not to resist. Some, like Chum, were visiting aged relatives, and others swore they were on their way to Sonora where new mines were opening. Many of them avowed they were strong Union men. The Official Records do not spell out the details on what happened to this party, but we do know that Dan Showalter took the oath and was released making his way to

Texas later fighting for the Confederacy. Showalter, we learn, had been a member of the California Legislature and had killed a fellow member named Percy in a duel. We also learn that Showalter had never set a foot on southern soil until the war. He was a Pennsylvanian by birth "proud to fight...with a people who have contended so gallantly for their liberties against such fearful odds."[4] There were many cases of regular officers "marrying south." Perhaps the best-known case was the Confederate defender of Vicksburg, John Pemberton, another Pennsylvanian, whose wife was from Old Point Comfort, Virginia. And on the Union side there was the example of George H. Thomas, a Virginia born West Pointer, "marrying north", his wife coming from Troy, New York. He won fame as "the Rock of Chickamauga." Thomas was yet another of the Union's heroes to have served in the Department of the West, serving at Ft. Yuma, one of the most remote stations in the country.

This might be proper time to list the General officers who bore the title Commanding General of the Department of the West during the period preceding and following the war:

    Albert Sidney Johnston from Jan. 15, 1861 to April 25, 1861[5]
    Edwin V. Sumner from April 25, 1861 to Oct. 26, 1861
    George Wright from Oct. 26, 1861 to July 1, 1864
    Irvin McDowell from July 1, 1864 to July 27, 1865
    Henry Halleck from July 27, 1865 to 1869

McDowell and Halleck were senior Major Generals when appointed, the latter having been General-in-Chief during much of the war. Johnston and Sumner were Brig. Generals, and Wright, a Colonel when appointed, was promoted to Brig. General in the Volunteers three days after his elevation to Department commander. In addition to his term in this office of two years, eight months, six days—he refers to it in his farewell communiqué as three years—he spent another ten years in various districts throughout the West in Oregon, Washington

Territory and California. "I point with pride to the happy and peaceful condition of this country. Entrusted as I have been with a high and responsible command, far removed from the seat of the General Government, I have during the whole period held in my hands the power of peace or war. Had I for a moment yielded to the insane demands of a radical press and its collaborators I should have filled my forts with political prisoners to gratify personal hatred, causing such an outburst of indignation at such a course as to render it almost certain that civil war and bloodshed would have followed."[6]

Promotions came fast and furious for many during the Civil War period. The need for some kind of military experience was such that any recent graduate of West Point was welcomed back to active duty at their old rank, and often with an attractive promotion. Many regiments were raised in the north by political figures who would then command troops in the field—often with disastrous results. Others might be raised by a school principal who would then be recommended to the state governor to be their commanding officer, a position that might entitle them to a rank of colonel. In an earlier chapter we featured a citizen soldier, Fielder Jones, who managed to land right in the thick of fighting and slowly climbed the promotion ladder all the way to Brevet Brigadier General by the war's end.

During the war, advance in rank went to those considered in the front line—the main theater of the war. Sheridan leaves the Department of the West as a Captain and in active fighting in the Army of the Cumberland is promoted to major general. Wright is left to guard the Pacific west and is finally promoted as a Brig. General of Volunteers. Here is a regular officer being offered what would be called today a reserve officer's commission. If this was not humiliation enough, the office of commanding general of the Department of the West was to be offered to an officer who eventually turned it down—Gen. Mansfield. How did Wright feel about this treatment? A letter to his brother-in-law, General

Sumners says it all. "I am crushed...officers of my own regiment and gentlemen who won their spurs under my command now rank me."[7] He was placed in an awkward position, somewhat mollified by being named by Lt. General George McClellan, the new general-in-chief back in Washington as Commanding General of the Department. In retrospect perhaps he was better off than his brother-in-law, who had the dubious distinction of being the oldest corps commander on the Union side at age 64. He saw plenty of action at Antietam and Fredericksburg under McClellan with results that could hardly be called glowing, confirming once again that war is best fought by the young. The average age of brigadier generals in 1861 was thirty seven and as the war progressed there were many appointed to that rank who were in their early thirties and even twenties. Wright, when finally made a general, was months shy of age 60.[8]

GENERAL GEORGE WRIGHT

Promotions aside, it could be argued that Wright was the ideal man in the ideal spot. By the time he was named Department head he had already spent nine years in the various Districts north and south. During his command of the Department of the West, two governors in Oregon and California, charged with having "strong sympathies with the rebels," were replaced by strong Unionists—Leland Stanford in California and Addison Gibbs in Oregon, both of whom gave Wright their wholehearted cooperation. Washington, desperate for troops for the war in the east, began moving what regular troops were stationed in the Department to what was considered the main theater of the war. Most of these transfers had happened during the period Sumner was in charge of the command. By the time Wright had inherited the Department he had a command stripped of all but a few of the experienced regulars. More and more the Federal forces in the west depended on volunteers. What volunteers that were raised in the west came mainly from California. Until volunteers could be raised in the northwest it was necessary to transfer five companies of the 4th Regiment of California volunteer infantry. A year end report in 1861 shows that the District of Oregon had thirty-six officers and 620 enlisted men with headquarters at Ft. Vancouver, six garrisons in the Washington Territory and three in Oregon. The primary duty of these small garrisons scattered over what today are three states and part of a fourth—Washington, Oregon, Idaho and western Montana—was to contain Indian uprisings, to protect emigrants arriving in great numbers all during the war years and, in the case of Eastern Washington, to protect miners. In 1864, by way of example, 40,000 emigrants traveled west on the Platte River road, half of them from Missouri where secession support was strong. On the trail the shared dangers of survival were of more immediate concern than the war that was left behind, but once settled, the new arrivals were not bashful in making their sympathies known.

When it was proposed during the war that 5,000 volunteers should be raised in the west for the proposed invasion of Texas—

the civilian population opposed it with a near unanimous roar. Leave the west unprotected—never! Yet in fact, with little fanfare, the Department during Wright's tenure, responding to orders from the War Department, did raise a force under Col. James H. Carleton, a forty-eight year old professional who commanded a force including the 1st California Infantry Regiment with elements of the 2nd California Cavalry, the 5th California Infantry and the 3rd Artillery. The column left southern California in the spring of 1862 and helped General Edward R. S. Canby to nudge out of New Mexico, Sibley's Texans, who for a brief interval had prevailed in the Southwestern lands that so recently had been a part of Mexico. The battles at Valverde (a Confederate victory) and at Glorietta Pass (a Union victory engineered by volunteer recruits from frontier Colorado mining towns) are principally remembered as the westernmost battles of the Civil War. In point of fact the Confederates were defeated not so much by Northern arms, as by the destruction of a poorly protected Confederate supply depot. The Colorado troops circled sixteen miles through what appeared to be impassable mountains, descended on the depot destroyed seventy-three wagons—all of the Confederate's ammunition, food, baggage, saddles, tents, clothing and medical supplies. And if that wasn't enough they went on to kill or maim 500 horse and mules. It was a blow that ended Confederate hopes of conquering the southwest. Instead of victory the Confederate force faced the prospect of a long agonizing withdrawal across deserts and mountains. As Shelby Foote observed, "It was one of the great marches of all time, and one of the great nightmares ever after for the men who survived it. They had no guide, no road, not even a trail through that barren waste, and they began the ten-day trek with five days' poor rations, including water."

In time Carleton was rewarded for his efforts with a brevet promotion to Brigadier General and made the commander of the Department of New Mexico. It was an achievement that the west could be justly proud of even if it had been originally designed to protect mail and supply routes to the west.

This movement of the California column across the great desert during the hottest month of the summer season speaks well of those who planned and executed this expedition. It was the driest season that had been known during the past thirty years. Just to get across the desert and have troops available to aid General Canby was a military achievement of the highest order. Wright, the desk bound general back in San Francisco, gets little credit for this achievement, but from his field commander he did get a set of the colors that were hoisted over the forts that the California column had restored to the Union cause. Not the sort of information that makes headlines, the steady arrival of supplies shipped from San Francisco to Ft. Yuma. A train of about forty wagons plied between Ft. Yuma and Tucson. A contract had been signed to keep the column supplied with fresh beef at nine cents a pound! Back east, in the citadels of the military mighty, where new and higher military drafts were eliciting riots, the fact that this effort had been largely done by California volunteers was duly noted and appreciated.

The attempt to raise a regiment of volunteers in Oregon and the Washington Territory was a continuing concern for all the officers in command of the Department. Mention has already been made of the dependence of the Northwest on volunteers from California. Finally the District of Oregon was able to report the organization of a regiment of mounted troops under the command of Col. Thomas R. Cornelius, but getting them trained and battle ready was slow work. A report to the District headquarters at Ft. Vancouver in October 1861 contains this evaluation: "The company of Oregon Cavalry ordered to be mustered makes no progress and cannot be counted on for the defense of the frontier at present."[9] Note the disparity between the hoped for regiment and the company in training at this point. How keenly the loss of the regular non-commissioned officers shipped off to the main theater of the war is felt. Slowly both Oregon and the Washington Territory were able to achieve some success in raising a volunteer force. But the dependence of the region on the volunteers from California lasted through the entire war period.

The generals in command in San Francisco were constantly getting complaints from settlers about Indians who had been moved to reservations and had slowly filtered back to their old homelands. We have a copy of a letter that Gen. Wright wrote to a C.L. Murdock of Del Norte County, California. The General assures the correspondent that he will call the attention of the commanding officer in Redding to the situation, and then with what seems a touch of sardonic humor asked the question, "Where would you advise me to put these people? If they are taken back to the reservation, how can you be sure they won't return? Is there an island off the coast where they may be settled?"

On another occasion in a letter to William Dole, Commissioner for Indian Affairs in Washington, General Wright says: "A fruitful cause of our Indian Wars has been the encroachment by the white people on their lands before the Indian title had been extinguished and when treaties have been made for the purchase of Indian lands our people have at once proceeded to occupy them and dispossess the Indians before the treaties have ever been ratified. Indians cannot understand how it is that one party to a bargain can avail themselves at once of all its benefits, while they themselves are left to await the ratification and tardy fulfillment of its stipulations by the Government at Washington."[10]

After the war Major General Henry W. Halleck, former General-in-Chief of the Army, assumed command of the newly created Military Division of the Pacific, which consisted of the Department of California (consisting of the states of California and Nevada and the Territories of Arizona and New Mexico, and the Department of the Columbia (consisting of the state of Oregon and the Territories of Washington and Idaho). McDowell, who had displaced Wright earlier, now was displaced by Halleck, and became the commander of the California Department. Wright was scheduled to become commander of the Columbia Department, where he had commanded before the war.

Wright was ordered to the Department of the Columbia to take up residence at Vancouver Barracks where he had lived before the war. He and his party departed for his assignment on the *Brother Jonathan*. On July 30, 1865, just north of Crescent City, the old passenger ship was hit by a storm and battered on the rocks just north of the city.[11] A cemetery in the Del Norte County seat preserves the memory of this tragic loss. George and his wife Margaret were buried in the State Burial Ground in Sacramento City Cemetery, where a monument still stands to mark his identification with California and the Pacific Coast.

Many believe that the west enjoyed the blessings of peace and was spared the horrors of war because of Wright's good judgment, his sense of fair play for all, and his wise management of resources and personnel. That he was highly regarded by his contemporaries there is no doubt. This is not to say he did not have his detractors. Some felt he was too sympathetic with the Indians, "all palaver and no action" was the way they put it. But from his early years in the Northwest we know that when military action was required, the Ninth Infantry that Wright commanded could deal quickly and decisively with Indians bent on exterminating the white settlers. When it was learned that he and his wife had drowned enroute to his Columbia command, reports were passed along by telegraph all over the west expressing regret that the old Vermonter had ended his long years of service. The President himself is reputed to have written him a letter expressing the thanks of the nation for the job he did, a letter he proudly carried in his tunic pocket and was lost in the turbulent sea.

CHAPTER TEN

The Stagecoach Era

THE STAGECOACH, WHICH WAS developed in England in the seventeenth century, was a ponderous vehicle. It had seats for nine passengers inside; second-class passengers sat in a large basket-like contrivance in the rear; third class passengers sat on the roof hanging onto a rail. Four to six horses were changed at stage stops twenty miles apart. The average speed was four miles per hour.

A parallel development was the mail coach. A four-horse coach was used, driven by an armed coachman, accompanied by a guard. Horses were changed every six to eight miles, with speeds of eight miles per hour. At first only four passengers were carried, bur later changes were made for passengers to be carried in the boot and on the roof. This was the true ancestor of the stagecoach as we have come to know it in North America.

By the time the United States had won its independence from the mother country, regular coach service was being offered to passengers traveling from Boston, to New York and Philadelphia. Independent feeder lines served the larger cities and town from border to border. In New York State two men who had some experience in organizing the carrying of parcels on the growing network of railroads, Henry Wells and William Fargo, formed an express company specializing in the Albany to Buffalo run. In 1850, with the help of John Butterfield, another experienced express man, the trio formed the American Express Company and extended their service west to Cincinnati, St. Louis and Chicago. Gold had been discovered in California in 1848, but the partners bided their time until their organization was complete and then on the pages of the May 20, 1850 issue of the *New York Times*, they ran the following announcement:[1]

Wells, Fargo & Co. California Express
Capital $300,000
A joint stock company
Office 16 Wall Street

This company, having completed its organization...is now ready to undertake the general forwarding agency and commission business; the purchase and the sale of gold dust, bullion and specie, also packages, parcels and freight of all description in and between the City of New York and the City of San Francisco, and the principal cities and town in California, connecting at New York with the lines of the American Express Company.

Three thousand shares with a par value of $100 were issued. Those who invested in this initial offering would look back on the purchase as the best investment they ever made. During the life of Wells, Fargo & Co. it provided multiple functions. It was first an express company. In that role, with its parent company, The American Express Company, it utilized the fastest means of conveyance, be it rail, ship or stage. Secondly, and most important to western miners, it provided portable bank service. A miner who had an active claim could not take time off to travel to the nearest assay office to sell his gold dust. If he did he ran the risk that when he returned he would find that his claim had been "jumped." Now with a Wells Fargo agent readily at hand he could dispose of his dust, get a receipt and be sure he would get honest payment. The third function the company provided can be summed up in a single word—Security. In its announcement in the *Times* the item stressed "energetic and faithful messengers furnished with iron chests for the security of treasure and other valuable packages accompany each express upon all their lines." The company provided armed guards.[2] And lastly, from an economic point of view the least important function, was to be the passenger services their coaches would provide.

In 1852 when the company finally opened its office in San Francisco it would be seventeen years before the first transcontinental train would make its first run. In the interval Wells Fargo and rival companies provided overland service.[3] The company was never free of competition. Two of the largest competitors were the Adams Express Company and Page, Bacon, a banking firm. As late as 1854 Wells Fargo was running a poor third in terms of gold shipped back east by way of Panama. First to depart the field was Page, Bacon whose parent bank in St. Louis had closed its doors. When the news reached San Francisco on February 22, 1855 the San Francisco branch was forced to close its doors. Both Adams and Wells Fargo endured the same kind of panic driven by the rush of depositors. Only Wells Fargo survived. On February 25 they posted the announcement: "Wells, Fargo & Co. have completed a balance of their accounts this day, and find to the credit of their house above every liability $389,106.23, and ask of their friends a few days to convert some of their assets to resume payment." In this same year (1855) Wells Fargo paid two dividends, each of five percent. By year's end the firm had forty-five express offices reaching from Portland, Oregon to San Diego. In any move to a new gold digging or town you were much more likely to find a Wells Fargo agent than a recognized peace officer or a minister of the gospel!

One by one stage companies yielded the field to Wells Fargo. Ben Holladay, owner of the successful Overland Express and Stage Company, saw the railroad gradually creeping west and decided to unload. He sold his interests to Wells Fargo for $1,500.000 cash and $300,000 in Wells Fargo stock. He would reappear on the transportation scene in the Northwest where he joined forces with William Ainsworth, the Columbia River steamboat "king" to create a north to south, Portland to the Bay Area line. Holladay pushed his line south to Roseburg, when his rail empire began to unravel. Wells Fargo was rapidly becoming the express colossus of the West.

Travel along the West Coast

From its earliest days the firm had the good sense to buy the best coaches. The concern they turned to was Abbott, Downing and Co. of Concord, New Hampshire, a company that had been in the coach business since 1826. Three hundred men worked twelve to fourteen hours a day in the Concord plant, each man a specialist in his own field. The two founders took the English mail coach as their model and adapted it to the rough roads of North and South America. The precision and care in construction were matched by the selection of materials that were chosen. White ash, elm, basswood, hickory and oak were joined to make an oval shaped body. Wheels were capped with iron rims. The Concord coach was built close to the ground for sharp curves, with a light upper body structure and heavy underparts, with a springing arrangement made of heavy leather straps to absorb the shocks of the rough roads. How many of the Concord stages were purchased from the company is not known. What we do know is that Wells, Fargo was the company's largest customer. In 1867 for example, thirty coaches were assembled and shipped to the famous stage company. The final touch on each stage was the hand-painted panels on the doors—one was a view of Mount Washington and the other the Old Man of the Mountain, New Hampshire's famous landmark immortalized in prose by Nathaniel Hawthorne.

How did they ride? Short answer—the bigger the load the better they rode. Before the advent of rail service west of Omaha, filling the coach with passengers and freight was never a problem. The stage left the key city with a full load of passengers, baggage and packages. After rail service was extended to the west coast, first along the central Union Pacific route and later along the Northern Pacific St. Paul to Portland route, stages continued to serve sparsely settled areas well into the early twentieth century when they were replaced by trucks and automobiles.

Let's take the testimony of two frequent riders of the Concord stage, the first from Daniel Tuttle, a missionary Bishop of the Episcopal Church serving in Montana, Idaho and Utah, and Mark Twain, who after spending years on the Mississippi decided it was time to head west.

First from Bishop Tuttle: "My experience in stage coach travel are a vivid part of my Rocky Mountain experience. I have traveled more that forty thousand miles in that way. Most of the times I have enjoyed that mode of travel, many times I have grimly endured it." Tuttle tells the story of a stage that pulled into a Wells, Fargo & Co. office to discharge passengers. A large crowd was assembled, as the incoming and outgoing coaches were great events for the town. At the stop the only passenger threw open the coach door, leapt on the ground, ran hurriedly across the street and turning a handspring, stood on his head with his heels up against the supporting wall. "What's the matter?" he was asked. "Well, friends, I'll tell you what it is. This standing on my head is the only position which I haven't been in during the last twenty-four hours."[4]

Tuttle was consecrated as a bishop May 1, 1867 and left for the west shortly thereafter. He was able to travel by train as far as North Platte, Nebraska, at the time the western terminus of the Union Pacific. He had never been further west that Niagara Falls and now he stood at the western end of the rail line, forced to wait five days before he could obtain passage on a stage. Because of Indian uprisings it took the Bishop and his party the better part of a month to make the trip to Salt Lake City by way of Denver. Once established there he had to move on to Boise, Idaho and to Virginia City, the capitol of the Montana Territory. One of the worst stage trips ever was a trip from Salt Lake to Boise that normally took three days and nights of travel. "Near all the way I was alone and in a jerker instead of a stagecoach. A jerker was a small canvas-covered affair, seating four inside and one outside with the driver, and drawn usually by only two horses. When the wheels struck an obstacle it did not have the easy roll and swing of the coach, but, as the name implies, jerked the passenger unmercifully on, or oftener off, his seat. To be alone in a jerker was to be in extreme discomfort."[5]

"Of the stage drivers I want to put on record words of grateful appreciation. The California and Rocky Mountain stage drivers of the early days were a unique class of men. Their duty was only to sit on the box and drive; stock tenders harnessed and fed the horses. Yet the drivers knew their own horses and had names for them, and they always took care to see that they were well looked after. Going round curves or down a mountain-side, with his foot on the brake and the six lines in hand and with his eyes keenly watching the road as it stretched in front, the driver was such an example of marvelous skill as is a pilot in troubled waters."[6] On many a ride the Bishop would sit along side the driver for the sake of steadiness and support. Twice he was involved in accidents where the stage tipped over.

As for Mark Twain's reaction to stage travel we have only to turn to one of his many stories that describe the early West. The narrative, "Roughing It" begins in July 1861 when he and his brother, Irion, departed St. Joseph, Missouri for Carson City, Nevada, where the brother was to serve as Secretary for the Nevada Territory. He went intending to stay three months. In fact, he stayed six years.

"The first thing we did on that glad evening that landed us in St. Joseph was to hunt up a stage office, and pay the hundred and fifty dollars apiece for the tickets per overland coach to Carson City."[7] There were just three passengers in this stage. The rest of the space was occupied by mailbags, scattered over the forward passenger seats door to door. The combined weight was more that the coach could bear and a through brace broke and repaired on the spot by the driver and conductor. The excess weight, roughly half the load, was deposited along side the road for another coach to pick up later. Five hundred and fifty miles west of St. Joe their wagon broke down and this time the repairs took the better part of a day. Even with these delays on the morning of the twentieth day they reached Carson City, Nevada. "It had been a fine pleasure trip; we had fed fat on wonders every day; and we were now well accustomed to stage life, and very fond of it. So the idea of coming to a standstill and settling down to a humdrum existence in a village was not agreeable."[8] While his brother took up his duties as the Secretary of the Territorial Governor, Sam (let's call him by his given name) partook of the local life becoming at various times, a prospector, a speculator and a reporter for the *Territorial Enterprise.* Always he would write stories about the people he met. The best of these were sent back east and published in some of the leading magazines of the day. When he finally did return to the east he found that he was known and was much in demand as a lecturer.

As for Wells Fargo, as we noted earlier, their express business was flourishing. They realized that their days in the passenger trade were numbered. The principal rail systems were forever developing feeder lines. One by one the sparsely populated towns that had been served by the stage were now served by rail. The company experimented with a profitable new sideline—the shipment of perishable goods from the West Coast to the East. The company had contractual agreements with the Northern Pacific, the Union Pacific and the Southern Pacific. In the latter years of the nineteenth century it began to invest heavily in still another transcontinental carrier—the Santa Fe. To make the passenger run pay, one of the Wells Fargo executives hit on the idea of attaching a refrigerator car to the passenger train and making the Los Angeles to Chicago run in fast time. It proved to be an immediate success and West Coast producers clamored for daily service. In short time the Santa Fe was running an all refrigerator express train over the same track bed, hooking up with the Erie at the Dearborn station. The Erie was the only Chicago to New York railroad the company had a contract with. The arrangement prevailed down to the First World War when for reasons of national defense the Wells Fargo express was shut down as a separate entity and its assets were transferred to the parent company, the American Express Company. What "national defense" had to do with this exceedingly strange business decision is beyond comprehension. For some time the company was getting adverse publicly. First there was the matter of excessive dividends being paid. The muckraker press ran articles critical of the commissions and rates charged. Backers of a national parcel post system felt the express company stood in the way. John Wanamaker, a merchant whose stores in Philadelphia and New York are fondly remembered, served as Postmaster in the Benjamin Harrison Administration, 1889–1893. He became the spokesperson for those who felt the express companies were blocking this needed development. The early years of the twentieth century were a period of trust busting. Agree with this view or not, Wells, Fargo and its allied express companies were perceived as a monopoly.

    The American Express Company is very much alive. The principal products these days are traveler's checks and credit cards. You'll find it listed in the New York Stock Exchange. Wells Fargo continues to exist as a bank. On March 18, 2001 the company observed its one hundred fiftieth anniversary. The home office is still in San Francisco where the company has a history room and museum containing the paraphernalia of the stagecoach era. In 1996 the bank bought out the First Interstate Bank that only a few years before had purchased the First National Bank of Oregon. Wells Fargo is a major presence in the banking business in the West.

Using the oratorical devise employed by Evarts at Gold Creek, Montana we might rephrase the question he asked of assembled miners and cowboys: "Where would Wells Fargo be without the help of New England and New York?" Yes, New York State must be added, for although the elder of the two partners was born in Thetford, Vermont, he and his New York-born partner grew up in the Empire State, and it was in this state they established their express business with their New York to Buffalo run. The answer to the question would be much the same that Evarts got. Where would Wells and Fargo be without their eastern connections? No place. As a matter of record, these two founders never did stray far from their comfortable New York headquarters. For all of their identity with the west, the fact is Wells made one business trip to the West. He traveled by way of Panama before railroad service across the isthmus was completed in 1855. Wells made his exploratory trip well before that date so he endured a rough trip through jungle trails. He took a ship to San Francisco, looked over the terrain where the new company would operate was satisfied with what he saw and returned to the east, again by way of Panama.

With so much historical emphasis on travel overland by covered wagon and stage, it may come as a surprise to learn that the most popular mode of passenger travel and freight transportation between the two coasts was by ship. Two to three thousand persons passed through the isthmus each way every month. In 1847 Congress passed the Mail Steamer Act authorizing annual subsides for a line of ships sailing twice a month from New York and Chagres, Panama, and a ten-year contract to the Pacific Mail Steamship Company to provide three ships for the once-a-month service between Panama and San Francisco and Astoria. The three ships produced were *The California, The Panama* and *The*

Oregon produced during the May to August period of 1841. Within months of their launching President Polk, in a message to Congress, widely quoted in every newspaper, announced the discovery of gold in California. That announcement alone was enough to provide the Pacific Mail Steamship Company with passengers far beyond their ability to safely handle.

As for Fargo, the record indicated he made a trip west to a vitally important conference held in Omaha in 1869. As a result of that conference Wells Fargo bought the Pacific Express and obtained an important contract to carry express on the Union Pacific. The price was exorbitant. The Crocker interests controlled this first of the transcontinental railroads and demanded $5,000,000 for the Pacific. Fargo really had no choice. It was either sign the agreement and pay the price or get out of the express business. Eventually the two original partners yielded leadership positions to younger well-prepared men and pursued other interests. Fargo became interested in journalism and became the publisher of a Buffalo newspaper. Wells became interested in the founding of a college for women—Wells College in Aurora, New York.

Frequent mention has been made of the disadvantage the Northwest endured prior to the completion of the Northern Pacific in 1883. When a prospective settler reached the end of the rail line, the usual route to Astoria, Portland and the Puget Sound region would be by sea. But many a traveler preferred the relative safety of the overland route. Several stage companies provided local transportation within the Washington Territory, Oregon and California. In California, Sacramento became the hub of stagecoach travel.[9] From this state capitol the traveler could book a southbound stage for San Diego; an eastbound stage for Virginia City and Omaha, a western jaunt to San Francisco, and a northern bound stage to Jacksonville, Oregon where connection could be made with other stages servicing towns and villages along the Willamette Valley. The time required, for the seven hundred mile

Sacramento to Portland trip, was seven days during the dry weather, during the rainy period often twice that time. To stock the line, known as the California and Oregon Stage Company, twenty-eight coaches, thirty freight wagons, five hundred horses, fourteen district agents, seventy-five hostlers to care for the stock, and thirty-five drivers were needed. Except for the St. Joseph to Sacramento route that Mark Twain and his brother took, this was the longest stage run in the United States. One of the Concord coaches can be viewed in the Wells Fargo History Museum located at SW Fifth & Jefferson in Portland, one of seven museums run by the company in locations in Alaska, California, Minnesota and Oregon.

Inquire about free admission museums at www.wellsfargo.com.

CHAPTER ELEVEN

The Villards and the Northern Pacific

HENRY VILLARD IS A NAME THAT brings to mind great projects, all of them wrought here in his adopted land. In Bavaria in 1848 a revolution was being waged. On one side, as the head of the provisional revolutionary government was his uncle, Friedrich Hilgard, on the other side was his father, a judge, who remained loyal to the throne. Young Heinrich chose to support his uncle and the losing revolutionary cause. Unable to speak English and with twenty borrowed dollars, he arrived in New York a scant five years after the failed revolution. He changed his name from Heinrich to Henry, became successively a journalist, a teacher, a railroad magnate, a publisher, a founder of the Edison General Electric Company and a philanthropist.[1]

In the Northwest his name will be forever associated with the completion of the Northern Pacific. His first job as he landed on our shores was as a reporter for one of the many German language newspapers. He first worked in New York, later in Illinois and Wisconsin where, at age twenty-one, he edited the Racine *Volksblatt*.

The thrill of seeing his own thought in print suggested a literary career, so it was back to New York where the publishing world was centered. By this time he was bilingual, and wrote pieces in both English and German—but the income was very, very minimal. So the thought occurred—why not get regular employment, and do the literary work on the side. He had seen enough of country schools in the Midwest to feel that he could fill the requirements. Back home in Bavaria he had graduated from the gymnasium in Speyer and had gone on to study in Munich and Wurzburg. That translates to high school plus a year or two of college. My father taught in a one room rural school in upstate New York. He was a high school graduate—period. It was his very first job, not counting the work on the family dairy farm. The first order of business was to lick the biggest boy in the school. If you failed, pack your bags and look elsewhere.

He stayed long enough to put himself through a business college in Elmira and then he was off to New York at the dawn of the twentieth century.

In Villard's case he heard about a vacancy near Lebanon County in Pennsylvania. Luck was with him, the School Commissioner was a very kindly, elderly gentleman who spoke excellent German and took a personal interest in Villard's case. Did he have a teacher's certificate? No. No matter, he would examine him right then and there. "He made me sit down, and, for an hour and a half, put me through a series of questions in arithmetic, grammar, history, and geography, three-fourths of which, under his kind leading, I answered correctly. Then on the payment of one dollar, I received a certificate pronouncing me duly qualified to teach any district school in the State of Pennsylvania,"[2] The next morning he walked the six miles to Jonestown, a neat, clean place. The population, with the exception of a single family, was entirely made up of Pennsylvania Germans that had settled in this region generations ago. By evening the school board met and he was hired for two terms of three months each at thirty dollars a month plus board. The board part was to be provided by the farmers whose children were his pupils.

The most irksome part of this arrangement was that in order to take advantage of the free board he had to move from week to week. He seldom had any privacy and often shared a bedroom with the hired man. Finally his good friend, the village doctor and school board chairman, talked the board into a different arrangement where he could live with one family and have a room to himself.

On Saturdays he went to school, lit a fire in the stove and kept up on his literary output. He fired off articles to the larger papers. The *Staats-Zeitung* published some of the sketches he sent in. This German language paper in New York can be looked upon as the grand daddy of the Knight Ritter chain of papers of today. Today the *San Jose Mercury* is probably the largest paper of the group. But the foundation stone was Victor Ritter's *Staats-Zeitung und Herold*.

By the summer of 1858, with schools closing for the summer Villard returned to New York where he wrote articles for the paper on a space basis. The paper, in addition to its daily issues had a weekly edition with a very healthy circulation in the mid-West. His first steady employment with the paper was to travel through the region collecting on old subscriptions, get new ones, and at the same time write articles describing the lives of these recent arrivals from the German homeland. The pay was fifteen dollars a week plus expenses. Villard soon discovered he wasn't cut out for the circulation side of newspaper life, but his once-a-week newsletter ran from one-and-a-half to two columns and was highly regarded by the editors back east.

The public press at the time was filled with the approaching contest for the Senate seat in Illinois. Would the *Staats Zeitung* be interested in having him cover the campaign? The answer came back, yes, they would. Actually he covered the debates for two papers, his own and for the Philadelphia Press, an English language paper. Villard is quite frank that his sympathy in this debate was with Douglas. He was the leader of the Democrats who had opposed the pro-slavery followers of President Buchanan. By the seventh and final debate Villard writes that at times there seemed to be nothing in favor of Lincoln. "He had a lean, lank, indescribably gawky figure, an odd-featured, wrinkled, inexpressive, and altogether uncomely face. He used singularly awkward, almost absurd, up and down and sidewise movements of his body to give emphasis to his arguments. His voice was naturally good, but he frequently raised it to an unnatural pitch. Yet the unprejudiced mind felt at once that, while there was on one side a skillful dialectician and debater arguing a wrong and weak case, there was on the other a thoroughly earnest and truthful man, inspired by sound convictions in consonance with the true spirit of American institutions. There was nothing at all in Douglas's powerful effort that appealed to the higher instincts of human nature, while Lincoln always touched sympathetic chords. Lincoln's speech excited and sustained the enthusiasm of his audience to the end."[3] Villard covered four of the joint debates, six other speeches by Lincoln and eight by Douglas. The summer of 1858 was very hot in Illinois, which had at the time a population of about a million and a half. He traveled almost continuously over bad county roads and poorly constructed rail beds. More important to his future he traveled with some of the top reporters and editors of the day. His ambition from the start was to become a correspondent for one of the English language papers. And it was during the coverage of these debates that he formed a lifelong friendship with Horace White of the *Chicago Tribune*.

He had access to both of the candidates, but a chance meeting with Lincoln at a flag rail stop twenty miles west of Springfield gave Villard what he considered one of his most precious recollections. The train was late and a thunderstorm compelled them to take refuge in an empty boxcar, there being no buildings of any sort. From nine to half past ten on a hot summer's evening Villard had his private audience with one of the great figures of American history. Lincoln talked of his own early misgivings about his abilities, and his chances of securing a majority in the State legislature. He expressed surprise at Villard's fluent use of English after such a short residence in the country. The two talked about all sorts of subjects, religion included. Within two years the two protagonists, Lincoln and Douglas, would be rivals again, this time for the Presidency.

Villard's real aim, to establish a contact with an English language paper, was achieved when he went to work for a Cincinnati paper which sent him to Colorado to cover the Pike's Peak gold rush in 1859. The following year he was hired by the Associated Press and assigned to the capitol of Illinois, Springfield, which by this time was almost a second home to him.

He was there for the election of 1860, and accompanied Lincoln and the presidential party to New York and Washington, where he formed a news syndicate and became telegraphic correspondent first for the *New York Herald*, later for the rival *New York Tribune*. His first war coverage was the battle at Bull Run in Northern Virginia. In time Villard became one of the best-known journalists covering the war, an ardent abolitionist with undisguised Northern sympathies. For three years he reported on some of the major battles of the Civil War—Shiloh, Fredericksburg, Charleston and Missionary Ridge, forming contacts with field officers that would prove valuable in future years. Most of the general officers were happy to have Villard with them, hoping, of course, he would report the battle in a favorable light. Before Sherman's famous march to the sea, the North's Nashville to Chattanooga to Atlanta route was blocked by able defenders who seemed destined to check every Union move. An earlier and failed attempt to move along this route was commanded by General Rosecrans. The Southern heroes of that earlier engagement were Generals Polk, Longstreet and Bragg and nameless others who, with raids beyond counting, interrupted the flow of supplies to Union troops. One Union commander emerged as the hero of this 1863 engagement, Virginia born General George H. Thomas, known to history as "the Rock of Chickamauga" who held his position south of Chattanooga in spite of the Confederate breech of the line and the retreat of adjacent forces.

Here is a little first hand flavor of the scene as recorded by Villard after the defeat. He had just returned from a front line review of the battle as viewed from Missionary Ridge. "The Northern papers had been full of all sorts of accounts of the course of the two days of battles, the causes of our defeat, and the behavior of Generals Rosecrans, McCook, Crittenden, Negley, Davis, Sheridan, Wood and VanCleve. Charges that the first three had sought safety in flight from the battle-field had been freely published all over the loyal States...There was so much contradiction and partisanship in the printed versions that I resolved to ascertain the truth and to write a review of the battle. I began at once to gather material for it. Generals Rosecrans and Garfield expressed their readiness to place at my disposal all the information they had. General Garfield, knowing that he was safe with me, took me freely into his confidence."[4] Shortly after, Garfield won a seat in Congress, proceeding under orders from Washington to deliver in person to the War Department Rosecrans report of the Chickamauga battles, and to make such verbal explanations as might be called for.

"I could but lament his departure, for our relations had become so friendly and even intimate that he was always ready, not only to give me all the army news, but to talk our situation over with me in the frankest manner. I was but too conscious that I should probably not again be able to form such a genial and professional profitable connection in that army."[5] Garfield, be it observed, was public relations wise, an attribute that would help carry him on to governor of Ohio and ultimately the presidency, one of three Union general officers so honored.

Sherman, who was soon put in command of the Army of the Cumberland, was a horse of another color. He hated the press and at one time said that he would willingly agree to give half his pay to have his name kept out of the public prints. Aware of his views, Villard felt it the better part of discretion to keep away from the general for the time. And here—with Sherman on the attack in the very first stages of his victorious battle of Atlanta and the subsequent march to the sea at Savannah, the campaign that literally broke the back of Confederate resistance, we abruptly leave the scene of the fighting with its first person singular account, and turn to a third person singular account doubtless written by his son when he edited his father's notes and prepared the memoirs for publication in 1904.

What we do know about this transition from war correspondent to international financier is that recurrent fever forced him to leave the western battlefields for medical treatment. By May he was healthy enough to cover the war, this time in what he felt was the main theater of operation, the battle for Richmond, headed by a general who had won his spurs in the west, General Grant. Lincoln, after all these years, had found himself a commander to match the wisdom and courage of Robert E. Lee. The campaign was just nicely begun when Villard received an urgent call from his family in Bavaria. When he arrived in his homeland most of his time was spent with his ailing and widowed father and sister. By March 1865 he sailed from Liverpool, expecting to arrive in time to witness the final struggle between Grant and Lee. Arriving in Boston he learned that Richmond had been taken, Lee had surrendered, and—most devastating of all—that Lincoln had been assassinated.

At war's end, Villard continued in the journalistic field, becoming the Washington correspondent of the *Chicago Tribune*. Soon he was sent back to Europe to cover the war between Prussia and Austria. This time he took his bride, Fanny Garrison, with him. By the time he got to England the determining battles had been fought and peace negotiations were under way. His paper, this time the *New York Tribune*, found other stories for him to cover—the World Exposition of Paris in 1867, the eruption of Vesuvius, along with interviews with famous people of the time. This was pretty tame material to one who had covered the war in America.

Soon he was casting around for a new chapter in his life. It came as a result of his now close ties with his family in Germany. During one of his stays there, he proposed the establishment of a mortgage bank providing a special charter could be obtained in one of the older eastern states. In due time application was made to the Massachusetts legislature. The application failed and nothing more is heard of the subject. But the relations with financial circles in his homeland were about to payoff in ways beyond his wildest dreams. To put it in a nutshell, English and German investors had been flim-flammed by Ben Holladay to invest in his Oregon & California Railroad. The German investors were the hardest hit. The issue before them was—should they exercise the rights of bondholders to take possession of the railroad, or make some kind of advantageous compromise. The latter course was decided upon. Villard and other members of the group set off for a meeting in New York. It was soon discovered that Holladay's reputed wealth was fiction.

Villard was commissioned on behalf of the bondholders to proceed to the west coast and to see for himself what the prospects might be for this partially completed rail line. With him he took Richard Koehler, a knowledgeable German railroad engineer, who was to serve as the resident financial agent for the bondholders. The year was 1874. They traveled by rail to San Francisco and then by

HENRY VILLARD

stage most of the distance between the Bay area and Roseburg, the terminus of the O & C at the time. What he saw of Oregon on that trip to Portland filled him with the greatest enthusiasm.

Villard and his associates proceeded slowly to transfer ownership from Holladay to a firm representing the bondholders. Villard soon became the president of the Oregon Steamship Company and of the Oregon and California Railroad.[6] Next he planned to buy out the extensive facilities of the Oregon Steam Navigation Company. John Ainsworth, the president and chief stock holder of this company that had long dominated river based traffic on both the Columbia and the Willamette Rivers asked $5,000,000, fifty percent in cash and fifty percent in stocks and bonds. Villard jumped at the offer and the deal was sealed on May 23, 1879. It became known as the Oregon Railway and Navigation Company. By 1883 this company had spent over $20,000,000 in building some five hundred miles of rail bed largely along the south bank of the Columbia into eastern Oregon and Washington with the object of connecting eastward with either the Northern Pacific or the Oregon Short Line extension of the Union Pacific.

It is time now to introduce the reader to the Northern Pacific, a railroad whose name will be forever identified with Villard. It began July 4,1864 with a stroke of a pen by Abraham Lincoln on a federal charter for a railroad that would connect the Great Lakes with the West Coast. The readiness of the federal government to issue such a charter can best be explained by recalling that in 1853 the government had spent over a million dollars in search of the best and most economical rail route to the Pacific Coast. Three routes were proposed—a southern route roughly along the 32nd parallel favored by the then Secretary of War, Jefferson Davis; a central route backed by Illinois Senator Stephen A. Douglas; a northern route between the 47th and 49th parallels favored by a former typographical engineer and Governor of the Washington Territory, Isaac I. Stevens. The survey produced a political stalemate. [7]The work was not in vain, however, as two of the three routes were developed roughly along the suggested lines. The proposed northern route was to begin at Duluth on Lake Superior and its western terminus was to be Tacoma on Puget Sound. It slowly took form with the largest land grant ever given a railroad. First it reached Fargo and then Bismarck. By the time Villard appeared on the scene it was very much in his interest to route the connecting link through the Columbia River valley. He proceeded to do this in a scheme known at the time as the Blind Pool. He raised $8,000,000 in cash with no mention of what the money was to be spent for, an action without precedent in Wall Street history. With these resources he bought up Northern Pacific securities, and demanded to be a part of the Northern Pacific management.

By October 1881, he was on the board and elected President. By September 8,1883 at Gold Creek in the Clark Fork Valley, 55 miles west of Helena, Montana, the two rail beds of the Northern Pacific were joined. This event in railroad history is overshadowed by the joining together of the Central Pacific and the Union Pacific at Promontory Point, Utah on May 10,1869. But Villard proved himself something of a impresario. Three thousand invited guests converged on this out-of-the-way point to witness yet another last spike being hammered into an awaiting tie. The celebration organized for the occasion included an ex-president, the still popular Ulysses S. Grant, distinguished guests from Germany, England and the Scandinavian countries. From the United States came several members of President Arthur's administration, former cabinet members, important members of the Senate and House, governors of seven states and prominent international bankers. Among the celebrities was William Maxwell Evarts, back in private practice after a four-year stint as Secretary of State in the Hayes Administration. Evarts was widely recognized as one of the great orators of the day.

Large crowds gathered at this out-of-the-way spot in Western Montana. Most of this gathering of ranchers, cowboys, miners, sheepherders and Indians had never seen General Grant and this was their chance to see the great war hero. It must have been a humbling experience for the orators of the day, Mr. Evarts and the Secretary of the Interior, Robert M Teller, who were frequently treated to cries of "We want Grant."

Finally the General, sensing that this was a situation rapidly getting out of hand, arose and made a few humorous remarks. After speaking and the driving of the spike, the main line of the Northern Pacific was declared open and it was on to Portland for another celebration, for the city of Portland had become the western terminal point of the Great Lakes to the Pacific line, thanks to Villard's efforts. It was a proud moment for Villard and for Portland. One of Villard's most ardent admirers during periods of success and moments of apparent failure was the historian and fellow railroader Joseph Gaston.

"The coming of Henry Villard to Oregon in 1874 was the fact of largest importance to the development of the Northwest. On his first visit to Oregon, the author of this book (Gaston) accompanied him on a trip throughout the Willamette valley and discovered that he had thoughts, if not plans, for a field of action far beyond the confines of the state. Quickly getting under his full control the existing Oregon roads, he went straight at the work of his vast plan of an Oregon railroad system having transcontinental power and influence.[8]

Gaston had been involved in railroad ventures long before the arrival of Villard. He was one of the group who had endeavored to put forward a "westside" road from Portland to the California line only to be edged out by Ben Holladay. In 1878 he built a narrow-gauge railroad connecting Dayton to Sheridan, with a branch to Dallas, in Yamhill and Polk counties, Oregon. This enterprise was managed solely by Gaston with the support of farm interests.

He goes on to say of these connections, the main line east to the Great Lakes (and eventually to Chicago), to Tacoma to the north, and to Salt Lake City to hook up with the Union Pacific, "the grand conception was his in origin and execution; although hampered by doubters and opposed by powerful enemies, he triumphed over all obstacles and made its success the most enduring monument of his fame as one of the most forceful characters and honorable men of his day and generation." This reference to "doubters" and "enemies" refers to the period following the completion of the main line when fellow board members voted to accept Villard's resignation as Northern Pacific president. Why would they take such action? In order to complete the railroad Villard's expenditures exceeded receipts by almost $8,000,000, and shortly the amount rose by another million and the end was not yet in sight. To meet these expenditures, second mortgage bonds were issued to the extent of $20,000,000 with the result that the Northern Pacific securities depreciated in value. In the face of these adversities Villard resigned effective January 4, 1884. Thus in a period slightly in excess of three months, Villard went from hero to bum. And yet none of his plans for growth and expansion were halted. The southward expansion that had been halted at Roseburg in 1872 was resumed and was completed as far as Ashland in 1884 when insolvency forced a stoppage. Eventually this line would pass into the hands of the Southern Pacific and little old Ashland, whose claim to fame to this point had been as a part of the Chautauqua Circuit, was now the scene of a golden spike ceremony presided over by Charles Crocker, one of California's "Big Four," who noted that now Portland would be united with New Orleans and by this act Oregon had become a part of the longest railroad in the world.[9]

What a contrast this represented. For fourteen years, beginning with the completion of Central Pacific line connecting the Midwest with Oakland and San Francisco in 1869, the Northwest had no direct rail line to the east or even to California. Travelers to the northwest could, during that period, travel by rail to the Bay Area where they had a choice of taking a ship to Portland, Tacoma and Seattle, or travel by stage north through the central valley of California and the Rogue River Valley to Roseburg and continue to their destination by rail. Beginning with 1883 the same traveler was faced with multiple choices. In addition to the Northern and

THE VILLARDS

Southern Pacific, there would soon be a Union Pacific connection known as the Short Line, leaving Granger, Wyoming and running west through Pocatello, Idaho and Huntington, Oregon. In 1893 the Great Northern, Jim Hill's railroad, reached the Pacific. If it were not for Villard's more varied career—if the choice were to be made on the basis of railroad prowess alone—Hill would be the author's clear choice for inclusion in this book. As one observer notes, "in no other case have the conception, construction, and operation of a great American railway system been so completely the work of one man as was the construction of the Great Northern system the work of James H. Hill."[10]

The northernmost of all of the American transcontinental railroads, the Great Northern, found itself squeezed in between the Northern Pacific and the boundary line with Canada. No large cities are to be found in this region. After leaving St. Paul, Minnesota the next city of any size is Grand Rapids, North Dakota, then Havre and Great Falls, in Montana, Spokane and the Inland Empire in Eastern Washington, and on to Seattle and the Puget Sound area. Joint control by the Great Northern and the Northern Pacific of the Chicago, Burlington and Quincy Railroad gave both of these railroads entry to Chicago, the rail center of the entire country.

The final of the east to west rail beds was completed in 1909 when the Chicago, Milwaukee, St. Paul and Pacific pushed west from its base in Kansas City and Omaha into the Black Hills of South Dakota to Harlowton, Montana where the line became electrified for its run into Puget Sound. The nation now had seven carriers serving the transcontinental trade. The Santa Fe and the Southern Pacific traversing the southern route, the Western Pacific and the Union Pacific serving the central route, and now three carriers vying for the northern trade—Northern Pacific, Great Northern and the Milwaukee. In an earlier chapter we noted the unique position New York state found itself as commercial activity, once confined to the eastern seaboard, began to expand to the old northwest—the present day states of Ohio, Michigan, Indiana and Illinois. The only east-to-west break in the Appalachian range was the Mohawk River, soon to be developed into the Erie Canal and at a later date to become the route by which the New York Central made its New York to Chicago run. On the west coast the Columbia and Snake Rivers played much the same role. It was the sole east-to-west break in the mountain system incorporating the Sierras to the south plus the Cascades to the north. For much of the time of British and American occupation of the Northwest, the Columbia was the vital link, and commerce was largely dependent on river navigation.

Just as the great central valley of California soon became the heart center of agriculture of that state, so the Willamette Valley and the Inland Empire of eastern Washington became the centers in the northwest. The rail lines serving the area would be foremost among those urging settlers to come. The maintenance of a steady flow of immigrants was from the start recognized as an ever present necessity. Agents were placed in the chief ports of entry on the east coast where pamphlets extolling the virtues of the Northwest were distributed. Under Villard's influence, agents were appointed to Great Britain, Norway, Sweden, Denmark, Holland, Switzerland and Germany. In the year that the Northern Pacific completed its Duluth to Portland run, 632,590 copies of the railroad's publications were distributed in the major European languages. To insure that prospects who were headed for the Northwest were not enticed to settle elsewhere, agents were assigned to Omaha and Topeka, key way stations to the west. In the period before the completion of the northern route all immigrants would pass through San Francisco where agents gave settlers every kind of assistance to encourage them to continue their journey. It was quite a promotional network. In the end it paid off, because without settlers to take up the land there would be no crops planted, no freight to haul, no profit to be made.

In 1876 the Centennial of the Country was observed. The display of northwestern products created a sensation. This, with an almost total crop failure in California, gave the most important wave of immigration yet experienced. Overland migration by wagon still endured well into the railroad age, averaging roughly 10,000 a year as late as 1877. Some few still came by ship to Panama and thence up the coast to ports in California and the northwest. With the passage of years rail traffic grew dramatically.

1883 was the beginning of through service to the northwest. The monopoly the Northern Pacific enjoyed lasted roughly a decade. During that short period Villard had to satisfy the bondholders, and the commercial interests of three very competitive cities—Portland, Tacoma and Seattle. Here is an excerpt of an address Villard made before the Tacoma Board of Trade, October 7, 1881.

"We propose to deal with the Northern Pacific, to conduct the enterprise as a business enterprise for the benefit of the stockholders, having due regard at the same time for the interests of the public. Now, you may be aware that it is the purpose of the management of the Northern Pacific...to connect the Washington Territory branch from Kalama with the city of Portland. You will all admit that it is a very natural thing to do, to bring about this connection...We intend to make that connection at the earliest possible moment, and I hope and expect that it will be the first means of making Tacoma a wheat shipping point. It is claimed that it is far less expensive to bring sea-going vessels to Tacoma than to Portland. If that is a fact, wheat will come here as soon as it can be brought here as conveniently, as expeditiously, and as cheaply as it can be brought to Portland. You cannot expect wheat to come here unless you have facilities, in the first place for storing and handling it, and in the second place capital to attract it. That is, there must be money power here to control the movement of wheat."[11]

Villard touched upon a very tender issue to Portlanders in this speech. Portland was a river port. During the period when waterborne traffic was king, the trade of the Columbia and the Willamette had made it a great center. Now, with the dawning of the age of larger and larger cargo ships, Portland found that the hundred miles from the sea with a wild and tempestuous bar at the mouth of the river a distinct disadvantage. Seasonal variation of the water level could vary from a low of ten feet to forty feet when the snow pack of the Cascades melted. The wise master of an ocean going ship would take on a river pilot to get his ship over the bar and up river safely. Puget Sound, already a gateway to Alaska, has many natural harbors, excessive depth and minimal need for pilotage. English shipmasters went public expressing their displeasure over the high cost of using the port facilities of Portland. One correspondent claimed the total charges for towage, pilotage, and literage to and from Portland was $4,115 compared with $400 to and from Tacoma. While this may well have been an exaggeration, still Portland recognized the damage this kind of publicity could do. Plans were made to deepen the channel from the ocean to Portland. From that day to this dredges have been engaged in an ongoing task of keeping the river traffic moving.

Villard's speech mentions the Kalama line, the purpose of which is to connect the port cities of the Washington Territory with Portland and connecting roads to the east. Kalama is a river port town some 25 miles down river from Portland. While the main line of the Northern Pacific was being pushed eastward along the south bank of the Columbia to Gold Creek, Montana, another crew had been working with corresponding speed on a Kalama to Tacoma branch. September 8, 1883, the day the last spike was hammered into place on the transcontinental rail line, was in reality a double celebration. Portland was at last connected with the east, which was the source of great elation, and at the same time connected to the Puget Sound, probably a contender in the shipment of grain to the markets of the world.

To the commercial interests of Seattle, Villard promised the eventual construction of what would be called the Cascade line—a line that would cut across the towering mountain range. Villard's words to his critics in Seattle, who wanted a direct road to the east right now, make good sense. Be patient with us. Wait until we have the necessary resources to accomplish this task. Eventually the line was put through. As noted, the Great Northern completed its rail line into Seattle in 1893, the last year of Villard's service on the Northern Pacific Board.

Villard's service in the northwest lasted from his first arrival at Roseburg in 1874 to the day of his departure as Chairman of the Board of the Northern Pacific. During that time he was the dominant factor in the transportation scene. Of all of the railroad builders none was so identified with the welfare of people as he was. One of the many friendships he formed in Oregon was one with Judge Matthew P. Deady, chairman of the board of the newly created University of Oregon. The University opened its doors in the fall of 1876 with a faculty of five, eighty students, ninety-seven preparatory students and no library. The first crisis came in 1881 when there was fear that creditors would seize the heavily mortgaged Deady Hall. The indebtedness of the University at the time was close to $8,000. At this critical juncture Villard came to the rescue by donating $7,000 to liquidate the indebtedness. Other bequests followed. In 1883 he made a gift of $50,000 in Northern Pacific bonds, with the stipulation that $400 of the annual income should be used for the purchase of library books. Concerning this gift Deady, in his annual report to the Regents, observed: "It is noteworthy as being the only considerable contribution ever made in this state by private wealth to public use."[12]

When all those dignitaries who had come west on the special trains for the driving of the spike at Gold Creek reached Portland, Villard had his assistant Koehler bundle the party off to Eugene to see the University. The names of the party will hardly be remembered at this late date, but the party included a member of Parliament, a Naval Captain who had overseen the transport of Cleopatra Needle from Thebes to Central Park, New York, William Lloyd Garrison, of Boston, son of the famous anti-slave journalist and brother-in-law of Villard plus several German scholars and government officials. Looking back over the span of the first century of the University's existence, George N. Belknap calls this visit "a second installment of Villard's munificence."[13]

From this same period we have this description of Villard at fifty years of age: "He is five feet eleven feet tall, weights 210 pounds...He is bright, quick in speech and action, and possessed of a wonderful amount of magnetism. His frank hearty manner and clear, full voice are attractions in his favor difficult to surpass."[14] When the news of Villard's collapsed empire appeared in the press in early 1883, Deady wrote a letter of sympathy and regret to his friend, a letter deeply appreciated by the recipient who described it as the first of its kind he had received from Oregon. The University, on its part, did not forget its benefactor. During this down period, a new college building costing some $30,000 was to be called Villard Hall. Villard was restored to the Northern Pacific Board of Directors serving from 1887 to 1893, the last four years as chairman. In 1891 a sculptured bust was placed in the assembly room of the hall named for him. In 1899 Villard and wife made his last visit to the University coming by a special train provided by the Southern Pacific.

His productive years were far from over. In 1881 he had purchased the New York *Post* and *The Nation* magazine. The Post masthead proudly proclaimed the name of its founder Alexander Hamilton. Although never a leader in the circulation wars of the city, its list of editors reads like a list of who's who in American journalism. William Cullen Bryant, a revered poet, editor of the paper for a half century, was a Free Soiler and one of the founders of the Republican Party. Edwin Godkin was the editor of the foremost review in the country, *The Nation*. When Godkin sold *The Nation* to Villard he became editor of the *Post*, succeeding Carl Schurz, a former cabinet secretary, serving from 1883 to 1899. Horace White, Villard's lifelong friend from the days of the Lincoln-Douglas debates came aboard as an executive assistant about the time when Villard's son, Oswald Garrison Villard, was being groomed for leadership.

In 1890 Villard bought the Edison Lamp Company at Newark, New Jersey and the Edison Machine Works at Schenectady, New York and formed them into the General Electric Company of which he was the president. Villard knew how to pick a winner. He had, along with J. P. Morgan and others, been subsidizing Edison for years. Edison acknowledged that help. "In pioneering you have to have a man with nerves to adopt your ideas. I have found that man. He is Henry Villard." Villard was the first to attempt the application of electricity to railroads, hoping he could apply it to the Northern Pacific. In fact the Milwaukee in 1909 did electrify their line from Montana to Seattle in 1909. It also came into use on the commuter trains running undergound below Park Avenue en route to Grand Central Station.

In writing of his antecedents Oswald Villard liked to say that he was a compound of New England abolitionism, the German Revolution of 1848 and Northern Pacific shares. His grandfather was William Lloyd Garrison known to his countrymen as the Great Liberator. The masthead of Garrison's paper declared "I am in earnest. I will not equivocate. I will not excuse. I will not retreat a single inch. AND I WILL BE HEARD."[15]

Villard's mother exerted a tremendous influence on her son. She met her husband-to-be on a chance visit he made to Boston. When they married she gave birth to her son during one of Villard's visits to his homeland. It was to cost Oswald Villard dearly, this accident of his birth overseas, for during his editorship of the *Post* he pled the cause of neutrality during the Great War, 1914–18. He was accused by his foes as a spy, a traitor, a German propagandist. Others saw in these same editorials a voice for truth, honor and fair dealing.

Fanny Garrison Villard was as ardent in her support for women's suffrage as her father had been for the cause of the enslaved Negro. Many of the leaders of the suffrage movement were personal acquaintances. She was always proud of the support her husband gave this movement. "It gives me joy to remember that not only my father, but also my good German-born husband believed in equal rights for women."[16] She had reason to be proud of the support her son gave the movement. He helped organize a Men's League for Women's Suffrage and marched down New York's Fifth Avenue braving the jeers and the rotten eggs. Oswald Villard, it can honestly be said, never ran away from a controversial subject. He wrote hard-hitting editorials that offended many of his own colleagues. His pen was always busy. He was merciless in his exposure of the corruption of Tammany Hall, the New York City political arm of the Democratic Party. For much of his life, like his father before him, he could be categorized as liberal, a term he applied to himself in the title of one of his many books, *Fighting Years: Memoirs of a Fighting Liberal*. He is credited as having done much to guide Woodrow Wilson's thinking during his first administration.

OSWALD GARRISON VILLARD

Wilson's slogan for re-election bid in 1916—"He kept us out of war" echoed Villard's own neutralist position. When America entered the war in 1917, many neutralist papers changed their position, but not Villard. Loss of advertising and circulation followed and made the position of the *Post* so precarious that he was forced to sell in 1918. But he hung on to *The Nation* and was its editor and publisher until 1932. Like the *Post*, *The Nation* still exists today. The *Post's* survival as the sole afternoon paper in the New York market is something of a marvel. It outlasted the *New York Sun*, the *World-Telegram*, and the Hearst paper, the *Journal*, all casualties of the great newspaper strikes of the mid-60s. These days the *Post* is owned by Rupert Murdoch whose journalistic empire is scattered over three continents. I very seldom see the paper and can make no judgment call. As for *The Nation* I do buy an occasional copy. It bears no relationship to the fine publication Oswald Villard published. If you are shopping around for alternative journalism, give it a try. It still can be found on some of the newsstands and public libraries.

Oswald Villard at one time owned *Yachting Magazine* and *Nautical Gazette*. After he divested himself from ownership of the newspaper and its companion magazine, he continued to write for *Scribners, Harper's, The Progressive,* and *The Christian Century*. Over the years he received honorary degrees from Washington and Lee, Lafayette, Howard Universities and one that pleased him greatly—a Doctor of Laws from the University of Oregon. He was one of the founders of the National Association for the Advancement of Colored People.

CHAPTER TWELVE

The Connectors

Chicago, Burlington and Quincy

The Burlington Northern Railroad (more recently restructured as the Burlington Northern Santa Fe) is actually an amalgam of three major railroads that have served the west for close to a century and a half. They are the Northern Pacific, the Great Northern and the Chicago, Burlington and Quincy whose rails stretch from Illinois to the states of Oregon and Washington. Enshrined in the present day title is the name of an eastern Iowa city, Burlington. There, on August 13, 1868 a bridge across the Missouri was opened for traffic. The structure was 2,237 feet long, fifteen feet, nine inches wide, carrying a single track and cost $1,227,044. At the time of its construction there were four rail routes, all of them east to west, across the state of Iowa. The lines were, from south to north, the Burlington and Missouri, connecting Burlington with Nebraska City, the Mississippi and Missouri line (soon to become a part of the Chicago and Rock

Island) connecting Rock Island with Council Bluffs, the Iowa Central Air Line and at the northern part of the state, the Dubuque and Pacific. The land grant legislation passed by Congress required that these roads be completed and finished by ten years. The date set for completion was December 1865 but as a result of the intervening war years, the date was extended.

Lured by the offer of public lands that might be secured for as little as $2.50 an acre in 160 acre plots, families from the east came to Iowa in droves. In June 1855 the land office reported that over 3,250,000 acres of Iowa public land had been occupied during the previous year. 190,000 people had been added to the state almost doubling its population. Guidebooks and pamphlets were published by the state, by counties and by railroads extolling Iowa as a land flowing with milk and honey.

The Chicago, Burlington and Quincy had originally started out with a track bed from Aurora, Illinois, on the Fox River to Quincy on the Mississippi in 1856. About the same time the railroad created what would be known as the Burlington route, a fifty mile track bed from Galesburg, Illinois, to a site on the Iowa side of the Mississippi, Burlington where a ferry system made connection with points to the west. The connection from Aurora to Chicago itself, a matter of a few miles, had to wait until 1864.

Gradually the pieces of the Burlington System were being put together. The next expansion would take place in Nebraska. By the year 1870 there were two railroads that could in any sense be called transcontinental. The foremost was the Union Pacific that connected Omaha and points east with Oakland and San Francisco. Slightly to the south, running through the state of Kansas was the Kansas Pacific running from Kansas City to Denver. There was a connector line from Denver to Cheyenne where the main line of the Union Pacific was intercepted. As the CB&Q pushed west into Nebraska it had to face the fact that land grants had already been sold by the older and better financed Union Pacific. Further, that the through traffic from the mid-west to the Pacific Coast would continue to be carried by the Union Pacific. Therefore the CB&Q had to depend on the local business. Bit by bit it pushed its rail lines west to Kearney and Beatrice in one direction and to Alliance, Nebraska and Billings, Montana in a northwestern thrust where connection was made with the Northern Pacific by 1894. Both the Northern Pacific and the Great Northern, as far as passenger service was concerned, terminated in St. Paul, Minnesota. St. Paul had become a transfer point second only to Chicago. Realizing the importance of this growing trade the CB&Q made what was doubtless its most financially productive extension and organized the Chicago, Burlington and Northern, a wholly owned subsidiary to link St. Paul with the Windy City.

The line began operation October 24, 1886 and was the means whereby the two northern railroads gained entry to what had become the most important transfer point in North America. The land department of the CB&Q sold lands well into the first decade of the twentieth century, Charles Russell Lowell, poet, critic, diplomat and onetime editor of the *North American Review,* wrote: "We are beginning to find out that he who buildeth a Railroad west of the Mississippi must also find a population and build up business." During the decades from the 1860s to the year 1910 all western railroads heartily subscribed to the words of one of New England's great poets-editors. Under the terms of the original Homestead Law of 1862, a maximum of 160 acres could be secured by any one settler. But when the grazing lands of western Nebraska were encountered it became clear that the acreage limit was too small. In 1904 Congress enacted the Kinkaid Law which made it possible for homesteaders to claim up to 640 acres in certain designated areas. The colonization work of the railroads thus continued into the twentieth century with railroads such as the CB&Q conducting personally conducted home seeker tours into these regions recently made available.

A brochure prepared by the railroad land office reads: "A well satisfied settler is a good asset. A misplaced man is a liability. Our interest does not cease with the location of the settler. We are deeply interested in his success. We have no financial interest in the sale of lands nor any lands to sell." (This was written well after the period when the railroads did have lands to sell). "Our sole interest is in the development and general prosperity of the country." The custom of running special excursion trains through the region continued for a number of years. These later trains were often co-sponsored by the state departments of agriculture and dealt with such subjects as the improvement of livestock, seed potatoes, poultry, sugar beets, soil care, hogs, hay crops and new developments in farming. The exhibits carried by these excursion trains reached over 30,000 ranchers and homesteaders in a single year and built good will for the sponsoring CB&Q.

It was at Chicago that the Erie picked up the cars from the west and began its "fast freight" run to the markets of the east. After the Civil War railroad engineers developed a great variety of special cars. Stock cars were developed to take care of the Kansas to Chicago run. Attempts at developing refrigeration cars predate the war years. It wasn't a western railroad that developed these cars. It was an eastern road, the Vermont Central that first developed such a car for the butter trade. Fifty of these cars were developed in the rail shops in Ogdensburg, New York in the early 1850s.[1] The butter trains left Ogdensburg on Lake Ontario every Monday morning and arrived in Boston by Wednesday noon. Twenty years later the Illinois Central developed a larger and improved version that became widely used in the shipment of fresh fruits and meat products.

Other cars, developed either before or just after the war include the storied Pullman cars. Pullman developed the first of these cars for the Chicago and Alton Railroad—a connector line that linked Chicago with St. Louis. After the war his shops turned out "The Pioneer" featuring carved woodwork, mirrors, and plush carpets. The price tag of this new model was $18,000—four times what the earlier version had cost! The Pioneer was first used when Mrs.

Lincoln, having heard about the car, asked if it could be added to the President's funeral train as it made the Chicago to Springfield run.[2] The development of dining cars quickly followed, and the Gilded Age of the American railroad had dawned.

Kansas Pacific Railroad

No part of the proliferation of western railroads should be written without mention of the Kansas Pacific. Two colorful characters are linked to its origin and development, William F. Cody, the famed Buffalo Bill of a somewhat later period, and Jay Gould, a stock manipulator we have met before in our study of the Erie Railroad. Let's begin with the development of the Kansas Pacific right after the Civil War. The eastern terminus of the railroad began at Kansas City and moved westward along the Kansas River and its tributary, the Big Smoky Hill linking Lawrence, Topeka, Manhattan, Junction City, Abilene and Salina with Denver to the west which was reached in 1870. These towns were to have considerable influence in the future of the region. Lawrence and Manhattan, university towns, Topeka the state capitol, Abilene, Dwight Eisenhower's birthplace and Russell, the political base of Bob Dole. For a time, all seemed well on this new line. Abilene became the place where the cattle trails met the railroad trails. In 1871, 700,000 head of cattle were shipped to the stockyards of Chicago. Alas, there were other problems. From the first there were the problems the railroad faced with the Indian tribes. A treaty with the Cheyenne, Arapahos, Kiowas and Comanches was achieved by the Indian Peace Commission in 1867. It stipulated that the land between the Platte and the Arkansas rivers were to be opened for white settlement. Another provision enabled the railroads to make suitable construction through the area. Still another provision required the tribes to retire to reservations in the Indian Territory. Although the chiefs and the headmen had been unanimous in support of these provisions, the young men of the tribes were bitterly opposed to what had been done. In time their elders came to feel that they had not understood all of the provisions. What resulted was called the Plains War of 1868. By this time General Sheridan had been assigned to the Division of the Missouri, and he moved his headquarters from Leavenworth to Fort Hays in the western part of the state.

It was estimated that the tribes could put together a war party of 6,000, while Sheridan had in his command a force of regulars numbering 2600 men, 1200 mounted plus 1400 infantry. With these few troops all of the posts along the principal rivers had to be garrisoned, emigrant trains escorted, settlements protected, routes of travel kept open, and the construction parties of the Kansas Pacific defended. This same small force was expected to provide small movable columns that were always on the go. They responded to over forty attacks on settlements involving the stealing of horses, burning houses, and the killing of settlers. Sheridan's appeal for reinforcements resulted in the assignment of seven additional troops of cavalry and a regiment of Kansas volunteers. The railroad town of Hays became the base of all operations. One of the scouts Sheridan was able to employ was Bill Cody. Cody served as a contractor for the railroad to supply fresh meat for the construction party. Cody, who had served as a scout for the Union in the Civil War, now turned his attention to the needs of Sheridan's forces, knowing the plains country as well as any white man alive, he carried dispatches back and forth through hostile country, at one point covering 350 miles in less than sixty hours. One of his more famous exploits was his hand-to-hand duel with Yellow Hand, a Cheyenne chief. The dime novels of the period soon turned Bill Cody into worldwide celebrity. By 1883 he had organized a Wild West Show that toured the United States, Great Britain and Europe. He made (and lost) a fortune in show business. One of the staples of the new motion picture industry that was developing in the early decades of the twentieth century was called simply—the western. In 1993–94 the United States Postal Service released a sheet of twenty stamps under the title *Legends of the West*. There you will find Buffalo Bill along with Annie Oakley, Chief Joseph, John Fremont, Kit Carson and Sacagawea. Thus in a matter of less than a decade the Kansas Pacific had managed to make the Kansas City to Denver connection and thence northward to Cheyenne to make a link with the Union Pacific. Therein lay the third and most dangerous obstacle—Jay Gould. This period, the latter part of the nineteenth century was a time of railroad mania. Investors the world over seemed keen on buying stock in western railroads. We have seen in the chapter on Henry Villard that his rise to fame was coupled with his ability to represent bondholders from Germany and Great Britain. In our own day we have seen investors, or should we call them speculators, clamoring for the initial stock options in start up software companies. Stocks that initially sold for twenty-five dollars would often be selling for twice the sum in a matter of months. That was a pattern of what may be called "railroad mania." In the case of the Kansas Pacific some of the original bondholders were the same investors that had made possible the completion of the Northern Pacific.

The troubles for the Kansas Pacific began when, having made a connection with the Union Pacific at Cheyenne, it found that the older and more dominant railroad refused to pro-rate with it. Pro-rating was close to a given in the sharing of profits. The railroad where the shipment originated was entitled to a percentage and the railroads who participated in the haulage (often several in number) were likewise entitled to a percentage of the rate the shipper was charged. The Kansas Pacific sought relief both in Congress and in the courts. The legal battle pitted Jay Gould, who controlled by far the largest block of stock in the Union Pacific, with Henry Villard once again appearing in his role as the representative of European bondholders who had invested in the Kansas Pacific. As a result of increased indebtedness, the lack of feeder lines and continuous pressure from the rival Union Pacific the Kansas Pacific defaulted on its mortgage bonds in November

1873. The railroad was then placed by the courts in receivership and for the next six years Henry Villard served as one of the receivers. During this period the stock of the Kansas Pacific sold for as little as nine to twelve cents on the dollar. The aim of Gould and his allies was obvious, to hammer down the value of the stock of the rival, which they did with unrelenting zeal. Much of the stock they had purchased cost $12.00 a share. And the slippery Gould pulled a maneuver that won him fame. The simplistic way of describing it is to say that he switched sides. Beginning in 1878 he began to make large purchases of the depressed Kansas Pacific stock. A year later he bought controlling interest in the Missouri Pacific, which gave him entry with eastern roads. In the same purchase he bought controlling interest in the Missouri Central, a narrow-guage line that ran west of Leavenworth along the Kansas River for 166 miles. He then added the Central Branch of the Old Union Pacific. He then turned on his former colleagues on the board of the Union Pacific. He offered terms. He would exchange shares on a two-for-one basis. The Union Pacific stock was selling for $50.00 a share. The stock he had acquired in the almost bankrupt Kansas Pacific probably cost no more than $20.00 and in some cases far less. In the end the Union Pacific directors blinked. On January 14, 1880 they caved in. The high price the company paid to free itself from competition would plague it for years to come. As for Gould, soon after the consolidation he sold his stock. It is said that he cleared over ten million dollars on the deal. That doesn't sound like a vast sum in these days. By the standard of the times it was considered a huge coup.

It is fair to add that, like the Erie before it, the Missouri Pacific and the Kansas Pacific lived on to provide connector service between railroads of the west to the markets in St. Louis and the east.

A claim can be made that the commerce clause of the Constitution made possible a united country. Article 1, section 8

THE CONNECTORS

in outlining the powers of Congress states that Congress shall have the power "to regulate Commerce with foreign nations, and among the several States, and with the Indian Tribes." Regulation of rates was first attempted at the state level as early as 1870. Since the Constitution had clearly delineated this as a responsibility of Congress, such attempts were quickly struck down by the courts. The first test of the commerce clause was provided by the great monopolies of the day, the railroads. A typical devise employed by the transcontinental roads was to charge low rates between cities where several lines competed for business, and high rates between points where they alone provided the service. When the Central Pacific (known as the Union Pacific) completed its roadbed from Omaha to San Francisco in 1869, they had the ultimate monopoly for well over a decade. Wells Fargo, as a carrier of goods and parcels, was literally forced to meet their demands. In the annals of railroad lore this meeting between the two giants is known as the "Surrender of Omaha." The power of the railroads to set rates was challenged by two politically powerful groups—the farmer groups in the west and the business interests in the east. Both felt the railroads were taking advantage of them. Congress felt the heat and during the presidency of Grover Cleveland passed an Act to Regulate Commerce in 1887. This act brought into being the Interstate Commerce Commission. The rate-regulating responsibilities of the Commission were gradually spelled out. Eventually the oversight of Congress gave way to an independent commission. Other regulatory agencies were created to insure fair rates and consumer protection. The Federal Trade Commission was created in 1914, the Federal Communications Commission in 1934, and the Securities and Exchange Commission in 1934. In each instance the model Congress used was the Act to Regulate Commerce.

CHAPTER THIRTEEN

Promotion of Immigration

THE PROMOTION OF IMMIGRATION was a concept thrust upon the trans-Mississippi railroads from the very first. Eastern railroads had been developed in settled areas with a high degree of productivity. Moreover many of them served areas where they supplanted the older waterways and canals. They were assured from the start of a profitable business and they found willing investors to assist in their expansion plans. This was not so with the railroads west of the river. Here the railroads were being pushed through new and sparsely settled communities. There would have been little incentive to invest in these railroads had it not been for the development of the railroad land grant. By this method large portions of the public domain were transferred to the railroad to promote the construction of the railroads. In 1864 a charter was issued and signed by President Abraham Lincoln. Under the terms of that charter a railroad was to build a line from Lake Superior to Puget Sound. In aid of that construction there was given to the railroad a federal grant of odd sections of the public domain within a limit of twenty miles of either side of the track in the states and forty miles in the territories, plus an indemnity limit of ten miles on each side of the primary grant. This made a strip sixty to one hundred miles wide (depending on whether it was in a state or territory).[1] The idea was simple enough. The railroad, in this case the Northern Pacific, would build the rail bed in fifty and one hundred-mile intervals and apply for the transfer of title. It was understood from the first that the railroad would then sell their lands to aid them in defraying the cost of building the next fifty to one hundred mile rail bed. Long before Henry Villard had any connection with the Northern Pacific, the railroad had formed its own land company. At first the office of this land company was in New York. It seems a curious place for a western railroad to center its sales activities. But New York had already become the port of entry for tens of thousands of immigrants.

Literature developed by the railroad was published in English and several European languages. During the early years of development the Northern Pacific track beds were being laid out across Minnesota. The land office found that Lutheran pastors were often an ideal means of attracting large groups of settlers. We read about a group of 245 Swedish immigrants that sailed from Gothenburg on March 31, 1871 and another group of 200 Norwegians who left the next spring. Another report tells about sixty Hollanders who left for the Northwest and an equal number of Germans. Another agent wrote that a party of 242 Finns was shortly expected to sail. Minnesota soon became a state with a generous spread of Scandinavians and Germans.

While all of this recruitment was going on in Europe, an equally important domestic migration from the eastern states was taking place. Some of the crops in the eastern states had been planted on marginal lands from the very beginning. A plow pulled through the glacial soil of a New England farm will yield as many rocks as it will potatoes. When those same farmers began to hear of the rich soil in Minnesota, all they needed was a little nudge from a land agent. These people were seen as good farmers and desirable settlers, and they came by the hundreds and thousands. My father-in-law's parents Abram and Sarah Elizabeth Reitzel were among them. In 1882 they moved west by rail from Sterling, Illinois to an area in the James River valley, South Dakota and homesteaded 160 acres. The railroads had developed a freight car they named an Emigrant Car. It was designed so that you could put livestock in one end and household goods and equipment in the other. In between, there was space for the person to live and to care for the animals—in this case two horses and a milk cow. Abram made the 500-mile journey in this car. His wife preceded him in a passenger car. The nearest town was Mitchell, named for the President of the Chicago, Milwaukee & St. Paul Railroad, who in 1879 had sent an engineer to the valley to locate a town site. The house they lived in didn't look anything like the cover of this book![2] Their first home on the prairie was a sod hut, eighteen by fourteen. Five years later the hut was enclosed with lumber and a lean-to added. Here the family enjoyed seven years of plenty followed by seven years of drought. Many of their neighbors simply gave up and moved on. The Reitzels stuck it out, raised a family of four boys and a girl. The deed to their quarter section was dated July 26, 1889 and was signed by direction of President Benjamin Harrison by the Recorder of the General Land Office. It had taken Abram Reitzel two more years than required before he could spare the $12.50, the cost of obtaining the title. In all they spent some eighteen years in the Dakotas. About the turn of the century they returned to Sterling, deciding that the fertile fields of Illinois provided good soil with which to provide the children (now grown to six) with a good education.[3]

This picture of active solicitation and response lasted to the year of the 1873 panic, which was caused in part by the enormous cost of the war and excessive railroad building. Eighteen percent of railroads in the nation wound up in receivership. Indeed, if any one thing triggered this panic it would be the failure of Jay Cooke, up until this point the principle financier of the Northern Pacific. This depression affected every aspect of the economy. For five years the economy of the nation was stagnant. Before the panic the Northern Pacific had reached Bismarck on the Missouri River. It wasn't until 1879 that it again became possible to push the rail bed west of the river. In 1881 the control of the railroad passed into the hands of Henry Villard, who from the first days of his presidency became intensely interested in immigration efforts. The number of agents in the British Isles was stepped up to 831 agents! Another 124 agents were appointed for Norway, Sweden, Denmark, Germany, Holland and Switzerland. The general land office was transferred from New York to St. Paul, Minnesota with an Immigration Office in Portland. In 1883 it was reported that the offices in St. Paul and Portland had received over 60,000 letters of inquiry in reply to which 2,500,000 pieces of descriptive literature were sent. Not all of these inquiries resulted in sales. As a matter of fact many of these settlers took up government land grants rather than the lands offered by the railroad. This was not a cause for concern. A railroad land commissioner observed: "It does not matter very much to the Company whether settlers locate upon our lands, or upon lands purchased from us, or upon government lands. What we want to do is secure the rapid settlement and development of the lands tributary to our line and I have observed that the very best class of settlers which we have secured are those who have been passed through a frontier experience in the older states, and who know just how to adapt themselves to the work of subjugating these prairies and of establishing new homes thereon."[4]

After the organization of the Oregon Railway and Navigation Company in 1879 extensive efforts were made to popularize the eastern portion of the Washington Territory, commonly called the Inland Empire, as well as the Idaho Territory and the Willamette Valley. Until this time the Northern Pacific had concentrated its colonizing efforts on the Minnesota and Dakota portion of their roadbed.

A Spokane newspaper situated in the heart of the Inland Empire, on March 28, 1882, stated that immigration up the Columbia River amounted to 2,800 per month, while overland roads were lined with teams conveying immigrants from Kansas, Nebraska, Iowa and Minnesota. A writer in the *Atlantic Monthly* for January 1883 described his journey to Portland and found one of the most interesting places in the city was the bureau of immigration of the Northern Pacific. There, looking into the tall case containing samples of the products of the fertile Northwest were Swedes, Norwegians, Germans and Irish, standing in wonder before this case, originally constructed for the Centennial Exposition in Philadelphia back in 1876. Later in that same year, 1883, for the first time the immigrant seeking to investigate the lands of the Northwest, could come by rail. Up until the date of completion, the Northwest had been isolated. Now, in the place of having to journey to San Francisco and then take a northern bound ship to Portland, Tacoma or Seattle, the settler could travel the whole distance by rail. The joining together at Gold Hill, Montana, of the eastern and western branches of the Northern Pacific was the harbinger of a new day for the Northwest.

CHAPTER FOURTEEN

Gold Creek, Montana

ON SATURDAY, SEPTEMBER 8, 1883 in the Clark Fork Valley, fifty-five miles west of Helena, the two rail beds of the Northern Pacific, one starting from Duluth 1198 miles to the East and the other from Portland, 622 miles to the West were joined. The event in history is overshadowed by the joining of the Central Pacific and the Union Pacific at Promontory Point, Utah, May 10, 1869. Henry Villard, the president of the Northern Pacific, used the occasion to prove to the world that he was something of a showman.

The orator of the day was William Maxwell Evarts, back in private practice after a four-year term as Secretary of State in the Hayes administration. Evarts was widely acknowledged to be one of the country's great orators. The United States Centennial Commission looked around for a speaker to address the throng gathered in Philadelphia, the site of the Declaration of Independence. By unanimous vote they chose Evarts, the grandson of Roger Sherman, one of the committee of five appointed to draft the Declaration.

Asked by a friend how long the speech would be, we get a sample of the Evarts sense of humor. Rattling off some of the events he had become famous for, he replied: "I spoke for four days on the Johnson impeachment trial, two days before the Geneva Tribunal and for eight days in the Beecher trial; no limit of time has been set for my oration, but there is the implied understanding that I shall get through it before the next centennial."[1]

Take those highlighted events he refers to beginning with the impeachment trial. In 1868 he became the chief counsel in the defense of President Andrew Johnson. It was a startling choice. Evarts was what might be called in our time a "Wall Street" lawyer. He was a graduate of Yale and of Harvard Law School. Johnson started out life as a tailor's apprentice and began his climb up the political ladder as an Alderman in Greeneville, Tennessee. Evarts was the only Republican. The others were members of the Democratic Party. Henry Stanbery, who resigned as Attorney General to give full time to the defense of the President, former Supreme Court Justice Benjamin Curtis, William Groesbeck of Ohio and Thomas Nelson from the President's home state. All were certified patriots, signifying in this instance that they had all supported the Union cause in the war. Evarts later wrote of his contacts with the President: "During the whole time of my association with him, (he) impressed one with the dignity of his manners, the sincerity of his patriotism and his unfailing confidence in the spirit and purpose of the great body of the American people."[2] Seven Republicans joined their Democratic colleagues in the Senate in securing acquittal. None of the seven ever held another elective office. In 1956 John F. Kennedy, in his book *Profiles in Courage* extolled the courage of these men in taking what they knew to be an unpopular position. Evarts, too, was a Republican who had played a very large part in defending the President. What would the cost be to him? To compound the problem, soon after the impeachment trial, Johnson named Evarts as Attorney General to close out his term—a period of eight months.

Two years later, in 1871, Evarts was appointed by President Grant to a committee of three to serve as counsel in the Alabama Claims Arbitration. The appointment of Evarts was actually opposed by the President. The first name Secretary Hamilton Fish proposed was Charles Frances Adams. Grant objected. A number of other names were discussed in cabinet and rejected for various reasons, Evarts and his lifelong friend Richard H. Dana, Jr. among them. Fish favored Adams who had just refused the presidency of Harvard. Finally, after offering all sorts of obstacles the president was cajoled into naming Evarts. Since the President gives no clue as to his lukewarm embrace of Evarts, we must assume that Grant knew there was a sizable group in his own party who found it difficult to forgive Evart's apostasy on the impeachment issue. The dispute between England and the United States centered on the cruiser Alabama built in England and used by the Confederacy to destroy commercial ships during the war. The case is remembered because of its profound effect on the practice and procedure of arbitration in the field of international law. The tribunal found Great Britain legally responsible for the losses caused by the ship and awarded $15,500,000 to the United States. Work on this committee required Evarts to spend much of his time in Washington and in Geneva, Switzerland, where arguments on both sides of the issue were presented. More important to Evarts personally was the friendship he formed with President Grant's Secretary of State, Hamilton Fish.

The Beecher trial in which Evarts claims he spoke for eight days needn't detain us for long. What it amounts to is that the greatest Protestant preacher of his time was involved in a suit brought against him for adultery. Two ecclesiastic courts exonerated him, and the civil case (involving Evarts) failed to reach an agreement. The newspapers of the day saw the trial for what it was—a sure-fire circulation builder.

The next national assignment Evarts faced was the contested election of 1876. Until the election of 2000, the Hayes-Tilden election was always sighted as the nation's closest election. In both these elections, one candidate won in the electoral college, the other candidate led the popular vote. By 1876 the Republicans had won four successive elections—two with Lincoln at the head of the ticket, and two with the North's leading military hero, Ulysses S. Grant. The scandals of the second Grant administration cost the Republicans dearly. In the election of 1876 they lost such northern states as New York, New Jersey, Indiana and Connecticut. As the votes were certified it became apparent that the results in Florida, South Carolina, Louisiana and Oregon would determine the election, and that Hayes could only win the election if every one of the four states went for Hayes. When the Republicans were looking around for their leading counsel, they choose Evarts.

Each contested state had a slightly different scenario. In South Carolina and Louisiana the government in office at the time of election was Republican supported by Federal troops. In other southern states home rule had been adopted, but in these states carpetbag governments still survived. It is also pertinent to remember that on the Electoral Commission that would count the votes, the Republicans prevailed eight votes to seven. The contested elections in the three southern states all went to Hayes, the vote in Federal Electoral Commission was eight to seven in each instance.

Oregon is of special interest. The state constitution did not provide for a returning board to forward votes to the College of Electors, but stipulated that the secretary of state should canvass the votes in the presence of the governor. This report showed that the three Republican electors received a higher total than any of the Democratic electors. The governor of state at the time was a Democrat, and in his report he certified one for Tilden and two for Hayes. Of the four contests the decision in the Oregon case was evident from the beginning. Hayes won all three of the Oregon electors and was declared the victor in the electoral college by a single vote.

What a spot to be in. Actually Hayes turned out to be one of the better presidents of the post war period. He let it be known from the beginning that he had no aspirations for a second term. This is a violation of rule number one in American politics, for in so doing the office holder turns himself into what is quaintly called a "lame duck." Hayes seems to have survived quite nicely, in spite of this indiscretion. The first thing the war hero and three-time governor of Ohio did was to name a powerful cabinet. Evarts was appointed Secretary of State. John Sherman became Secretary of the Treasury, Carl Schurz was the Interior Secretary. One of Hayes's first actions was to extend home rule to all the states that had participated in the Confederacy. To the radical wing of his own party this was seen as weakness. To much of the nation, it seemed only right that the south be returned to full participation in the federal government. Federal troops were withdrawn. His administration is credited with the first serious civil service reforms. On this issue, too, he faced the opposition of many of the leaders of his own party. To the victor belong the spoils was a kind of unwritten mantra which had governed political appointments from the earliest days of the republic, and it died a slow death. He was at all times a sound moneyman, something members of his party could all agree on.

A friend met Evarts just after he had been to a dinner at the White House and asked how it went. "Excellent," replied the Secretary of State. "The water flowed like champagne."[3] Lucy Hayes was a woman of great personal beauty, and as first lady she maintained a gracious and delightful hospitality while strictly adhering to her principles of total abstinence. Members of the Women's Christian Temperance Union looked upon Lucy Hayes with something close to adoration. Those who imbibed of spirits did not take kindly to Lucy's innovations. It is said that the chef in charge of state dinners took compassion and went so far as to fashion a box made of the frozen skin of an orange. When it was opened you found instead of an orange, a punch or a sherbet into which was added as much rum as the box would hold. This was known as "the life saver."

As for the period that Evarts served as Secretary of State, he had the good fortune to preside over the department when things were rather quiet on the diplomatic front. He conducted some delicate negotiations with Great Britain regarding fishing rights. Arthur Schlesinger observes "the Senate exercising its power in the realm with relish, freely rewriting, amending and rejecting treaties negotiated by the executive. Indeed, it ratified no important treaty between 1871 and 1898."[4]

The fact that Hayes did a good job during his single term is reflected in the results of the 1880 election when still another war hero from the state of Ohio, James A. Garfield was elected. Presidential historian Clinton Rossiter of Cornell University makes bold to rate the Presidents of the United States. Washington and Lincoln are at the top, Wilson and Jackson come next, Teddy Roosevelt and Jefferson follow. Then come Franklin D. Roosevelt and Harry Truman. No surprises here.

Just below them Rossiter lists six presidents who turned in creditable to unusual performances. The six were Grover Cleveland, James J. Polk, Dwight Eisenhower, Rutherford B. Hayes, John Adams and Andrew Johnson. This is what he has to say about Hayes: "A vastly underrated President, whose successful struggle to name his own cabinet, dogged devotion to civil service reform, seven stout vetoes of legislative riders, and dispatch of troops in the railroad strike of 1877 were all long steps forward from the Waste Land of Grant."[5] And Evarts had the privilege of serving two of this group.

After his service during the Hayes years, Evarts returned to his practice in New York to take up his old work as one of the great trial lawyers of his time. It was during this period that he accepted Villard's invitation to be the orator at the ceremonies marking the completion of the Northern Pacific. The likely reason for his acceptance? It was a chance to mingle with old friends in government and out. Along with the other eight hundred invited guests, Evarts made the trip to Chicago and boarded the train that would take him all the way to the mining country of western Montana. It was the perfect vacation for this gregarious Yankee. He probably looked upon the excursion as a lark, and sensed this was not the occasion for turgid prose. Quite aside from the official invited guests, there were thousands of settlers and miners from the region that had traveled to Gold Creek with but one thought—to see and hear their great hero, General U. S. Grant. Evarts and the others went on to Portland where still another crowd greeted these distinguished guests from the east and from Europe.

Several times during his long legal career Evarts was put forward by his friends for the position of Chief Justice of the Supreme Court. Both occasions involved Chief Justice Salmon P. Chase. The first serious chance Evarts had for this post was in 1864. President Lincoln had the choice between Evarts and Chase. For whatever reasons Lincoln chose the better-connected Chase. When Chase died nine years later Evarts name once again was mentioned on the "best qualified" list. As indicated earlier, Grant was not a great admirer of the New Yorker, and the Senate approved the nomination of Morrison Waite.

Evarts evoked one of two responses. His attractive qualities are set forth by Henry Adams: "Generous by nature, prodigal in hospitality, fond of young people, and a born man-of-the-world, Evarts gave and took liberally, without scruple, and accepted the world without fearing or abusing it. His wit was the least part of his social attraction. His talk was broad and free. He laughed where he could; he joked if a joke was possible, he was true to his friends, and never lost his temper or became ill-natured."[6] His less attractive qualities are set forth by James A. Garfield in a letter to his wife: "It was a pleasure to listen to the brilliant talk of a great lawyer. He gave me a minute account of the two journeys to Europe during the war that he undertook for Mr. Seward to prevent complications and perhaps war with England and France; and then he gave me the interior history of the part he took in the great argument before the International Tribunal at Geneva. It was really a great treat to listen to Mr. Evarts and to measure my mind by his. I suspect that no amount of brilliancy in a man can make his egotism altogether agreeable; for pleasant as it was to listen to Mr. Evarts, I could not forget that he was making himself and his own achievements the center of nearly seven hours of talk."[7] Ah, that fine line between confidence and conceit all of us know so well.

In 1885 Evarts, at the age of sixty-eight, was chosen by the legislature of New York to a six-year term in the Senate. The direct election of Senators by the people did not come until the ratification of the 17th Amendment May 1913. Article I Section 3 of the Constitution in its original form reflected the view that the House represented the people, while the Senate represented the states. He was appointed to two prestigious committees—Foreign Relations and the Judiciary. With his experience as Secretary of State and Attorney General these two assignments were right down his alley. He did a credible job as Senator. The problem was that great things were expected of him. Age was catching up with him, and the most damaging of all was the problems he was having with his sight. He was content to serve just the one term.

In his last years his winters were spent in New York and his summers in Windsor, Vermont. Evarts is best remembered as a transplanted Yankee. He was born in Boston, February 6, 1818. His father was editor of the *Panoplist,* a periodical founded by the orthodox Congregationalists in their dispute with Unitarianism. The liberal Unitarians had taken over that bastion of Congregationalism, the Divinity School Harvard College. The response of the orthodox party was to embrace Yale College and found Andover Seminary, as a "West Point of Orthodoxy." Young Evarts grew up in the thick of this controversy. After graduation from Boston Latin School the normal progression would have been to go on to Harvard. But not in these times of stress in what has been called the "holy commonwealth of New England." Evarts went off to Yale where his family had ties equally strong. His father was one of the founders of the American Board of Commissioners for Foreign Missions and a strong defender of the rights of Native Americans in the southern states. He and his committee sought just treatment for the Indians at the hands of the government. His father died when William was thirteen, a student at Boston Latin. At fifteen he enrolled at Yale where his father had graduated, a brother had been a student, a grandfather (Roger Sherman) had been treasurer, and a brother-in-law had studied divinity. One of his interests at Yale was the debating society, at which he excelled and which gave him invaluable training for the profession he eventually entered. On graduating he ranked third in a class of 104 and was selected as one of the commencement orators. After graduation he returned to Windsor to the home of a sister to teach Latin at the local school and to study law in the office of Horace Everett. Although by this time both Harvard and Yale had law schools, it was still the custom for a young candidate to read under the direction of some established lawyer. Many prepared for the law by reading in the office of an established barrister. When the year was done, Evarts applied for and was accepted by the law school at Harvard. During these years of preparation his vacations were spent at the home of his uncle, Samuel Hoar, whose two sons became surrogate brothers and formed a relationship that lasted a lifetime. One of the two Hoar brothers, Rockwell, became a senator from Massachusetts.

Many years later, Hoar in his book *Autobiography of Seventy Years* writes of his cousin:

"He was always a delightful orator. He rose sometimes to a very lofty eloquence. He had an unfailing wit. You could never challenge him or provoke him to an encounter without making an abundant and sparkling stream gush forth. He never came off second best in an encounter of wits with any man."[8] In a similar vein, Hamilton Fish became irritated by the endless number of Centennial celebrations that dragged on from 1875 to 1889. He gave it as his opinion that William M. Evarts "would yet be heard pronouncing an eloquent discourse on the centennial of the death of John Hancock's tom-cat."[9] To be sure we are speaking of a day and time when people expected a long discourse. If you attended a lecture series and the speaker spoke for less than an hour, you would have felt cheated. Phillips Brooks, one of the great preachers of the nineteenth century, frequently published the best of his sermons. All of them produced, in the idiom Hoar chose to use, "an abundant and sparkling stream" of words that buttressed and supported his central theme. As a skilled practitioner of the courtroom arts, Evarts knew better than most how long a summation of a case should be. What we are left with is a portrait of a great lawyer and advocate of the time before the days of specialists. In 1869 Evarts was the President and founder of the New York Bar Association. He was one of the founders of the Republican Party in New York State. In 1860 he was chairman of delegation to the National Republican Convention that chose Abraham Lincoln as the standard bearer of the fledgling party. Personally he had worked hard in support of the candidacy of New York's very capable senator, William Seward. The convention was held in the days before nominating speeches; hence Evarts' support for Seward had to be limited to the visits he made to the several state delegations. He made a vigorous appeal on behalf of a great statesman who had helped to found the party, and knew where and how to lead it. When it became apparent that Seward could not be nominated, he and the others in the delegation switched to Lincoln and supported the candidate vigorously in the fall election.

Evarts' response to the call to public service extended well over forty years. It began in 1849 when he was appointed Assistant District Attorney for the Southern District of New York and ended with his Senate term in 1891. If money were the primary consideration, Evarts would have chosen another path, and could have become wealthy in the process and at best would have been remembered as a great orator and courtroom tactician. Instead he divided his time between his practice in New York and service in the national capitol, in London, in Paris, and in Geneva.

In his retirement years he spent more and more time in Windsor, where he had received his first training for the law. He built a home and willingly cut himself off from the scenes of his past triumphs. One prominent visitor who dropped by shortly after the War with Spain was Thomas Reed, recently Speaker of the House, who thought the former Secretary of State might wish to be caught up on the new relationship with the Philippines. After listening for some time, Evarts said: "Reed, I don't think I care to hear more about the Philippines. I am not going there anyway."[10]

He was more than happy to talk to some of the clergy he knew from his days at Yale and Harvard. To one visitor who, finding him disinclined to talk, asked him if the affairs of the world no longer interested him. "No, the only world whose affairs interest me is the next one, and nobody who comes here appears to know anything about that."

He died on the last day of February 1901. Following a service in New York his body was taken to Windsor where his grave lies in the shadows of Ascutney. Evarts was never one to speak of his family. He had two sons and a daughter who were apparently devoted to their father. About his wife we knew even less. That must have been the way he wanted it, to keep domestic and private affairs life in the background.

What did Evarts say?

Harvey Scott, for forty years editor of Portland's *Morning Oregonian*, who was present in Gold Creek for the festivities had pencil in hand and kept notes of Evarts speech. Evarts made humorous allusions to New England as the source from which the Northern Pacific Railroad was chiseled. There was truth as well as humor in the allusion, Scott pointed out. The person who first advocated a Pacific Railroad was a Dr. S. B. Barlow from Massachusetts. Asa Whitney, another resident of the same state, who kept the idea alive, is sometimes referred to as "the father of the Pacific railroad." And three Vermonters all played important roles in its development: Edwin Johnson who was the chief engineer beginning in 1867; John G. Smith, the second president and Frederick Billings who was president of the Northern Pacific from 1879 to 1881. And most important of all, Henry Villard was married to a Massachusetts born and bred wife, Emily Garrison Villard. Evarts concluded this portion of his speech by asking the question: "What did Henry Villard do towards building the Northern Pacific railroad before he married his New England wife?" The well-coached response from the crowd was "Nothing!" Villard was delighted with this light touch.

CHAPTER FIFTEEN

Westward Journeys

THE WESTWARD TREK OF THE author's wife's family may prove instructive. The beginnings trace back to the colonial period following the French and Indian war. The authorities of the Province of Nova Scotia encouraged English speaking people from the New England colonies to take up the lands vacated by the expulsion of the Acadians.[1] Six to seven thousand migrated from New England to Nova Scotia in 1760–61 among them the Copps from the North Parish of New London, Connecticut. In the Maritime Provinces the paths of the Copps intertwined with the McCullys and the Dillons. All three had adjoining farms in Albert (formerly Westmorland) County.

The first move westward took place around 1822 when the McCullys purchased a farm not far from the Ohio River in Dillonville, Jefferson County, Ohio. There, John McCully died and his wife Mary moved to Guernsey County, Ohio, in the early 1830s where she remarried. The home she and John

McPherson acquired is said to have been sixteen miles east of Zanesville, an important city on the National Turnpike. The next stop was New London, Des Moines County, Iowa, some eighteen miles west of Burlington—a Mississippi city that was to give its name to a railroad still serving the northwest. Here, her two sons, David McCully and his brother Asa went into the mercantile business. In 1849 the two brothers and a friend, John Love, caught the gold fever, and they went to the California gold fields. They made a considerable amount of money, either from mining gold or more likely selling equipment to miners, and returned east by way of the Isthmus of Panama in 1851.

On March 21, 1852 they started out once again this time on a five-month journey across the plains reaching the Willamette Valley in August and built a home on the present day site of Harrisburg, Linn County, Oregon. Asa and his brother, David McCully, served as scouts of this thirty-wagon train. A log of the journey kept by John McKiernan and a reminiscence by Delilah Frances (McCully) Hendershott recorded by her daughter, Mary Frances Walton, in 1906 provide the details of the 1852 trek.[2]

DELILAH FRANCES HENDERSHOTT

"There were four yoke of oxen and three men for each wagon, three carriages a dozen women and fifteen children. There was one doctor, but no minister in the train. They brought 200 or 300 cows and some horses. The wagon boxes were deep and long, two storied. Provisions were packed in the under story and bedding on top boards laid over the provisions. Each family had two wagons. On the back of one was an extension leaf and on the other a mess chest the lid of which made a table. Our wagon carried a sheet iron stove.

"The first day they traveled 18 miles to Burlington. Crossed the Des Moines River after dark. The Missouri River was muddy and wide with full banks. Here Cousin Joseph got his leg broken. In watering a mule, his leg caught in a lariat on a saddle and he was thrown. The leg was not properly set and he died in a few days. He was about ten years old. They started to Ft. Kearney for medical aid, but he died before they reached there.

"They were all day ferrying the river at "St. Joe." Had three ferries on which to put wagons and swam the cattle—putting them in a quarter of a mile above where they were to come out. Only their noses and horns could be seen. They were thin and one mired down and died. He was eagerly seized by the Indians—the first painted and feathered ones we had seen, and they had a big dance around the fire while they cooked it. We camped there one night, and did not see another house except for forts till we got to Oregon.

"It was a long uneventful trip, there was no road and the wagons traveled along a space a mile wide. Had to carry wood and water across the desert places, and crossed deserts at night on account of the heat. Captain Asa went ahead on horseback to select the camping place for each night.[3] The wagons were placed to form a corral, with tongues outside. Tents were pitched in the circle and all cooking done in there being protected against the Indians. People slept on the ground or in the wagons. Had feather beds and blankets. The horses and oxen were driven in close in a circle around the wagons after grazing till dark. Outside of all were the sentinels to watch the cattle. At daybreak everybody was up—to milk the cows, get breakfast. Surplus milk was strained into cans on the backs of the wagons. The motion of the wagons churned into nutmeg-sized lumps of butter. At night the milk was thrown away.

"They brought some potatoes. After they were eaten up they had rice, beans, bacon and ham, dried fruit (apple and peaches) and lived well. Mixed bread at night and baked before starting in the morning. Sometimes they camped for half a day. Justice was meted out swiftly. A man killed his hired man. A jury was chosen, he was convicted and strung up to a gallows formed of wagon tongues before his wife.[4]

"One day, when camping on the fork of the River Platte for half a day of cooking, washing and grazing two Indians came up, pretending to be very friendly and wanting to look at the guns. They were very dirty Pawnees then at war with the Sioux. A cloud of dust appeared and they affected panic wanting to hide in the wagons from the coming Sioux. Uncle Asa would not allow it. When the Indians arrived it was 50 of their own tribe with whom they held a joyous pow-wow. Their arrow pouches were crowded full and they demanded a cow. If given one they would have followed the train and demanded more and so Uncle Asa decided to have it out with them. According to previous instructions the men of the train (in hiding) would pop off a gun at random. Indians, not being able to see either the men or the guns, were scared and started off both sullenly and reluctantly. They met some young men of the train out by the river hunting. One Indian rode up to Sam Reed (grandfather's hired man) and cut his necktie off with a long knife. These Indians were the only mean ones encountered and they never came back.

"Uncle Asa had hundreds of calico shirts which he sold to Indians for a dollar, or traded for fish, mocassins, beads or arrows. Saw a few Cheyennes. They were clean and traded beads or moccasins for blankets. Shooting into a herd of buffalo caused a stampede. Someone in another train shot into a herd that headed toward our train. As they neared it, the herd parted, and part went on either side, all except one old buffalo which jumped between the tails of the oxen and a wagon and on he went.

"Once Uncle Asa went to get out of the wagon tripped over the tongue and fell. Two wheels went over his shoulder, but he was not hurt much. There was no continual quarreling among the men. Many single men got their board for working until they found work in Oregon. Grandfather was ill for weeks with mountain fever and lazy Sam Reed let grandmother and Uncle John, a lad of 14, set tents etc. After grandfather.was thought to be about well, he ate a few dried peaches. It gave him colic and he nearly died. At this time Lila stepped into a pit of hot buffalo chip coals and severely burned her right foot till it was blistered all over. It left her lame for life.

"When the train came to the Sweetwater, (a river in Wyoming) the banks were full. Two wagon beds were pitched to carry freight and women and children. The wagons and the cattle were swum across. They camped on the bank after crossing on this rather dangerous homemade ferry. The Cascade Mountains were very steep and they held the wagons back with ropes. When crossing the John Day River (Eastern Oregon) they saw their first salmon.

"Got to Salem, Sept. 21st.

Those in the train were, four McCully families

Samuel, wife and four children

David, wife and three children

Asa, wife and little Alice Hamilton

Others in the train were John Starkey family, Dave Busey, Uncle James Hendershott, Wes. Briggs,[5] Sam Reed, Mr. & Mrs. McDonough and one child, Mr. McDonald, wife and three children. Each of the McCully brothers staked out a half section right on the Willamette except Uncle Hamilton McCully who was not married and so could take only a quarter section. They got red fur from Clark's sawmill to put up houses, floor, roof and siding and one window. All furniture was home made, and dug wells for water. They were thirty miles from the nearest store. One or two wagons went to Portland and filled orders for stores.

"The country was advertised as a Garden of Eden with sunshine and no snow. In February there came the first heavy storm which lasted for two weeks. Supplies got low and they were without flour for three days. Had only boiled wheat ground in a coffee mill, and no meat. The wagon brought back from Portland Chili flour which is said to be made of a fine wheat but is very yellow; also they bought a barrel of solid fat pork. All planted fine gardens in the spring. They gathered wild hay for straw ticks and used ropes instead of bedsprings. All were happy to have a home."

For most of this party, the Willamette Valley became their home. But some pressed on, settling in Josephine County in southeastern Oregon and in Crescent City, Del Norte County, California. The McCully family left their mark on the history of their adopted state. David and Asa, who had set up in the mercantile business in Harrisburg, were instrumental in the founding of the People's Transportation Company which ran a line of riverboats on the Willamette. Both brothers served their terms as president.

Asa, it should be noted, made a third trip across the plains. Having arrived in Harrisburg in August 1852 and seeing the desirability of establishing a mercantile business, he once again set sail for Panama, then across the Isthmus, the Gulf of Mexico to the east where he arranged for a load of goods to be shipped to the northwest by way of the Horn. Exactly where he made these arrangements remains unclear. One of the port cities of the East seems a likely possibility. What is obvious is that Asa McCully got around. Three trips across the plains in the space of four years. Were there others like him? Probably. In the year 1852 there were some 50,000 persons who crossed the plains to Oregon, California and points west. We know that Joel Palmer, who eventually became the Commissary General of the Oregon Territory, made two trips. The first trip was exploratory. Did this country live up to its advanced billings? Apparently his answer was, yes. He went back home to Indiana and before setting out a second trip over the plains he authored a road atlas. Here is the route, here are the landmarks, here is where you find good camping grounds, and here is what you should pack for the trek. It turned out to be a financial success. Eventually Palmer settled in Dayton, Yamhill County, Oregon where his home (now in the heart of the wine country) has been turned into a restaurant.

For a report of the third trip taken by Asa McCully we depend on a reminiscence by Wesley W. Briggs of Brownsville, Oregon. The train started out from New London, Iowa, the same starting point as the previous year. The McCully train in 1852 consisted mainly of family and friends. This group was large enough to break into two trains to travel by different routes. They had over 400 head of cattle that required large amounts of feed, that could be obtained with more certainty at two feed yards rather than one.

The memorable events of this second trip were first, a stampede by the cattle that took days to control. The cattlemen were unable to regain control of the herd until the frenzied creatures had spent their last strength. Some of the wagons were turned over and there was a scattering of bedding, cooking utensils and all manner of camp equipment. Some of the troubles with Indians seem almost a repeat of the 1852 crossing. Fifty Pawnee Indians appeared blocking any forward movement of the train. McCully had his wagons circle and placed his sharpshooters at the ready position. The Indians demanded an animal for slaughter. Captain McCully refused. McCully, with a revolver in either hand, rode out to the Indians and demanded that they clear the road and stack arms. Which they did in a very sullen mood. The train passed on without further untoward event. David McCully met the train with supplies, fresh horses and messages from their friends in the Willamette Valley.

After selling the steamship line to the Holladay interests, David McCully again returned to the mercantile business, this time in Salem. In November 1866, David, his wife Mary Ann, and a party of eight took a sailing ship from Portland to the Sandwich Islands. While there, the Consul of the Unites States arranged for a dinner and reception at which the reigning monarch, Kamehameha V and the Queen attended. The party returned home February 1867 by way of San Francisco and a coastal steamer. Much later David and his wife took a trip back east with a group of Oregon Pioneers. The year was 1883 and the excursion took the McCullys and their fellow travelers back east to visit familiar places and persons. The rail bed over which they traversed had been completed a month before. What a sense of satisfaction these pioneers must have experienced as they looked out the windows of their fast moving Northern Pacific train. It sped across the country where many in the party had vivid memories of their earlier trip with oxen and wagon. The McCullys found time to return to the place in Ohio where they had been joined in holy wedlock on May 7, 1840.

Through the influence of a son, Frank David McCully, David and his brother Asa became interested in farm properties in the northwestern part of Oregon. The two jointly owned 1,400 acres of land in Union County on which they raised large herds of cattle and sheep. In 1886 David organized the First Bank of Joseph, Oregon, and jointly with his son built the town's water works system. Young Frank was a chip off the old block when it came to starting various enterprises. In 1879 at the age of twenty he established Joseph's first general store. In 1884 a print shop was added, on land donated by McCully, and the Wallowa *Chieftan* was launched. He was also involved in the development of a stage coach line which connected the town with Elgin and the world beyond. It is no exaggeration to say that the McCullys, father and son, had a financial interest in just about ever aspect of the town's commercial life.

The *Chieftan's* editor, with support from his mentor, began a campaign for the separation of the Wallowa Valley from Union County. In 1886 McCully ran for the state legislature and was elected on that platform. He headed for Salem and wasted no time in fulfilling his promise to the voters. The third bill introduced into the lower house of the legislature that year proposed the creation of a new county in the northeastern corner of the state. McCully had managed to get himself appointed to the Committee on Counties during that session and the bill went sailing through both houses of the legislature. On February 11, 1887, Governor Sylvester Pennoyer made it official with his signature and Wallowa County was now a distinct and separate county.

The town named for old Chief Joseph soon became the county seat. When death closed the career of the "father of Wallowa County" he was buried in an Indian cemetery along side old Chief Joseph. The pioneer generation of McCullys belongs to a fecund era that often produced seven to nine children a generation. Hence there are McCully homes scattered over the state from Jacksonville where John, referred to by the family as Uncle Doc, built a home, to Harrisburg, to Salem and far off Joseph. There are two McCully brothers who are frequently overlooked—Samuel, who divided his time between hotels and farming, and Hamilton who spent most of his adult years in Brownsville, just a few miles east of Harrisburg, where he farmed and operated a flour mill. In time Samuel's descendants pushed over the California line and settled in Crescent City. It was Samuel's daughter, Delilah Frances Hendershott, who wrote "The Crossing of the Plains" we just read. She is the great-great grandmother of the author's wife.

CHAPTER SIXTEEN

River Transportation in the West

THE COLUMBIA AND ITS TRIBUTARIES provide the Northwest with a great natural highway to the interior. For three decades steamboats searched out the navigable waters along the Columbia, Willamette and Snake rivers. What they soon discovered was not one continuous system, but a series of systems divided by impassible rapids and falls. The Columbia was soon divided into three separate navigable sections known to river men as the Lower, Middle and Upper rivers. Each section had its captive steamers and between sections there would be portage, often quite long. Every load proceeding up or down the river had to be loaded on to, or taken off, three times in a trip upriver from Portland to Walla Walla and the Palouse country. Portage was initially supplied by horse drawn wagons later replaced by portage railways.

It didn't take long for the cry of "an open river" to be heard. The people using this phrase were indicating that they wanted a river free of impediments from its mouth to its farthest reaches.

The goal would be achieved in time, but the first response of a constantly enlarging settler community was the organization of navigation companies. The Oregon Steam Navigation Company provided the glue that tied together some of the various elements of this highly profitable route to the interior. The Washington Territory first incorporated the company in 1860 and by the state of Oregon two years later, right in the Civil War period. These were the golden years for the Oregon Steam Navigation Company and their profits made their owners rich. Among the original shareholders there were three known to their contemporaries as "The Triumvirate." The most colorful of the three was Captain J. C. Ainsworth. Born in Ohio in 1822, at seven he lost his father and by his early teens began to make his living taking odd jobs on the Mississippi. Before long he became the master of a steamer serving St. Louis and points north. On his boat he had a young pilot named Samuel Clemens who was to make a name for himself under the nom de plume Mark Twain. When news of the discovery of gold reached St. Louis, Ainsworth with his good friend, William C. Ralston, decided to try their luck in the west. Ainsworth transferred his nautical knowledge from the Mississippi to the Sacramento River, while Ralston soon became one of San Francisco's leading bankers. By 1850 Ainsworth was off again, this time to Oregon to become the master of the very first built-in-Oregon steamboat, the *Lot Witcomb*. He asked Ralston for a loan of $50,000 that was quickly granted. When Ralston's partner returned from the east and found that his partner had made an unsecured loan he demanded the loan be rescinded. Much against his own personal wishes, a letter to this effect was sent. But Ainsworth had already made a profit on his deal and had returned the money before Ralston's letter reached him. The affair so disgusted Ralston that he severed connections with his partner and organized a new bank, the Bank of California. Another member of "The Triumvirate" was Simeon Reed, who had interests in the distribution of liquors and groceries, farm properties, and river navigation. Reed is best remembered these days as the donor of funds that led to the establishment of Reed College in Portland. R. R. Thompson, the third member of the group, controlled navigation on the upper river. He appears to have been a man of few words, but where matters of business were concerned his partners found him a wise counselor.

Traffic increased rapidly from 10,500 passengers and 6,290 tons in 1861 to 24,500 passengers and 14,500 tons of freight in 1862. Luck was with the Triumvirate from the first. About the time the company was organized, rich placer gold mines were discovered in Idaho, eastern Washington and western Montana. There was a rush of prospectors up the Columbia to these points. Growth in the interior was straining the facilities of the company to the very limit.

"These were the days when the Oregon Steam Company made money, hand-over-fist." as Henry Dosch, who we will meet in the chapter on Centennials Galore, recalled many years later. "They charged $60 a ton for freight from Portland to The Dalles. Fare was $20 and meals were a dollar. Frequently a steamer would make from $3,000 to $5,000 on a single trip. The record profit was made on May 13, 1862 when one boat made a profit of over $10,000."[1] Portage railways were added in 1863. In that same year what little competition the company had was diminished when the People's Transportation Company abandoned their Columbia River routes in return for a free hand on the Willamette.

The People's Transportation Company has a special interest for the author, since his wife is related to two of the company's founders, Asa and David McCully. The organization of the company was much like that of the older, stronger OSN. The settlers along the upper Willamette River wanted an outlet for their produce. The two brothers had a mercantile business in Harrisburg and they and others found it necessary to start a river transportation company that could keep a reliable schedule to and from the emerging center of commerce, Portland.

The People's Line, as it was frequently called, was organized in 1857 and had two fleets, one below the Falls of the Willamette and another above the Falls. Passengers and freight south bound from Portland to piers at Champoeg, Dayton, Salem, Albany, Corvallis and eventually Eugene, had to stop at Oregon City, unload to portage that would take them to Canemah above the Falls. There they would reload on to the little steamers that would take them to one of the numerous ports along the river. The first improvement made to this route was the construction of a breakwater at Canemah. Now steamers waiting to dock at Canemah did not run the risk of being washed over the Falls. The second improvement came with the completion of the canal and locks on the west side of the river. An attempt was made to dramatize the opening of this important appendage to river navigation. Guests included the Governor, a former Governor, the Mayor of Portland, the editors of the leading papers and others prominent in the business world. On a raw, windy, rainy New Year's Day 1873 the dignitaries squeezed on to the seventy-five foot long *Marie Wilkins*. At the Clackamas rapids the small steamer encountered difficulties. For a time it seemed that the craft would not be able to access the canal entrance, but persistence paid off. She arrived at the locks at noon where she was greeted by an enthusiastic crowd protected by shelters and umbrellas. The Governor made a speech praising the canal builders, following which the people broke open their packed lunches and made merry. It didn't match the opulence on display at Gold Creek, Montana, when the first northern transcontinental line was completed but people sensed that with this canal new markets would open up for the farmers of the valley. The canal had been financed by bonds issued by the State of Oregon. At first the maintenance and operation of the locks was entrusted to private contractors, and eventually would be turned over to the Corps of Engineers. The Willamette now presented a stream of continuous passage from Portland to Eugene. The dreams of an Open River were beginning to be realized.[2]

While the People's line did well, it never had the financial backing the Oregon Steam Navigation did. The periods that monopolized the river transportation scene on the Willamette were of short duration. Periodically it would face what appeared to be well-financed competition. The locks at Willamette Falls had just been completed when the formation of a new company was announced—the Willamette Transportation and Locks Company with a capital stock issue of a million dollars. The new firm proceeded to build and buy large steamers 140 to 163 feet in length. They announced that their aim was to transport wheat from Corvallis all the way to Astoria for $4.00 a ton. The new line lasted just over a year. During this same period the Oregon Steam Navigation Company announced that it was reorganizing as the Oregon Railway & Navigation Company with a capitalization of six million dollars.

As an artifact of their decade and a half presence on the river, here is a page one story published by the *Morning Oregonian* for Monday, April 17, 1865:

President Lincoln Assassinated!
Attempts to Assassinate Secretary of State
Seward Still Living
The Assassins Escape

Every newspaper in the country printed dispatches from the nation's capitol carried overland by telegraph authenticated by Edwin M. Stanton, Secretary of War. Copies of these newspapers carrying the story of Lincoln's death were carefully set aside and saved as something very special. In my family it was the *New York Herald* of the same date. In fact the front page of the *Oregonian* and the *Herald* carried the same dispatches from Stanton. Black lines between the margins of the story were used to maximize the sense of shared grief.

The *Oregonian* editorialized: "The nation bows under the weight of its grief and anguish. Through the fearful ordeal of battle by which it has been tried, it has borne up bravely, mourning indeed for the loss of its sons as they were snatched away by death, but its present bereavement is the most cruel and grievous of all, and an overwhelming sense of the calamity, oppresses every loyal and feeling heart. The nation's anguish is unutterable, and words are vain."

Other stories carried by the Portland paper were relegated to the inner pages. But the papers of that era carried advertising on the cover page. For people in the northwest this was still the pre-railroad period, so the departure and arrival of ships was of general interest to all. Here was an ad that advised that the *Brother Jonathan*, S. L. DeVolk, commanding, would leave Portland for San Francisco at 5 p.m., April 17. And here is another ad inserted by the People's Transportation Company in which Asa A. McCully, president, announces its new schedule. The *Reliance* will leave Canemah every Monday and Thursday for Corvallis, and on Wednesday the *Enterprise* would leave the same pier for Harrisburg.

The Northern Pacific was rapidly building its rail lines to the west. Both river transportation companies could clearly see that the advantages they had hitherto enjoyed would soon come to an end. The officers of the People's Transportation Company were the first to react. Part of the demands of running any business is knowing when to expand and when to call it quits. The officer and board members voted to sell their ten-boat flotilla and related properties to the Ben Holladay rail interests for $200,000. While none of the original investors became wealthy, at least they could console themselves in the knowledge that they had seen a need and had met it.

The Oregon Steam Navigation Company was soon presented with an inquiry from Henry Villard. What would Ainsworth and his partners sell their transportation company for? The cagey old riverboat captain made an inventory of everything the company owned. He came up with an estimated value of two and a half million dollars. He called together the members of board. This is what we have invested. Shall we sell it for this price? Thompson, always a man of few words, took a look at the proposal, studied for a time and finally said, "Ask for twice that amount." So they did. Villard and his associates jumped at the price and the deal was settled. On May 23, 1879 Villard became president of the Oregon Steam Navigation Company, now reorganized as the Oregon Railway and Navigation Company.

Ainsworth and Thompson went on to other projects. Largely for reasons of health, Ainsworth moved to Oakland, California. He and Thompson organized a beach resort in southern California, at Redondo Beach. Ainsworth had become interested in banking while still living in the Portland area. He formed the Ainsworth National Bank that in 1902 was merged into the United States Bank of Oregon. His son, John C. Ainsworth, became president of this bank and served in that position for twenty-nine years. As for his father, he seems to have found a second vocation in banking. In his latter years he founded a bank in his new home city, Oakland.[3]

With the completion of the acquisition the two companies were joined. For a time both aspects of the transportation business, rail and river, would be controlled by a single entity. Villard, acting on behalf of the German bondholders, had earlier taken over the Ben Holladay Oregon and California Railroad. Off in the future this rail line, which had reached Roseburg, would be extended to the California state line and would provide a north to south connection with the markets to the south. The vigor with which Villard and his associates pushed hard to connect the eastern and western branches of the Northern Pacific are told elsewhere. Here let us continue with the story of the western waterways. As the nation moved swiftly from the age of river transportation to the railway age, it is tempting to think that dependence on river transport was gradually disappearing. Nothing could be further from the truth. The People's Transportation Company was melded into the Holladay interests, which in turn were taken over by the Northern Pacific. And the Oregon Steamship Company was likewise folded in to the Northern Pacific. Each of these entities derived a portion of their income from river navigation. Two old names passed from the scene. In their place arose new navigation companies. Today it is the Shaver Transportation Company founded in 1880 based in Portland, the seventy-year old Tidewater Barge Lines based in Vancouver, and the Oregon City based Bernert Barge Lines that are the leaders in the Columbia-Snake maritime industry.

On the Columbia, two impediments to an Open River were removed. The first to go was the six-mile-long rock-studded channel through the Cascades. This time the project would be planned and built by the Corps of Engineers. In 1889 and 1890 eight western territories became states.[4] Add the three that were already states and presto—you have twenty-two new members of the United States Senate. It is truly amazing how an increase of that magnitude can increase a region's clout. In the earlier days of navigation on the Columbia, riverboat captains, seeking to avoid payment of portage, would occasionally slide through the rapids with boat intact. But it was at best a risky venture. In 1896 the

COLUMBIA RIVER LOCKS

Corps of Engineers at last completed the first of two canals and locks to circumvent the areas of potential disaster. By 1915 a second canal and locks at Celilo removed a final barrier when the *J. N. Teal* and the *Inland Empire* passed through the newly created passage. The ship *J. N. Teal* was named for Joseph N. Teal, who, with his father, had fought for an Open River for over three decades. His father had been instrumental in getting the state to approve the issuance of bonds to build the passage around the Falls of the Willamette, and the son had carried on the fight to remove the last obstacles on the Columbia.

That safe and unencumbered passage from Portland to Lewiston, Idaho was at last realized. Tugs and barges carrying wheat, potatoes, and other bulk commodities have been able to make this trip for close to a century. The scene up and down the far reaches of the river has changed drastically. The first of the great dams built to generate electricity came during the Franklin D. Roosevelt "New Deal" years. The Bonneville Power Administration was created in 1937 to market and distribute power at the lowest possible rates consistent with sound business principles, giving preference to public bodies and rural co-operatives. The latter provision gave rise to a large number of citizen-owned utilities. Over the years the Bonneville Power Administration created a power transmission grid distributing power to Canada and six western states.

Hydropower cost $10 per megawatt to produce, compared with nuclear at $60, coal at $45 and natural gas at $30.[5] The cost of electricity has been a major factor in attracting major industries to the northwest. During the energy shortage that peaked in 2001, there was an escalation of rates charged. Other regions, more dependent on fossil fuels, drove rates to heights never before experienced.

On the lower river between Astoria and Portland where the channel is forty feet deep there are twelve ports, three on the Oregon side, the remainder on the Washington side. Of these, five are rated as deep-water ports that have grain elevators, rail access and warehouse facilities. They are Astoria, Longview, Kalama, Vancouver and Portland. On the upper river from Portland to the Tri-Cities of Richland, Pasco, and Kennewick, where the depth is fourteen feet, there are four additional dams with locks at Bonneville (1937), The Dalles (1957), the John Day (1968), and the McNary (1954). Between the Tri-Cities and Lewiston, Idaho, there are four more dams with locks at Ice Harbor, the lower Monumental dam, the Little Goose dam, and the Lower Granite dam. The dams without locks in the upper Columbia between the Tri-Cities and Chelan-Douglas, generate electricity but are not a factor in water transportation.

The 465-mile trip up the Columbia-Snake river system from Astoria to Lewiston can take up to forty-seven hours. To Portland or Vancouver, both 105 miles from Astoria, the trip takes seven and a half hours. Almost half of all the wheat grown in the United States moves to market by means of the Columbia-Snake River. Containers filled with bulk grains are transported on this river highway to worldwide markets. In the year 2000 the value of this water borne cargo was estimated to be $13.9 billion.

The agency that dredges and maintains this river system is the Corps of Engineers, which can boast that it is the world's largest engineering, design and construction company. In 2001 the Corps had some 34,000 civilian employees with another 650 military men and women spread over eight departments and forty-one districts. The district responsible for the Columbia-Snake system has been headquartered in Portland since the first engineer, Major Henry W. Robert was assigned in 1871. Over a span of 130 years the Corps has surveyed local rivers and rapids, provided dredging and rock removal, embankment protection, built harbors and deep draft ports. Flood control is always a primary concern on any waterway. The Columbia-Snake river system has faced two major floods in recent years. The worst flood came in 1948 when Vanport, a wartime housing project located on

Portland's northside, took the lives of thirty-nine people and flooded 650 blocks in the downtown area. The Corps set about building a sea wall and reservoirs. The flood control thus provided saved the city a repeat performance during the flood of the winter of 1995–96. To keep the Willamette from flooding downtown Portland, the Corps of Engineers coordinated the operations of sixty dams throughout the Columbia basin. Releases from dams on the lower Columbia were manipulated to take advantage of the limited storage capacity available. In a massive community effort volunteers and emergency workers extended and reinforced Portland's seawall. Fortunately the wall was never needed as reduced releases and carefully managed flows at all of its projects allowed the Corps to keep the river below the sea wall top. After the danger was past it was estimated that this coordinated control prevented more than 3.2 billion in damages.[6]

The challenge facing the Corps today is twofold: can the need for power be balanced with the need to protect and enhance salmon runs, and second will the federal and state authorities allow a deepening of the channel in the lower river to forty-three feet from the present forty feet? The diminished number of salmon returning up river to their spawning grounds has been a widely shared concern of environmentalists and citizens for years. Millions of dollars have been spent to improve the present system.

Every dam has its fish ladder and the number of returning salmon is zealously counted. The most extreme measure suggested is that some of the dams must be torn down. There seems little support for this drastic measure, especially in view of the fact that the northwest is heavily dependent on hydropower generated by these same dams.

The second concern involves deepening the channel of the lower river by three feet. Where does the pressure for this development come from? From overseas shippers. The overseas shipment of bulk foods is now handled almost exclusively by ships registered in Korea and Japan. Some of the newer and larger deep-draft vessels can no longer make it up the lower river to the ports of Portland and Vancouver. One of the Korean firms, Hanjin, has already indicated that it will cease serving the ports in the year 2002. This depth of channel has been a problem for river ports from the very first.

Tacoma with its deep-water facilities on Puget Sound seems on the surface to provide an ideal solution until you examine the details. Is there a water route from the upper Columbia to Puget Sound? There is. Could the small sized barges designed to operate in fourteen feet depth make the trip by way of the ocean to Puget Sound? Short answer—no. River barges are not designed for such a task. There are sea barges that operate between Seattle and Alaska. Could shipments be transferred from river barges to sea barges? Yes, but the added cost of such a procedure would price the grain out of the market. Could the grain be shipped by rail? Yes, and once again the added cost of shipping by either truck or rail would make western wheat non-competitive in the world market.

Hanjin's regional manager in Portland put the matter this way: "It's a global decision. It's not lack of support from Portland. In fact our vessels have been full. But the world is a bigger place." To finish the rest of that sentence, one might surmise the ending to be, if our customers can find grain of the same quality at a cheaper price they will buy it. The newly appointed Executive Director of the Port of Portland has been quoted as saying: "The wheat farmer of Eastern Oregon, the athletic apparel company in Portland, and the tire distributor in Prineville share a direct reliance on these deep draft vessels to keep local products competitive and the regional economy robust."[7]

CHAPTER SEVENTEEN

The Automobile Era

THE CENTENNIAL OF THE AUTOMOBILE was widely observed in 1996. In the United States the Postal Service issued a set of five stamps honoring Locomobile, Pierce Arrow, Cord, Packard and Duesenberg. The observance marked the beginning of automobile manufacturing in Europe (Damlier-Benz) and here in the United States (Stevens-Duryea). There had been efforts that preceded that date as bicycle and carriage makers pioneered in efforts to link the combustion engine to a form that the consumer could relate to—the horseless carriage. It took a bit over a decade for the automobile to reach the Main Street of small town America. The first auto sold and the first purchaser to buy was grist for the mill of the local weekly. Not everyone was enthusiastic over the idea of motorized travel. For starters there were the owners of the 14,000,000 horses in the country along with the blacksmiths, harness and carriage makers plus the local merchants who catered to their needs. There were horse lovers who felt there was no sight so beautiful as a team of high-stepping steeds in full stride. Those early cars were noisy, smoking, chattering vehicles that fouled the air and scared the daylights out of horses.

Manufacturers were scattered from Connecticut to Wisconsin with the heaviest concentration in Ohio, Michigan and Indiana. New York had a modest share of this newly emerging industry. The famous Thomas Flyer, the winner of the first New York to Paris race in 1908, was produced in Buffalo, as was the Pierce-Arrrow, one of the great luxury cars of the pre-depression period. The air-cooled Franklin claimed Syracuse as its home base. Rochester produced the Cunningham, another highly regarded car the style-conscious public favored, along with the North East Electric Company, makers of generators, starters, and ignition systems. Ohio soon became the home of the automotive tire industry. Goodyear, Goodrich, Firestone, General, Fisk were all based in Ohio. For a time Indianapolis and Cleveland rivaled Detroit for distinction of being the automotive capitol of America. Peerless, Chandler, Winton and White were all made in Cleveland. Marmon, Duesenberg, Stutz, and Premier were all assembled in the Indiana city. The development of the prestigious Indianapolis 500 race stands as a symbol of the city's tie to the automotive era. During the first decade of the twentieth century, with Henry Ford's Model T leading the way, motor vehicle production rose from 4,000 to 187,000 annually with over 400.000 cars registered by 1910. It was the birth of a new industry. Census officials, wondering how to categorize this phenomenon, choose not to list automobile manufacturing as an industry but instead lumped it under the omnifarious title "miscellaneous."

As every car buff knows, Michigan came to dominate the field. The shorthanded way of referring to the entire industry was to use the name of the automotive capitol—Detroit. Several makes were made in nearby places such as Flint and Lansing. The combination of Ford, Dodge Brothers and General Motors along with the automotive supply firms that provided everything from axles and brakes, to special body shops and spark plugs made Detroit the place to go for a good job. It also helped that many of the inexpensive cars of the period were made there. Ford and Chevy, eventually to be joined by Walter P. Chrysler's Plymouth, all had models for under $600. A used car could be found for $100. It would have a few years on it but it would run. Cars in that price spread made them affordable to a mass market.

The big leap in motor vehicle registration figures came after World War II. By way of example, Oregon, which had 399,000 registered vehicles in 1940, saw the figure rise to 716,000 in 1950, 971,000 in 1960 and 1,457,000 by 1970. To switch from state to federal census figures, by 1980 there were 155,000,000 automobiles, trucks and buses in the United States. By 1990 the figure was 186,000,000 and by 1998 it had climbed to 211,000,000. When G.I. Joe and G.I. Jane came home from war, high on their agenda was completing their education, marriage, starting a family and buying a home and car. I bought my first home in Millbrae, California, for $13,600. I cashed in some of the war bonds I had purchased during my service days and moved in with $600 down plus closing costs. Our monthly mortgage payments for amortization and tax were slightly less than $100. I'm told that this same house today, given its close proximity to San Francisco, would probably fetch $400,000. I sold it for a figure somewhat less than that—$15,000 after three years of occupancy.

One of the unintended results in this growth of the automobile was in the design of the garage. The home my parents first built in New York in 1912 had no garage. It wasn't needed. My father walked to the nearby railroad station and at Grand Central Station changed to the subway that took him to his work at Maiden Lane and Nassau Street in the heart of the financial district. The home my parents purchased in White Plains, built in 1927, had a one-car garage. The car was never used for commute purposes. It was public transportation all the way, bus, rail, subway. The house my wife and I live in now has a double car garage. Fairly typical for our time. The only time I use public transportation, I'm ashamed to admit, is for the occasional trip to Seattle. Edith Wharton, author of the Pulitzer Prize winning novel *The Age of Innocence* was once asked why she preferred the car, "Because you can go when you want to." Within a few miles of our home I know of at least two five-car garages. One day the doors of one of these barn-like sheds were wide open and I spotted a vacation motor home, three cars and a riding mower. By their toys, you shall know them!

In the early years of the evolution of the automobile, the price was a real obstacle for most buyers. $1,500 doesn't seem like a lot these days. But in 1900 to 1910 it was a year's wage for many. Floyd Clymer, the automobile historian, says that over 2,200 makes of cars were once manufactured in the United States.[1] Most of them were handcrafted before production lines were introduced. When I was young my aspiration was to become an automobile manufacturer. I even had a name picked out—the Hillson 6. I developed a series of drawings for the various models—roadster, two sedans and touring car. In my teens I was a backyard tinkerer operating on a thirteen-year-old model T Ford. There wasn't a repair job that I couldn't handle, and parts were as handy as the nearest Sears or Ward's catalog. Sad to record, the Hillson 6 never made it to the drawing board and won't be found in Clymer's list.

As a part of the automobile centennial, the Portland *Oregonian* ran a list of cars that stood out in the first half century.[2] This is their pick:

- Model T Ford—no surprise here. At one time half of the cars produced in the United States were Model T Fords. Assembly line methods of production pioneered by Ford put this car within reach of millions. The last of 15 million of the T's rolled off the lines in 1927, at which time the model A was introduced.
- 1912 Cadillac—the first car with an electric self-starter. It put women behind the wheel for the first time.

THE AUTOMOBILE ERA

- 1916–1932 Jordan—credit Ned Jordan's marvelous ad for this pick "Somewhere west of Laramie."
- 1932 Ford V-8—my car during the war years was a slightly newer version of this car.
- 1934 Chrysler Airflow—An eye-catching design used in both Chrysler and DeSoto models. Engineers praised the design, but buyers shunned it.
- 1936 Volkswagen—the first import to make the list. Introduced in Europe, it wasn't until after the war that it took off in America. Some of the old Bugs are still cherished. It was my son's first car. I would rate it in the same bracket as the Model T.
- 1936 Cord—All the Cords and Auburns deserve to be on this list. Problem is they are so rare you seldom see one outside of a Concourse.
- Pre-War MGs—a wonderful sports car roadster with wire wheels. This import came from England. When one passed, heads turned.
- The Military Jeep—first made by Bantam, then Willys and Ford, it was the workhorse of World War II. As a Signal Officer in the Marine Corps I had one with mounted radio gear. I remember being able to listen to all of the St. Louis World Series of 1944. We were in the Solomon Islands and picked it up from an armed forces radio station.
- 1947 Tucker—Only a few were made, but people talked about some of its new safety features.
- 1949 Nash—almost bought one of these. It came down to a choice between this car and a Studebaker. I bought the Studie. The Nash was the first mass produced unit body construction, which would be widely copied.

A week later Boone followed up with a second list covering cars from the second half century.[3] Without editorial comment, they are:

- The Volkswagen Beetle made both lists, the only car to do so.
- 1953 Corvette, 1955 Chevrolet V-8, Austin Mini, Mercedes Benz 300SL, the Jaguar XKE, 1964 Ford Mustang, the AC Cobra, Datsun 240Z, Honda CVCC and the Chrysler Minivan. Note the high percentage of imported cars. In the first half century American car manufacturers had the domestic market pretty much to themselves. Now they were forced to compete with cars from Europe and Japan.

Not happy with these lists? What car and model would you add? To the first list I would add the 1911–12 Mercer Raceabout. The versions I have seen were all painted in a bright yellow with a bulb for a horn and a round window shield to keep the mud out of the driver's face. It was the number one sports car of its time, and today these babies are priceless. I would also include at least one steam car and an electric—say Stanley Steamer and the Detroit Electric. In 1906 the Stanley Steamer was rated the fastest car in the world when it achieved a speed of 127 miles per hour. The use of steam predates the combustion engine by at least a century. The development of the steam engine took place principally in the British Isles with the pioneer efforts of Watt, Neucomen and a namesake, William Murdock. Earlier we took note of the application of the steam engine to transportation on the Hudson. Robert Fulton applied a British-built engine to a riverboat and in 1807 made the New York to Albany run in the Clermont. The first crossing of the Atlantic in an all-steam boat took place in 1838 when the Great Western made the Bristol to New York run in fifteen days. Steam applied to a locomotive dates from 1829 with George Stevenson's Rocket. Steam applied to agriculture was bound to follow with the opening up of the prairie west of the Mississippi. When the steam engine was stationary and applied to such tasks as the threshing of grain, the ginning of cotton, the cutting of lumber and other belt work it was a great boon. But mounted on four wheels and used as a mobile plow it was expensive and cumbersome. Rusted hulks of these old monsters with their huge flywheels still can be seen in agricultural museums.

Reynold Wik, an agricultural historian, writes: "Before anyone had seen an automobile, approximately 75,000 farm engineers were operating their steam engines in the grain growing regions of the nation."[4] When the automobile came along at the end of the nineteenth century, and more specifically the truck and the tractor, it found a ready acceptance in the rural areas. The great stumbling block was the cost. Gradually the American farmer was forced to become a capitalist. Special applications to be attached to the tractor poured forth from the factories largely located in the mid-west. Plows, disc plows, harrows, seed planters, reapers—the list goes on and on. Each one was presented as a labor saving device. And it was—fewer and fewer people were needed to produce the food for the market.

One of the great boons to the farm family was the addition of the car. The sense of isolation fast disappeared. Going into town on a Saturday in the horse and buggy age was a great social event, but it often took hours to get there. Now with one of these new cars the family could cover the same distance in minutes—provided, of course, that the roads were ice free and dry. Roads, axle deep in mud, were the common lot in spring. Soon a cry went up from urban dweller and the farmer alike—we want good roads! It was a cry that legislators at the county and state level paid heed to. Soon construction crews laid down all kinds of improved roads. The most common were gravel, macadam and concrete. In 1916 Congress passed the Federal Road Act that allotted $500,000 with the intent to promote the farm-to-market transportation. It seems a paltry sum by today's standards, but it established a precedent. Now good roads were a concern at every level, town, city, county, state and federal. And to make sure that legislators were listening, the nation's automobile owners formed automobile clubs, the most prominent of which—the American Automobile Association—provided maps, travel guides, emergency services, a rating system of motels and travel lodges, and perhaps most importantly, a lobby at the state capitol.

At the time of America's bicentennial the Associated Press asked leading journalists to name the most important developments during that time frame. Two hundred seventy-two replied. They gave first ranking to the Revolution, the drafting of the Constitution, the Civil War and World War II. Henry Ford and the rise of the automobile was rated tenth ahead of the New Deal, the Louisiana Purchase, the Vietnam War, the 1954 Supreme Court decision outlawing school segregation, the development of television, aviation and the electrification of the nation.[5]

The mention of the Detroit Electric appended to the list of early cars, was included for two purposes. First, this car was a favorite of women. It was the favorite of Mrs. Henry Ford. For one thing the "bird cage" (that's what the public came to call it) didn't have to be cranked. It was also relatively silent. It produced no exhaust fumes. The limiting factor was the range that it could go on one charge of the battery. In the early models, a charged battery permitted a range of twenty-five miles. In the last models, the range was increased to well over a hundred miles. Moreover the electric car owner needed to provide space in the garage for the charger. With its limited range the electric car was essentially an urban vehicle. The ads featured people dressed as if they were headed for the opera. Detroit Electric production ended in the mid-twenties. The last one I saw in operation was in Greenwich, Connecticut in the fifties. It was chauffeur driven and the lady in the rear had probably exceeded the biblical three score years and ten. She had the look of someone who, when presented with the news that her favorite car was now an orphan declared, "Well, I'm keeping this car going as long as I live." Apparently she had the checkbook to do just that. Greenwich at the time had the reputation of having the highest per capita income in the nation.

The second reason I included electric cars is that these cars— or at least a hybrid electric—gasoline version, are making a come back in the motor world. Two imports, the Toyota Prius and the Honda Insight, are selling near the $20,000 price mark and feature a small gasoline engine with batteries that power an electric motor. The fuel mileage is impressive. The lighter weight of the two, the Insight, can deliver 68 miles per gallon on the highway, 61 mpg in the city, with the more conventional looking Prius delivering 52 miles per gallon on the highway, 45 mpg in the city. As the cost of gasoline inches up and the concern over global warming becomes widespread, consumers are beginning to look to these models as part of the answer. The advantage these cars have over the old electric cars of the early period is that they are charged while in motion. Yes, there is a downside to these lightweight models. It's the safety factor. If you tangle with a lumber truck in one of these models make sure you have filled out your donor body parts chart.

Tractors, once fueled by steam, in the twentieth century were fueled by gasoline. Much like the passenger cars, there was a wide price variation depending on the horsepower you needed to operate your rig. On the low side in 1926 was the Fordson priced at $495. The Fordson could pull two 14" plows at an average speed of 2.75 mph and weighted 2562 lbs. At the high end, the Caterpillar Company had a ten-ton model that could pull seven 14" plows. The price tag was $5950. Allis-Chalmers, Case and John Deere had models in mid-range that would pull three or four plows for $1300 to $1500.[6] Comparative prices for today's John Deere tractors would be $15,000 for the low end model and $80,000 for the 140 horse power 7410 model capable of pulling four to five plows. The farmer with limited acreage would be content with the low-end models. On the rangeland in west, Minnesota, Iowa, Nebraska and Kansas the choice would be one of the larger models that could pull multiple plows

Trucks, too, come in all sizes and all prices. Light trucks—those made by manufacturers of passenger cars—have seen increased sales in the 1985–2000 period. In 1999 over six and a half million of these quarter to half a ton trucks were sold with Ford alone producing 2.4 million. The heavy trucks with their trailers you see along the freeways now carry just over 70 percent of all freight shipped in my home state of Oregon.

The names of some of the rigs you are likely to see on the highway are Freightliner, Kenworth, Peterbuilt, Cummins and Mack. The Cleveland-based Mack Company switched to a diesel engine and is still competitive in today's market. The White Company, another Cleveland automaker, had a curious beginning. It was an established manufacturer of sewing machines. In 1900 White decided to enter the automotive field. It produced both steam and gasoline passenger cars, and at one time claimed to be the largest producer of commercial motor vehicles in America. The passenger line was given up but the firm continued producing a truck line well into the 1980s. In 1928 White made a one-ton, two-ton, three-and-a-half ton, and a five-ton truck. The price for the five-ton model was $4,500. Compare that price with the 2001 Cruiser Class Freightliner (with sleeper) for $90,000. The Business Class Freightliner suitable for local deliveries carries the more modest price tag of $34,000 to $54,000.

The *New York Times Almanac* has neatly categorized the age of the railroad and the age of the automobile as follows:[7]

- 1865–1915 the Golden Age of the railroad. During this half century the rail network grows from 35,000 miles to a peak of 254,000 miles.
- 1940 By the eve of World War II, automobiles, large buses, trucks, planes and pipelines have become competitors of the railroad.
- 1945–1970 Railroads invest huge amounts of capital to modernize their aging fleets. Diesels replace the steam engines.
- 1970–1975 Nine first-class railroads, representing one fourth of the industry, file for bankruptcy protection. Amtrak was created by Congress with the passage of the Rail Passenger

THE AUTOMOBILE ERA   229

Service Act and began service in 1971. Gradually rail service was curtailed. The first cutbacks came in the east where competing lines served the same region. A good example would be the New York to Buffalo run served by at least four carriers.

For years beyond counting, the railroads had counted on a combination of passenger service plus freight to end each year in the black with a good dividend for the stockholder. Trying to run a railroad on just passenger business would be a risky move in the best of times. With the government having to subsidize Amtrak the pressure built to terminate the less profitable routes. One by one, small cities lost their rail service. One of the economic facts of life in Twenty-first Century America is that in order to attract industry you must have public transit. If you lost rail service you'd better hope you have bus service. And most important, your community must be within an hour or two of a major airport.

The 2000 census figures reveal that the country has topped 281 million. The recent census continues two trends that have been evident for some time. First, small cities and towns are losing population. What small industry they once had, has relocated, often absorbed by large corporations in distant cities. Many of the shops along the Main Streets of these bypassed towns are shuttered. Fewer people are left to shoulder the burden of supporting the infrastructure, and the few that are left are older. Second, the shift of population from the East and North to the South and Southwest continues. Florida, Texas and California reaped the large gains. Nevada has grown by 66 percent, Arizona by 40 percent, Utah by 30 percent, Montana by 20 percent. California by the year 2000 had a population of 34,000,000. After World War II, I moved from New York State to California. By the 1950 census New York was still our largest state with roughly 14.8 million. California was second with just over 10.5 million. In the 1960 census New York hung on to its lead, but by 1970 the roles were reversed—the Golden State had become our largest state. In the last half century the state has more than tripled its population. California's economy now exceeds that of France!

The surprise in this list from the Bureau of the Census is Nevada. The state was added to the Union during the Civil War. With its silver mines booming the state soon had a United States Mint in Carson City. Later it became the gambling and divorce capitol of the country. An aunt and uncle moved to Reno after World War I. My uncle soon established his dental practice and both husband and wife camped and fished in the region along the Truckee River. In the early 20s they moved up into the Sierras where they built a home in Quincy, California. They found the fly-fishing in the Feather River and its tributaries equal to or better than what they had known in Nevada. My very first train trip took me to this "frontier" town. There wasn't a paved road in town. Basque shepherds would drive their sheep right down the main street of Quincy to go from one grazing spot to another. An unforgettable memory is driving on the mountain roads in the Fordyce's Studebaker Big Six. With my aunt at the wheel on the narrow twisting roads carved out of a mountainside we would meet a loaded lumber truck coming down hill. The rule of the road was that the up-coming vehicle must back down to a turn out, giving the driver of the lumber truck an opportunity to pass. My appreciation of my aunt's ability as a skilled driver knew no bounds.

One more story about the Fordyces of Quincy. In the mid 1920s they decided it was time to replace their trusty Studebaker. They arranged with the local dealer to pick up a new model in South Bend, Indiana, home of the automobile maker. The plan was to pick up the new car and ship it back to Quincy by rail. While they were at it, they extended the trip by a few hundred miles and drive from Quincy to St. Thomas, Ontario, my uncle's hometown, and then back to South Bend. I relate this story to give the reader some idea of what constituted an interstate road in the 1920s. Basically what it amounted to in the western states was a hodgepodge of roads connecting one small town with another and maintained by the state and county. Between Reno and Iowa the only paved roads to be found were in the larger cities they passed through. The remainder of the road net was what we would call a dirt road. My aunt kept a log of this trip, and made entries day by day. On the worst of days they would make less than 100 miles, and such days were frequent. Quincy to South Bend is a trip of roughly 2,200 miles. Add another 200 miles to reach St. Thomas, Ontario, and you are looking at close to a month of travel. Directions given by helpful service station attendants were often vague and resulted in an occasional wrong turn that cost miles and time. Each daily entry would catalog how many cars they had met on that day, and the make of the cars. No surprise, Ford Model T cars were predominant. At the time the Ford Motor Company controlled 50 percent of the domestic new car sales, General Motors controlled 30 percent and the rest of the industry scrambled for the remaining 20 percent.

With the Bicentennial of the Lewis and Clark Expedition in 2003, much is made of the overland trails that led west from places like Independence and St. Joseph, Missouri. These trails led to the Washington Territory, Oregon and California. Oxen, horses and mules provided the power to move these heavily laden wagons. We have already examined the stories of some of the principal trailblazers. Now we turn to stories of the first highways of the automobile age. Reference has been made to first legislation for a federal highway system in 1916. That legislation was modified in 1921 and 1925 and a year later the construction companies were hard at work. The first of the great east-west highways was the Lincoln Highway.

The Pennsylvania Turnpike, begun in 1940, triggered the erection of a series of state toll roads linking the east coast with the midwest. The best remembered of the early roads is Route 66 of "You'll get your kicks on route 66" fame. The road connected Chicago with Santa Monica just north of Los Angeles. From the first, the planners of this route set out to connect the rural and urban cities and towns along the way. St. Louis, Oklahoma City, Amarillo, Flagstaff and Albuquerque were some of the cities traversed. Some of the smaller towns had no prior access to a major highway—places such as Funk's Grove, McLean and Litchfield all in Illinois, or Carthage, Missouri and Riverton, Kansas and Clinton, in Oklahoma.

The diagonal configuration of Route 66 was of particular significance to the trucking industry that by the late 1920s had come to rival the railroads for primacy in the haulage business. The route that was chosen traversed flat prairie land before reaching the Rockies in New Mexico and Arizona. The mild climate of the southern route was an attractive added feature. Route 66 recently observed its 75th anniversary. In its formative period it attracted westward bound settlers and travelers. Some of the old filling stations, drive-in theaters, motels and cafes still exist. The *Christian Science Monitor* made a list of the 1920s style buildings that still exist along what remains of the route.[8] Want to stay in a classic landmark hotel? The Blue Swallow Motel in Tucumcari, New Mexico is your place. How about a burger at the oldest cafe in Amarillo? Try the Golden Light Cafe. Want to see a 1936 Fina Tower art deco filling station? Shamrock, Texas is worth a stop.

Service stations are a particular interest of mine. These days the stations handle just one brand of gasoline—Chevron, Texaco, Shell, Phillips, whatever. The stations look as if they were all designed by a common architectural firm. Once you've seen one, you've seen them all. Several covered islands with eight or more pumps offering three grades of gas. In most states it is pump-it-yourself or a stiff surcharge if you want the attendant to do it for you. In some extreme cases I've run into, there is no attendant—I repeat, none. Insert your credit card, push this button and that lever and maybe the darn thing will work. This is progress? I go back to the time when you pulled along side a pump and the attendants came on the run. They filled your tank, washed your windows, checked the oil, and checked the tires. And, oh yes, if you wanted a local map of the area it was free.

THE AUTOMOBILE ERA

Route 66 once laid claim to being the Main Street of America. It was started during the prosperity of the Coolidge years and finished by unemployed young men during the early Roosevelt years. The depression came in 1929 and lasted until the eve of World War II. John Steinbeck in his famous social commentary *Grapes of Wrath* calls Route 66 the Mother Road. 212,000 people migrated to California to escape the rigors of the dust bowl. Many of the westward bound settlers came to the central valley of California to escape the despair of planting crops and seeing them whither and die. To them and to their children this route represented the road to a new life.

When the depression gave way to the war years, Route 66 helped to facilitate the greatest wartime mobilization in our history. From 1940 to 1945 it was as if the nation was a gigantic checkerboard that had been tilted. Military and naval bases were expanded or built from scratch. Factories to provide the nation with the sinews of war were scattered up and down the west coast. The island hopping war in the Pacific depended on Liberty ships built in the Bay Area and Portland to provision this vast effort that eventually spread from Australia to Okinawa. Many of the workers in these newly conceived factories, male and female alike, traveled over this route. It is estimated that the federal government invested some 70 billion dollars in capital projects in California alone, the largest share of which was spent in the San Diego-Los Angeles corridor and would become the economic base of the port-war era.

After the war the triumphant commanding general of the European theater was elected to the Presidency. President Eisenhower had served as General Douglas MacArthur's chief of staff in the Philippines during the pre-war period. In that role he became increasingly aware of the heavy dependence of that command on both the naval supply lines and the over-continent rail and truck lines that crossed America.

During his years as supreme commander of the Allied Forces in Europe he became impressed with the speed and safety of

Hitler's autobahn. In his second term, at his urging, Congress passed the Federal Aid Highway Act of 1956 which provided the means to finance the cost of a national highway system. Many of the four-lane highways used to travel east to west and north to south date from this period. By 1970 all segments of the system were complete. The new highways practically wiped out old Route 66. I-40 that runs from Wilmington, North Carolina to Barstow, California, where it hooks up with I-15 for a run into Los Angeles, practically wiped out old Route 66 from Oklahoma City west. Flagstaff, Arizona, zealously clings to a section that runs through that city. Central Avenue through the heart of Albuquerque is another place that proudly hangs on to the older designation. Oklahoma has done the best job of perpetuating the memory of this old arterial. An unbroken stretch can be driven from Vinita to Catoosa where it joins I-44 through Tulsa, emerges south of that city all the way to Oklahoma City and beyond, all under its own designation on the highway posts. For those interested in planning a vacation through this region, enjoying the artifacts left from this earlier time, check the web address in the endnote.[9] Most of the states and communities through which this road passed realize they have a valued piece of Americana and are anxious to preserve it.

From the time of Henry Clay to our own day, internal improvements have been a hot item on the legislative agenda. Whoever presides over the House Committee on Transportation, Republican or Democrat, can usually count on the support of all the members of his committee when it comes to maintaining the great, but now aging, Interstate Highway. Federal grants to state and local governments from the Highway Trust Fund and Federal Transit Administration produce roughly $25 million a year.[10] Not a princely sum, by any means. Addition funds come out of the general budget of the Department of Transportation. A source of great concern as a new century dawns is the condition of our bridges. Of the 583,414 bridges in the United States 29 percent or 172,686 are rated either deficient or obsolete. In addition to the federal highway system there are state, county and city road systems. These roads are smooth and predictable, often two lanes as compared to the four-lane federal system. They connect the small cities and towns not served by the interstate connectors.

When Eisenhower reflected on his years in the White House he wrote, "Its (the interstate highway system) impact on the American economy—the jobs it would produce in manufacturing and construction, the rural areas it would open up—was beyond calculation." How right he was. Here are a few facts gleaned from the Bureau of Census reports for 2000:

- 1,813,000 are involved in trucking and warehousing in 1999.
- 2,406,000 are involved in auto dealer centers and service stations.
- 1,186,000 are involved in auto repair shops, services and parking.
- 767,000 are involved in auto and truck insurance.[11]

Those are just a few of the measurable statistics. Add to these figures those who maintain our highways, state police who enforce weight and speed regulations, employees of the parts stores and the tire dealers. I've heard estimates as high as one in every seven employed persons are involved in some way with automobiles and roads.

What lies ahead in the transportation field? We can begin by pointing out that the automobile industry has had what amounts to a quality revolution during the past twenty years. Ralph Nader's 1965 exposé of the Corvair, "Unsafe at Any Speed" set off a widespread concern with automobile safety that continues to this day. Little by little car makers produced models that were more efficient, more reliable, less polluting, lighter and quieter. In many instances they were forced to make these changes because of the imports. Seat belts, airbags, collapsible steering wheels have all made driving safer. Computers were incorporated into the automotive field resulting in more fuel-efficient cars.

Motorists who got-out-and-got-under grouse about how it's impossible to repair these new models. My particular gripe is changing bulbs in the head and taillights. It once was so simple. You dropped by the automobile supply store, picked up the bulb size you needed, brought it home and changed it with a screwdriver in five minutes, max. Now the bulbs are halogens that have pressurized gas inside and require careful handling. If the lens holder isn't broken you can still replace it yourself providing you have a headlight screwdriver. If the protective lens is broken you still might be able to buy a replacement and install it yourself. If any portion of the area had been struck or dented, reach for your checkbook. This is going to cost you big time.

On the bright side, if you've invested in a good car, 100,000 miles on the odometer is a common occurrence. I have friends who own a Mercedes-Benz with over 300,000 miles on it and it is still running like a top. Top quality tires will give you 50,000 miles and up provided, of course, you keep them inflated and rotate. Even before the introduction of the hybrid gasoline-battery cars numerous models have been delivering mileage in the high twenties. The good news is that although more and more people are driving, the total death toll from traffic related accidents has dropped substantially.

But we still come back to those bumper-to-bumper traffic jams that are the common experience of today's commuter. We will never be able to build a road net that will solve the predictable problems commuters face during the early morning hours and the drive home in late afternoon. If you want to see gridlock, take on traffic around any great city at these hours. So how do we get people to use public transit? Only one way—make it cheaper and faster and they will come. There are all kinds of experiments going on. Some are very simple and have been around for some time such as the HOV lanes. Two or more passengers and you can travel in this fast lane. Park and ride lots scattered throughout the commute area. Drive your car to a parking lot and take the bus into the city center. Some of the larger cities, with federal, state, and regional governments cooperating, have built rail routes that allow the passenger to travel from a station near his or her residence to the inner city and the airport. Atlanta, with the busiest airport in the country, has such a system.[12] With the center of the system not far from the State Capitol downtown, branches cover the far reaches of the city. Portland, Oregon has a system very much like it. Attempts are being made to tie in with Vancouver, Washington, just north of the Columbia. When finished it will extend from Gresham to Forest Grove and from Lake Oswego to the airport and beyond.

Smaller cities are equally concerned with automotive gridlock. A scaled down version of the rail service features the Flexliner, a diesel powered unit with separate engines in each car. Run separately and they have the look of a trolley, linked together they have the look of a streamliner. In an attempt to contain costs many projects attempt to use the existing rail lines. Over the country as a whole there has been an explosion of commuter rail projects during the last decade. More and more people are coming to realize that it is impossible to keep up with peek period commuter needs. Philadelphia and Detroit are cities that are trying to lure commuters back to the city. How would you like being able to walk to work? Or how about a ten-minute bicycle ride? I haven't lived in New York for years and years, but recall some great neighborhoods only minutes away from the theater district by subway. Most would agree that these are all great ideas. Out of earshot we add, you take the public transit and I'll take my car. The pessimists say the only way you'll ever get people off the highway and into public conveyance is to charge what Europeans have to pay for gasoline. Try running for office on that platform. So be realistic. Public transit is not a replacement for existing transportation patterns. But it does give us some viable options. I look back wistfully on the days when I rode on the New York Central's Harlem Division express from White

Plains to New York. I had thirty-five minutes to read and digest the morning news. When I reached Grand Central Station I had a ten-minute walk and I was hard at work on my job at West 41st. If it rained I could always use the cross-town shuttle on 42nd Street

    To end this chapter on an upbeat note, Amtrak is increasing its ridership at a steady pace. In 1990 40.2 million people booked rides. By 1999 that figure rose to 79.8 million. Thus Amtrak will have doubled its ridership in ten years. Freight trains are holding up their share of the haulage business. In 1998 freight railroads in the nation moved 1.38 trillion ton-miles of freight, more than ever before, setting new safety records in the process.

1931 PHAETON

CHAPTER EIGHTEEN

National Parks

ONE OF THE GLORIES OF THE age of railroads was the tour package the various lines would put together for the summer traveler. In 1927 the Union Pacific and the Chicago and North Western put together a fourteen-day tour featuring two national parks in two weeks starting and returning to Chicago, all expenses paid. The cost per person occupying a lower berth was $219.96. Two persons occupying the same lower birth was $201.96. Choose the upper berth and you could lower the cost by seven dollars.

The cost included rail transportation, sleeping accommodations, all meals, and sightseeing trips by buses—the works. How you got from your home city to the Chicago and North Western Terminal was a choice left up you. If you were coming from the southeast you might arrive at the LaSalle Street Station, take a cab to one of the finest railroad terminals in the country, dedicated to the life and spirit of the west, and settle back in your lounge to enjoy the first days of the trip through prairie and plain. By the third day you would have arrived at the western gateway of Yellowstone Park. After breakfast you hop aboard the Pierce-Arrow bus and set forth on a five-day automobile trip. Old Faithful Inn is the hotel where you will stay during this portion of your trip, with side trips to various sights within the park arranged day by day. Then it is on to Salt Lake City. The headquarters here will be the Hotel Utah. The ever present bus—an oversized touring car, with the top down accommodating a driver and eleven passengers—will take you on a tour of the city and visit the Tabernacle in time for an organ concert. Then on to the Great Salt Lake where time is provided for those wishing to experience the buoyancy of these waters.

On the ninth day you will arrive at Greeley, Colorado. Here you will spend four days in the Rocky Mountain National Park.

The bus will take you west to Estes Park and then back across the Continental Divide to Grand Lake Lodge and a circular tour of the park. You will arrive in Denver in the afternoon of the twelfth day. It's dinner at the Albany Hotel and then by 10:00 p.m. you will reboard the train for the trip back to Chicago.

Every one of the major railroads had its own tour depart-

REO TOUR BUS

ment. The Chicago & North Western Railroad had tour representatives in nineteen cities. Its partner in this enterprise, the Union Pacific, had seventeen. Some of the larger offices had as many as a dozen employees who would prepare and furnish, without charge, schedules, and routings for clubs, sororities, and organizations. Tours of the National Parks lives on into the present age. While most of the visitors to the parks come in automobiles, bus tours are still widely patronized. On a recent trip to the southwest to visit Bryce Canyon, Zion National Park and the Grand Canyon, the author observed tour buses everywhere. Some feature tour guides who speak in one of the foreign languages. One bus I encountered was booked by a travel agent in Germany. They wanted to see the west where John Wayne made all of those wonderful westerns.

Amtrak in partnership with the National Park Service has already started to bring to life the Lewis and Clark Corps of Exploration. During the summer of 2001 passengers between St. Louis to Kansas City on the westbound *Kansas City Mule* and the eastbound *Ann Rutledge* were able to retrace the early portion of the expedition's trail along the Missouri River. This use of the train, as a mobile classroom through commentary and the distribution of literature, may serve as a model during the entire three-year observance.

The Amtrak train that most closely follows the original path of the expedition would be the *Empire Builder*. The train runs between Chicago and Seattle. At Spokane, you can continue on to Seattle or stay on the Lewis and Clark trail and head down the Columbia River gorge to Portland. One of the advantages of the *Empire Builder* is that its passes through Glacier National Park. For the better part of an hour you can have "the best seat in the house" as you pass through this park that lies astride the Continental Divide. This may not match those open tour buses of prior days, but as you stretch out your legs sitting in your lounge chair you can imagine yourself as a pampered later-day explorer.

Amtrak's *California Zephyr* approximates the old central route of the Union Pacific. The tracks head west from Chicago to Omaha, the old base of that railroad, and thence west through Denver, Salt Lake to Emeryville, across the Bay from San Francisco. No National Parks along the way on this route, but the passage over the Sierras with its many tunnels more than makes up for it.

CHAPTER NINETEEN

Lewis and Clark Bicentennial

THE LEWIS AND CLARK Bicentennial Exposition is scheduled to take place during the years 2003 and 2006. The commemoration will be observed by all the states and communities spread out along the original trail. The kick-off event was held in Charlottesville, Virginia, at the mountaintop home of the President who authorized the Corps of Discovery. The last events will be tied to the return journey in 1806. Most of us usually think of St. Louis as the place where the trek began, but that honor belongs to Louisville, Kentucky and Clarksville, Indiana where Lewis joined Clark and the combined expedition set off for the Missouri. All the states and countless towns and cities along the original route will be involved in the celebration. A century ago, on the occasion of the centennial, it was largely a Portland, Oregon affair. It was a bold step for this young city to take. There was no assurance that federal funds might be allocated, and this exposition did not have the advantage of being named an international exposition.

But the aura of greatness, associated with this term, *exposition,* was in the air. It all began, say the historians of the movement, with the Great Crystal Palace Exhibition held in London in 1851. Prince Albert, the consort of Queen Victoria, became convinced that exhibitors from all over the world would send their wares to London. Oh, did he turn out to be right. 13,000 exhibitors showed up—650 of them from the United States. Everything about the Crystal Palace exposition was a success. Over six million persons came from all over the world. And then came the imitators. New York decided to have its own Crystal Palace in 1863. The exposition was held on the grounds presently occupied by the New York Library Building on Fifth Avenue and 42nd Street. The British model in every way overshadowed it. The roof leaked in rainy weather, the attendance dwindled, the exhibitors were unhappy and the event closed in debt. Not an auspicious beginning.

Next came the Philadelphia Centennial Exposition of 1876. This event was the first major international exhibition held in the United States. It was held in Fairmount Park Philadelphia, and was opened by President Ulysses S. Grant in the company of Dom Pedro II of Brazil on May 10, 1876. It was a great success. 167 buildings housed 30,000 exhibits and over eight million persons attended. The crowning event took place in Independence Square where a vast parade passed in review before General William T. Sherman after which the Declaration was read in Independence Hall and the orator of the day, William M. Evarts, gave his speech. The exhibits included dramatic evidence that a new mechanical age had dawned. The telephone, air brakes to be applied to trains, the duplex telegraph, sewing machines, and the typewriter were all on display.

The success of the Centennial Exposition in Philadelphia became the lodestar that ushered in a plethora of expositions. First came the Columbian Exposition in Chicago in 1893. It was to commemorate the 400th anniversary of the first voyage to

America by Christopher Columbus. It may be a stretch to link Columbus with Chicago, but a ten million dollar guarantee may have had something to do with it. That was what the city fathers put up to get the exposition. That, plus the fact that the city had become the acknowledged rail center of the United States certainly played a part. Although the exposition got started a year late, it produced a great show featuring "the White City," a display of electric power applied to all kinds of appliances. Electricity lighted the fair, it drove elevated trains that circled the fairgrounds and with thousands of electric light bulbs, it lighted the Tower of Light, the fair centerpiece. 21,400,000 attended the fair. It also has the distinction of being the first American exposition to make money.

As the twentieth century began, the exposition craze really caught fire. In 1901 Buffalo hosted the Pan-American Exposition. In 1904 the Louisiana Purchase Exposition was held in St. Louis. My grandfather Barton attended this event and may have worked on one of the many buildings erected for the fair. In 1905 Portland hosted what it was pleased to call "The Lewis and Clark Centennial and American Pacific Exposition and Oriental Fair." Quite a mouthful, that title.

In 1907 the Jamestown Exposition was held at Hampton Roads, Virginia to commemorate the 300th anniversary of the oldest permanent English settlement in America. Seattle followed in 1909 with the Alaska-Yukon Exposition commemorating the development of those northern territories after their purchase from Russia in 1867. George Berg, my wife's maternal grandfather, was the Art Director of this fair. In 1915 the Panama-Pacific Exposition was held in San Francisco commemorating Balboa's sighting of the Pacific in 1513 and the completion of the Panama Canal in 1914. Chicago held a second world's fair in 1933 and called it "A Century of Progress." It was held right in the middle of the Depression and still made money. In 1935 San Diego, not to be outdone by its larger neighbors to the north, staged something called a California Pacific Exposition. Then came the "biggies"—two fairs, one on the east coast and the second on the west coast. The one on the east coast was called simply "The World of Tomorrow." It ran for two years, 1939–40. I had a press pass that I used frequently. The Trylon and the Perisphere served as the symbol. In the latter building the world of tomorrow was laid out for the observer to behold. There were great shows in the Midway. Some of the international exhibits contained restaurants where you could sample the culinary specialties of a country like Lithuania or Poland for less than what it would cost today for a fast food burger with fries. I was at the Fair the day King George V and Queen Elizabeth arrived, accompanied by one of those great bands the British seem to specialize in. (The Queen Mum, as she was affectionately called, was born at the beginning of the twentieth century and died in the second year of the twenty first.) The western version of the world's fair was held in San Francisco for just the one year. The railroads of the period ran ads that headlined "See Both." And doubtless many people did. It commemorated the completion of the Bay Bridge. An island was created out of landfill and dredging midway between San Francisco and Oakland. When war began the buildings were hastily converted to war use.

That's as far as I care to go in the list of Expositions except to comment on one held in 1898 in Omaha, Nebraska. The Trans-Mississippi Exposition was a celebration of westward expansion, the theme of this book. As a lifetime collector of stamps and covers, I consider the commemorative issue of 1898 to be my number one favorite of all United States issues. Like the Columbian issue that preceded it, the Trans-Mississippi issue was reissued for collectors in 1998. The engravings include: Farming in the West; Fremont on the Rocky Mountains, Remington's drawing entitled Troops Guarding Trains, Heaton's painting Hardships of Emigration, Western Mining, Western Cattle and the Mississippi River Bridge.[1]

Now let us focus on the person who ties together this list of expositions with the first Lewis and Clark Exposition held in Portland in 1905. That person would be Henry Ernst Dosch. Like Henry Villard, Dosch came to this country from Germany. He was born in Mainz on June 17, 1841. His father was involved in the failed attempt to throw off domination by Prussia. Many of the most talented and liberal minded Germans had to flee for their lives and a number of them found a haven in the region around St. Louis. During the Civil War the loyal support of this group, estimated to be as high as 10,000, tipped the balance in favor of the Union in the border state of Missouri. Dosch was one of that number. He had come to America only the year before the war began. He came here with impressive credentials, having graduated from an engineering school. He passed the examination for a reserve commission in the German army and was given a passport that entitled him to a year off before joining the German army. Instead he went to America and enlisted in Fremont's bodyguard. He was wounded in an action at Springfield, Missouri, was discharged and then reenlisted in the 5th Missouri Cavalry. Dosch was involved in the defense of an arsenal that Southern sympathizers were attempting to seize. During his time in service Dosch rose to Sergeant Major and acting Adjutant of his regiment.

In time his enlistment was up and he joined a comrade who suggested they head for Omaha where a train was loading, taking supplies to Salt Lake City. They went to Omaha where they were offered $20.00 apiece if they would serve as bullwackers and drive four yoke of oxen. It took the train, of which they were apart fifty-eight days, to make the Omaha—Salt Lake march. They reached Salt Lake in the summer of 1863. His comrade elected to stay in Salt Lake, but Henry pushed on to Virginia City where, being stone cold broke, he took the first job offered—a pick and shovel road job. Here his knowledge of engineering paid dividends. He helped his crew lay out the road so it would provide an easy grade for a horse to climb. The boss man came by and asked the foreman, "Who laid out this road?" The foreman pointed to Dosch.

Shortly he found himself hired as an express rider for famed Pony Express. His life on that 33-mile run from Virginia City to Lake Tahoe by way of Carson City was every bit as dangerous as any assignment he had while in service back in Missouri. In later years he recalled those days. "One of the saloon men in Virginia City came to the door to see me start out on my run, a man stepped out and shot the saloon keeper through the heart. Instantly the bar keeper shot the murderer, who also fell fatally wounded, but before he cashed in his checks, he shot the bar keeper and also killed him, so inside of sixty seconds there were three dead men."[2]

The dust stirred up by the hoofs of his mount as they traveled at rapid speed over the alkali dust was damaging his respiratory system, so Dosch wisely decided to search for work in San Francisco. After several pick and shovel jobs he wound up with a firm that had branches in Placerville, California, Portland and The Dalles in Oregon and Walla Walla in Washington. He drew The Dalles assignment.

So, like many before him, he made the trip north by steamer arriving in Portland on April 9, 1864. He was put in charge of buying gold dust. He bought over $50,000 in gold dust in a single month that was then sent under guard to the mint in San Francisco. Of The Dalles, Dosch claimed that there was more action in a single day than there was in Portland in an entire month! The firm where Dosch worked sold miners their equipment on the way up river to the mines and then purchased the gold they found as they made the down river journey. Once again the middleman who sold supplies and managed to get the miners up river to the mines in Idaho and Montana, were reaping a harvest.

After putting in a year at The Dalles, Dosch struck out on his own running a merchandise store at Canyon City. His stay there is not as notable for his success as a merchant as it is his success in finding a wife. Marie Fleurot was born in France and came to Portland in 1857 where she studied at St. Mary's Academy for eight years. Her father and mother ran the French Hotel in Canyon City. One day, after Dosch had lived in the town for five years, one of the buildings caught fire. The winds helped spread the fire down through the canyon and at its end 255 buildings were destroyed. Neither the Fleurots nor the Dosches had insurance and a new life had to be fashioned. Late in 1870 the Fleurots were hired to manage the socially exclusive St. Charles Hotel. For Henry, with a wife and child to support, it meant taking the first job he was offered as a janitor and porter for a boot and shoe distributing company at the pricely wage of $40.00 a month. He became bookkeeper of the firm at a wage of $150.00 a month, and eventually part owner.

In 1890 they sold out and Dosch became wealthy enough to give the rest of his life to community causes. He bought a seventeen-acre tract at Dosch Station. He called the place Villa Eichenhof for a place back home.

There he began experimenting with walnuts. He soon found the Franquette and Mayette varieties of walnuts were best suited

HENRY DOSCH'S GROWN CHILDREN

to the Oregon climatic conditions. He helped organize the Oregon Horticultural Society.

His great love was for his adopted city and he deserves a great deal of the credit for making possible the exposition of 1905. His first venture into the world of expositions and fairs was at Chicago's Columbian World's Fair of 1893. He lobbied with both the governor and the legislature for the appointment. The Oregon exhibit took seventeen gold medals taking the highest honors in the grain exhibit. He received no salary for his work, indeed he had to pay some of the expenses out of his own pocket.

Finding the experience richly rewarding, he went on to the Trans-Mississippi Exposition in Omaha held in 1898. At this exposition the Oregon exhibit featured lumber. As a result, some of the engineers who attended contracted to buy Oregon lumber for railroad trestles and river barges. Next, it was on to Buffalo for the Pan-American Exposition in 1901. Once again, Oregon's agricultural exhibits garnered medals and blue ribbons. He then took an exhibit to far off Charleston, South Carolina. He clearly remembers the size of some of the huge logs that were exhibited there. One was originally 115 feet long and 3-foot square. It had to be cut back to 74 feet in order to navigate through a curved tunnel in Montana. The same train carried another log 20 feet long and 9 foot square. It had 365 rings on it showing that it was that many years old. An official from Germany saw this exhibit and came to Oregon and placed the first of many orders to be shipped to industries back home.

The most interesting of all of Dosch's travels on behalf of his home state was the trip he made to the 1903 Osaka Fair in Japan. This time the expense of his travels to both Osaka and St. Louis (the following year) were picked up by the sponsoring Portland committee.[3] The Japanese government had already committed $900,000 for a display at the Louisiana Purchase Exposition to be held in St. Louis in 1904. Would they be willing to spend an additional $200,000 and transfer the exhibit to the Lewis and Clark

Exposition to be held in Portland, Oregon, the following year? To his everlasting credit he pulled it off; a large portion of the exhibit in St. Louis made its appearance in the Oriental Exhibits Building in Portland in 1905—one of the more popular buildings positioned near the Fair entrance.[4]

While in Japan, Dosch made friends with two influential Japanese. Japan was about to go to war with Russia to settle long-standing disputes regarding Korea and Manchuria. In anticipation of that war they had begun to buy rice from Cochin China (now a part of Viet Nam). It was polished rice from which the vitamin B-1 was missing and as a consequence the Japanese soldiers were coming down with beriberi. As a result of Dosch's suggestion to his two Japanese friends they switched to Louisiana rice and the thiamine deficiency was abated. Japan went on to win that war with Russia in 1905. A year before the exposition in Portland was to open, Dosch was at the St. Charles Hotel, New Orleans. His objective was to secure a promise that Louisiana would participate in the Lewis and Clark Centennial. In the lobby three Japanese caught his attention. "Are you not Colonel Dosch? Do you remember telling Baron Komura about Louisiana rice?" Yes, Dosch remembered.

HENRY DOSCH

The Japanese continued," I have just dispatched a shipload of rice and am planning to contract for the entire crop."

Some years after the Russo-Japanese war was settled, Japan bestowed upon Dosch the title of Baron and the decoration "Order of the Rising Sun" and "The Order of the Chrysanthemum," honors he shared with Presidents Theodore Roosevelt and Howard Taft. But the greatest honor, Dosch insisted, was the part he was able to play as Director of Exhibits at the Portland Fair.

Of course the success of the fair did not rest entirely on his shoulders. Two acknowledged leaders of Portland deserve mention. The first was Henry Corbett, president of the First National Bank and a one time United States Senator. Corbett not only chaired the commission appointed by the state, he also pledged $30,000. As an established figure he was able to attract other sizable pledges. The Northern Pacific pledged $20,000 and Weinhard Brewery still another $10,000. Hotels, restaurants, and streetcar companies quickly followed with support.

The state legislature responded to appeals in 1903 voting $450,000 for exhibits at the show, and after a full-bore lobbying effort by the three western states the federal government made its pledge to erect a $475,000 for a building and exhibits. Sixteen states came through with buildings and exhibits. Nine European nations signed up for exhibits plus the Japanese exhibit previously mentioned.

Considering that the city sponsoring this event was roughly fifty years old, it was a bold venture to even make the effort to hold such a fair. Corbett's death before the exposition opened was a blow, but Harvey Scott, the northwest's best-known journalist and president of the Oregon Historical Society took over and the plans never missed a beat.

Every fair has its special events. One featured the end of the first transcontinental auto race. On June 21, 1905 the winning team of Dwight Huss and Milford Wright drove their Oldsmobile into the fairgrounds. They had started out from 59th

Street and Broadway in New York City and forty-four days later they arrived in Portland. No one recorded the number of blow outs they incurred, but given the condition of the roads of that period I'm sure changing tires may well have been a daily chore.

When the gates to the exhibition closed on October 15 the directors reported that paid admissions totaled 1,588,000 with perhaps another 900,000 free admissions to the press, exhibitors and others. After all the books were settled it was proudly reported that the fair had made a profit. But best of all, it was a successful venture that people talked about for years.

The planned Bicentennial of the Lewis and Clark's original Corps of Discovery will be a far different affair than the exhibit a century ago. That exhibit concentrated on a single site. The event planned for 2003–6 will be multi-sited. Signature events are planned to commemorate important events along the trail. The first, as noted, was held at Jefferson's home in Monticello, Virginia. The event in St. Louis is scheduled for the spring of 2004. The National Council in charge of planning the commemoration is hoping that the King of Spain and the President of France can be persuaded to attend.

Signature events are presently being planned for Fort Leavenworth, Kansas, Omaha, Nebraska, Great Falls, Montana, on the lower Columbia River near Fort Clatsop on the Oregon side of the river and at Station Camp on the Washington side. Events associated with the return trip celebrations will be held at Billings, Montana, and New Town, North Dakota the home of Sacagawea. The Dakota-Lakota tribes of South Dakota are planning a celebration, as are the Nez Perce tribes in Idaho. Maybe the biggest surprise in the list is the celebration in the late fall of 2006 in Philadelphia. The connection? Many of the plants the explorers collected and sent back after their first winter at Fort Mandan, North Dakota still exist at the Academy of Natural Sciences in Philadelphia.[5] This will provide a chance for people living in the east to claim a part in the observances.[6]

The 1905 centennial exhibition was more of a fair based on the model of the Crystal Palace, with buildings and exhibits concentrated on a relative small site. The Bicentennial will be scattered along a trail well over 2,500 miles long. This observance will offer the visitor choices. There will be sites where the visitor can get out and retrace the steps of Lewis and Clark, and for the more sedentary there will be roadside interpretive centers. One can readily see that some sort of transportation will be mandatory. The young and vigorous may cover parts of the trail by bicycle. The family car is a more likely option. Special bus tours offering travel, meals and lodging will be offered. It will be very difficult to size up the number of people who take part in this Bicentennial. Each of the signature events will require careful planning. And each committee should be lucky enough to have just one person like Henry Dosch. His son, Arno, once summed up his father. "He was always more interested in the general welfare than in his own personal fortune." He loved to travel and often would be away for months at a time. But when home, he was at his office, Room 150 of the Court House, every working day until his death in 1925.

At least one of the buildings made its way back east to Monticello, New York where it was reassembled and named Sho-Fu Den. My college roommate, "Doc" Osborn and his wife bought it in the late 1950s and I had the pleasure of staying there on my way back to Hobart College, Geneva, New York, for my twenty-fifth anniversary.

ENDNOTES

Chapter 1

1. Everett Dicks, *Lure of the Land*, (Lincoln, NE: University of Nebraska Press, 1970) 157.
2. Everett Dicks, p. 355.
3. Alan Wexler and Molly Braun, *Atlas of Westward Expansion* (New York: Facts on File), p. 215.
4. John Keegan, *Fields of Battle* (New York: Vintage Books), p. 109-110.
5. John Keegan, p. 137.
6. Patrick Connors, *The National Road Pictorial History* (Monongahela, PA: Historic Towns Publishing, 1997), p. 4-5.
7. Alan Wexler and Molly Braun, *Atlas of Westward Expansion* (New York: Facts on File), p. 63.
8. Alan Wexler, p. 63.
9. Alan Wexler, p. 64.
10. Contact the New York State Canal Corp., P.O.Box 189, Albany, NY 12201-0189.
11. Contact the United States Military Academy, West Point, NY.
12. P.H. Sheridan, *Personal Memoirs of P. H. Sheridan* (New York: Charles Webster & Co. 1888), p. 24.
13. Bernard Bailyn, *Voyagers to the West* (New York: Alfred A. Knopf, 1986), p. 14-16.
14. Everett Dicks, p. 157.

Chapter 2

1. William W. Campbell, *Life and Writings of DeWitt Clinton* (New York: Baker & Scribner, 1849), See Address to the Alumni of Columbia College.
2. William W. Campbell.
3. Joseph Brant's mother was the second wife of Sir William Johnson, Colonial Secretary for Indian Affairs. When his father died shortly before the outbreak of hostilities, Brant (1742–1807) became the leader of the Iroquois Confederacy consisting of Mohawk, Oneida, Onondaga, Cayuga, and Seneca later joined by the Tuscaroras. Brant took the British side in the conflict and fought in the Oriskany and Saratoga campaigns and organized a devastating raid on the Cherry Valley. All but the Oneidas and Tuscaroras sided with the British. After the war he settled his own tribe, the Mohawks, in Ontario.
4. Three of the colleges that Clinton makes reference to are Columbia, Union and Hamilton. Several of the academies mentioned were later chartered as colleges by the Regents of the state. Geneva College (now Hobart) in western New York held its first graduation in 1826 and is the likely fourth college.
5. Leuchtenburg and Wishy, *History of the United States during the Administration of Jefferson and Madison*, (Englewood, NJ: Prentice-Hall, 1963) Vol.1, p. 37.
6. Gouveneur Morris was a member of the Constitutional Convention, twice served as a financial advisor to the Federal Government and also as a U. S. Senator. Van Rensselear was a none-too-successful general in the War of 1812. He headed a prominent old Dutch family. A New York county and the engineering school bear the family name. William North was an aide to Baron Steuben, Inspector General of the Continental Army, and twice served as Speaker of the state Assembly and as a U. S. Senator. Peter Porter was Clinton's opponent for governor in 1817. Hosack's *Memoirs* adds the

name of a seventh commissioner, Simeon DeWitt, Surveyor General of the State of New York and a revered figure in the world of North American cartography.
7. History of Elections for President, 1796–1860. See appendix, Election 1812.
8. David Hosack, *Memoirs of DeWitt Clinton*, 1829. Philip Schuyler fought in the French and Indian War. During the Revolution he was a Major General in charge of the Army in New York. One of the great parks in the City of New York contains the mansion of his mother, Cornelia Van Courtlandt. Schuyler twice served as a U. S. Senator. His daughter was the wife of Alexander Hamilton. Weston, also mentioned, was the English Canal engineer who was hired to supervise this early attempt at canalizing the Mohawk River.
9. Life and Writings of DeWitt Clinton.
10. Klein and Howard, *The Twilight of British Rule in Revolutionary America* (Cooperstown, NY: New York State Historical Society, 1983), pp. 43–6.
11. Klein and Howard, pp. 54–5.
12. John Keegan, Fields of Battle, the Wars for North America, 1992, pp. 184–5.

Chapter 3

1. There were two ways to get to the Northwest Territory. One was the way Sherman, Hillhouse and others from Connecticut took, by way of New York's canals and rivers. The other was through Pennsylvania to Pittsburgh thence west by the Ohio River. New Englanders favored the New York route. The Pennsylvania Dutch and Scotch Irish immigrants favored the Pittsburgh route. The better-educated Yankees became surveyors, lawyers, judges and legislators in the new state. Almost every leading jurist of the day was from Yale.
2. John Sherman, *Recollections of Forty Years in the House, Senate and Cabinet* (Chicago: Werner Company, 1895), p. 831ff.

3. Michael Fellman, *Citizen Sherman* (New York: Random House, 1995), p. 311ff.
4. The correspondence between John and his brother William was published in 1894 as the *Sherman Letters*.
5. Sketch of the Life and Public Service of Hon. James Hillhouse of New Haven, New Haven, CT 1860, p. 34–5.
6. Hon. James Hillhouse, p. 33.
7. Hon. James Hillhouse, p. 45.

Chapter 5

1. Richard H. Dana, *Two Years Before the Mast* (New York: Jr., P. F. Collier, 1909), p. 45.
2. Richard H. Dana, p. 62–63.
3. Robert F. Lucid, *The Journal of Richard Henry Dana, Jr.*, vol.I (Boston: Harvard University Press 1968), p. xxxii.
4. Robert F. Lucid xxxii.
5. Richard H. Dana, *Two Years Before the Mast*, p. 415.

Chapter 6

1. Stephen W. Sears, *George B. McClellan, the Young Napoleon* (New York: Ticknor & Fields, 1988), p. 392.
2. Stephen W. Sears, p. 392.
3. Edward Hungerford, *Men of Erie*, (New York: Random House, 1949).
4. Edward Hungerford.
5. Frances H. Kennedy, *Civil War Battlefield Guide* (Houghton Mifflin, Boston, MA, 1990), p. 107.
6. Letter from Indiana State Archivist to author dated May 20, 1998.
7. Freeman Cleaves, *Rock of Chickamauga* (Norman, OK: University of Oklahoma Press, 19xx), p. 136.
8. Letters to Indiana Adjutant General urging promotion for Lt. Col. Jones.
9. Fielder Allison Jones was a baseball star of the early part of

the twentieth century. He was born in Shinglehouse, PA in 1871 while his uncle was still living. Jones played two seasons for Alfred College and after a brief minor league career played the outfield for the Brooklyn teams, two of which won pennants in 1899 and 1900. When the American League was formed in 1901, Jones was among those Charlie Comiskey was able to persuade to jump leagues to build his Chicago White Sox. In that first year the White Sox won the American League pennant. By 1906, Jones was the player-manager and in the company of Billy Sullivan, another ex-National Leaguer, led the Sox to a second American League pennant and in the only World Series between two Chicago teams, beat the Cubs 4 games to 2 for the coveted World Championship. What made the series memorable was the fact that the Chicago Cubs in 1906 won 116 games a record that would stand for 95 years until tied by the Seattle Mariners in 2001. And what made it even more remarkable was that the victory was achieved by "The Hitless Wonders." The Sox version of a rally would be a walk, a stolen base, a bunt sacrifice advancing the runner to third, and a sacrifice fly! After their playing days were over, Jones and Sullivan moved to Oregon where Sullivan became an apple grower and Jones became active in the lumber business.

Chapter 7

1. McCallum was the general superintendent of the Erie Railroad. After the War he lived in semi-retirement serving as a consultant for many railroads, the Union Pacific among them. His principal assistants were W. W. Wright, a pupil of Haupt at Gettysburg College and an assistant engineer of the Pennsylvania Railroad, and Adna Anderson, who later became chief engineer of the Northern Pacific.
2. *Reports of Brig. Gen. D.C. McCallum to the Secretary of War* (Washington, DC: Government Printing Office, 1866), p. 34.

3. Reports of Brig. Gen. D.C. McCallum, p. 16.
4. Reports of Brig. Gen. D.C. McCallum, p. 30.
5. K.W. Munden and H.P. Beers, *The Union, a Guide to Federal Archives Relating to the Civil War* (Washington, DC: National Archives and Records Administration), U. S. Military Telegraphs came into being during the war and enabled the Commander in Chief, the Secretary of War and General Halleck to maintain contact with all theaters of the war. President Lincoln was an avid reader of these telegraphic communications and is said to have spent many a long evening at the Washington office.
6. Sherman's *Memoirs*.

Chapter 8

1. U.S. Grant, *Memoirs and Selected Letter*.
2. U.S. Grant.
3. Oregon Historical Quarterly, March 1956, pp. 83-84. Attributed to Grace Cooper of the Benton Historical Society.
4. P.H. Sheridan, *Indian Fighting in the Fifties*.
5. Royal A. Bensell, *Bensell's Journal*, pp.203-204.
6. Royal A. Bensell.
7. P.H. Sheridan, *Indian Fighting in the Fifties*.
8. Shelby Foote, *The Civil War, Red River to Appomattox* (Vintage Books, NY 1974), pp. 554-555.
9. Thomas Buchanan Read, *Sheridan's Ride* (Greenwillow Books, NY, 1993), pp. 24-25.
10. Sheridan chose a picture of himself mounted on Rienzi for the cover of the first edition of his book.

Chapter 9

1. In 1985 both Partridge and Thayer were honored by the United States Postal Service in the Great American Series, Partridge on the 11-cent stamp and Thayer on 9-cent. Aside

ENDNOTES

from West Point, Norwich University provided more officers for the Civil War than any other military school—523 for the Union, 34 for the Confederacy.
2. *The Papers of Ulysses S. Grant*, Edited by John Y. Simon, Carbondale, IL: Southern Illinois University, 1967. Vol. I:1837–61.
3. War of the Rebellion, Ser.1 Vol. 50, pt.1, pp. 32–50.
4. WOR, Ser.1, Vol. 50, pt. I, pp. 32–50.
5. Albert Sydney Johnson was relieved by General Scott and became one of the Confederacy's four star generals, the others being Robert E. Lee, Pierre Beauregard Joseph Johnson and Samuel Cooper, Adjutant General of the United States who had "Married South."
6. Carl Schlicke, *General George Wright, Guardian of the Pacific* (Norman, OK: University of Oklahoma, 1988), p. 301.
7. Carl Schlicke 228–9.
8. E.J. Warner, *Generals in Blue* (Louisiana State University Press, 1964), p. xviii.
9. WOR Ser. 1, Vol. 50, pt.1, p. 666.
10. WOR, Ser.1, Vol. 50, pt.1, p. 967.
11. Burial of Gen. Wright and wife in Sacramento.

Chapter 10

1. Edward Hungerford, *Wells Fargo—Advancing the American Frontier* (Bonanza Books, NY, 1949), p. 6.
2. Edward Hungerford, p. 31.
3. Lucius Beebe and Charles Clegg, *U.S. West, the Saga of Wells Fargo* (Bonanza Books, NY, 1949), p. 11.
4. Daniel S. Tuttle, *Reminiscences of a Missionary Bishop* (Whittaker, NY, 1906), p. 91.
5. Daniel S. Tuttle, p. 91.
6. Daniel S. Tuttle, p. 92
7. Mark Twain, *Roughing It* (New American Library, NY), p. 62.
8. Mark Twain, p. 47.

9. Carlos A. Schwantes, *Long Day's Journey, The Steamboat and Stagecoach Era in the Northwest* (University of Washington Press, Seattle, WA 1999), p. 91.

Chapter 11

1. D. Joy Humes, *Oswald Garrison Villard, Liberal of the 1920s* (Syracuse University, 1960), p. 2.
2. *Memoirs of Henry Villard* (Houghton Mifflin, NY, 1904) vol.1, p. 80.
3. *Memoirs of Henry Villard.*
4. *Memoirs of Henry Villard.*
5. Oscar O. Winthur, *The Great Northwest* (Alfred A. Knopf, NY, 1948), pp. 283-5.
6. Joseph Gaston, *Centennial History of Oregon* (S.J. Clarke, Chicago, IL, 1912), vol. 1, pp. 704-5.
7. Luis Tuck Renz, *The History of the Northern Pacific Railroad* (Galleon Press, Fairfield, WA, 1980), p. 267.
8. Joseph A. Gaston, *Centennial History of Oregon*, pp. 529–30.
9. Oscar O. Winthur, *The Great Northwest*, p. 268.
10. Oscar O. Winthur, p. 270.
11. Villard in an address before the Tacoma, WA Board of Trade.
12. G.W. Belknap, *Henry Villard and the University of Oregon* (University of Oregon Press, Eugene, OR, 1976), p. 48.
13. G.W. Belknap, p. 24.
14. G.W. Belknap, p. 21.
15. D. Joy Humes, *Oswald Garrison Villard, Liberal of the 1920s*.
16. D. Joy Humes, p. 7.

Chapter 12

1. Jim Shaughnessy, *The Rutland Road* (Berkeley, CA: Howell-North Books, 1964), pp. 58–59 and 255.
2. John S. Stover, *American Railroads* (Chicago and London: University of Chicago Press, 1961), pp. 165–67.

Chapter 13

1. James B. Hedges, *Colonization Work of the Northern Pacific Railroad* (The Mississippi Valley Historical Review, Vol. XIII, No. 3, Dec. 1926), p. 313.
2. The United States Postal Service released a special brochure commemorating the centennial of the Trans-Mississippi Issue of 1898. Nine stamps highlight various aspects of westward expansion. The home presents an idealized and probably seldom achieved view of the aspirations of the pioneer settler.
3. Raymond J. Reitzel, M.D., *All in a Lifetime*, privately printed 1973, pp. 2–25.
4. Raymond J. Reitzel, p. 331.

Chapter 14

1. Brainerd Dyer, *The Public Career of William M. Evarts* (University of California Press), p. 267.
2. Brainerd Dyer, p. 82.
3. George F. Hoar, *Autobiography of Seventy Years* (New York: Scribner's, 1905) Vol._, p. 15.
4. Arthur M. Schlesinger, Jr., *The Imperial Presidency* (Boston, MA: Houghton Mifflin, 1973).
5. Clifton Rossiter, *The American Presidency* (New York: Time Reading Program, 1963), pp. 108–9.
6. Brainerd Dyer, *The Public Career of William M. Evarts* (University of California Press), p. 266.
7. Brainerd Dyer.
8. George F. Hoard, *Autobiography of Seventy Years* (New York: Scribners, 1905) Vol. ?, p. 17.
9. Allan Nevins, *Hamilton Fish* (New York: Frederick Ungar, 1957) Vol. II,, p. 902.
10. Brainerd Dyer, *The Public Career of William M. Evarts* (University of California Press), p. 267.

Chapter 15

1. Acadian is a term applied to the French-speaking inhabitants of Nova Scotia who were forced from their lands. Many of them relocated in Louisiana. Henry Wadsworth Longfellow's poem "Evangeline," memorialized these departed settlers: "Ye who believe in affection that hopes, and endures, and is patient, Ye who believe in the beauty and strength of a women's devotion, List to the mournful tradition, still stung to the pines of the forest, List to a tale of love in Acadie, home of the happy."
2. From McCully, Hendershott family records in the possession of Thae Ellen (Reitzel) Murdock.
3. The Delilah Frances (McCully) Hendershott account makes continual reference to Asa McCully as the Captain of the 1852 train. From other sources it seems certain that Asa's brother David was the Captain of this train, his bother heading up the 1853 train.
4. *The McCully Train*, Sanford & Sally Wilbur, Symbios, Gresham, OR 2000 p.80. David McCully gives us more detailed information. "Two partners got in a dispute over their property, one having furnished the mules, and the other the wagon. The owner of the mules unhitched them from the wagon, and was going to leave his partner alone on the plain with a sick man in the wagon, so the owner of the wagon shot the owner of the mules. A jury was called from the other two trains and a trial was had for the murder, and he was found guilty." David McCully, who was a member of the jury, wanted to bring the man to California or Oregon where a proper trial could be held. But the majority voted this motion down, and he was hanged.
5. Briggs, it seems well established, was a part of the 1853 train. These reminiscences were recorded a half century after the event.

Chapter 16

1. Fred Lockley, *Reminiscences of Col. Henry Ernst Dosch* (Fairfield, WA: Ye Galleon Press, 1972), p. 11-12.
2. The canal and locks at the Falls of the Willamette observed its 125th anniversary on New Year's Day 1998. In the earliest days the locks were operated by the People's Transportation Company but the financing was handled by a state bond issue authorized by the legislature in 1870. In 1915 the federal government bought the locks from the state and turned the operation over to the Corps of Engineers.
3. The Ainsworth family has left their mark in the greater Portland area. A home in Oregon City and the Jenkins Estate in Washington County, the home of a daughter and her husband are an ever-present reminder of their prominence. The Jenkins Estate was purchased by the Tualatin Hills Park and Recreation District and is used for weddings, memorial services, anniversaries and small conferences.
4. The eight states admitted in 1889-90 were Washington, Idaho, Montana, North Dakota, South Dakota, Wyoming, Utah and Colorado. The three existing states were California, Oregon and Nevada.
5. Comparative costs provided by Pacific Northwest Waterways Association, October 2001.
6. Water Resources Development in Oregon (U S. Army Corps of Engineers, 1997), pp. 20-21.
7. For a balanced view of the fish versus dams issue the reader is urged to read *River of Life, Channel of Death*, Keith C. Petersen, (Corvallis, OR: Oregon State Press, 2001). The author is the Idaho Coordinator for the Lewis and Clark Bicentennial commemoration.

Chapter 17

1. Floyd Clymer, *Early American Automobiles 1877-1925*, (New York: Bonanza Books, 1950), pp. 205-210.

2. These cars stood out in the first half-century, Jerry F. Boone, *The Oregonian* 12/6/1999, p. B4.
3. These set the tone for the last half century, Jerry F. Boone, *The Oregonian* 12/13/1999, p. C4.
4. *The Automobile and American Culture*, Lewis & Goldstein, editors, (Univ. of Michigan Press, 1983), Reynold Wik, *The Automobile and the American Farmer*, p. 37ff.
5. Ibid preface.
6. A.L. Dyke, *Dykes Automobile Encyclopedia* 15th Ed., (Chicago: Goodheart & Wilcox, 1928), pp. 996–7.
7. *New York Times Almanac*, NY 2001, pp. 215–19.
8. Ron Bernthal, *The Road Goes on Forever* (Boston: *Christian Science Monitor*, 4/24/01), pp. 17–19.
9. See web site of National Historic Route 66 Foundation at www.national66.com.
10. U. S. Census Bureau, Statistical Abstract of the United States, 2000 edition, table 1021.
11. U.S. Census Bureau table 684.
12. Air Transport Association of America reports that Hartsfield International Airport, Atlanta handled 8.2 million arrivals and departures in 2000.

Chapter 19

1. Trans-Mississippi Issue, Celebrating the 100th Anniversary (United States Postal Service, 1998), pp. 2–32.
2. Fred Lockley, *Reminiscences of Col.Henry E. Dosch* (Eugene, OR: Rainy Day Press, 1972), pp. 3–16.
3. Carl Abbott, *The Great Extravaganza* (Portland, OR: Oregon Historical Society, Revised Edition 1996), p. 43.
4. Part of the Japanese exhibit at St. Louis was sold to a Japanese-American medical researcher who had the building disassembled and shipped to Monticello, New York, in the Catskill Mountains. He named it Sho-Fu Den. Years later my college roommate, Melvin Osborne, purchased the

place and I spent a night there enroute to our 25th anniversary of our graduation from Hobart College.
5. The Natural Legacy of Lewis and Clark, by Jolene Krawczak in a Special Section of the *Oregonian*, May 24, 2001, p.AA1–AA4. Collecting plants was an important part of the Corps of Discovery.
6. For those wishing the latest information on the Signature Events of the Bicentennial, access the web site at www.lewisandclark200.org.

AFTERWORD

THIS BOOK BEGAN with a letter that I sent off to the Library of Congress. What was this Construction Corps of the U.S. Military Railroads that my maternal grandfather had served in during the Civil War? In reply I got a list of books of which the *Reports of Bvt. Brig. Gen. D. C. McCallum*, to the 39th Congress published by the Government Printing Office provided an answer. About the same time, I read David McCullough's *Brave Companions*. It was, as the jacket proclaimed, a series of good stories about interesting places and people, written by what many believe to be America's foremost historian and commentator. Where else can you find a good read about the bridge-building Roeblings, the builders of the Panama Canal, the explorations of Baron Alexander von Humboldt, artist-illustrator Frederick Remington, and the photography of David Plowden? On and on the author introduces you to first this well remembered figure and then another that history seems to have passed by.

I lay the book aside, and then as if the author was calling me to take pen to paper, I began to do research on people I have found interesting. At first I began by selecting people and places here in the Northwest. I soon found out that it is hard to pin down people to a given geographic region. One of the defining characteristics of Americans is their mobility, here today and move tomorrow. Allen Guelzo writing about Thomas Lincoln, Abraham Lincoln's father, described him as having "the western itch." If an itch it was, it was an irritant that many shared. Others would make a more rational case for the lure of cheap land. One hundred dollars cash could get a settler a quarter section of good farmland in Illinois. And how did this mass immigration move from the eastern states to the west? Most of the people in this book are associated in some way with transportation: canal building, riverboat travel, road building, bridges, stagecoach, rail and automobile. And the wars we fought intrude on the telling of this tale. The War of 1812 delayed western expansion for a bit, but oddly enough the Civil War did not. Western movement went on steadily right through those war years. I anticipate the reader will have lots of "why and why-not" questions. Why stop with railroads and automobiles? Why not air travel as well? Why not more stories about women? Why not stories about American Indians? Why no mention of the importance of religion on the frontier? Why no painter and artists? David McCullough ended his book by listing a series of persons for whom there exists no up-to-date biography. Who authored the Land Grant College Act? Who fought to end slavery? Who helped to end child labor? Who created the concept of a pension at sixty-five years of age? Who said, of free schools, "Intelligence is the primary ingredient in the Wealth of Nations"?

ACKNOWLEDGMENTS

One of the functions of this section of the book is to give thanks to those who made possible the gathering of data. The written sources are acknowledged in the endnotes. The circle of contributors—librarians, local historians, archivists, genealogists and descendants represent a special category the author wished to thank. The list includes:

Frederick Strong, historian for the Town of Woodbury, Connecticut, where the Sherman family lived from 1696 until Judge Charles Sherman left to oversee the distribution of the Fire Lands in the Western Reserve in 1791. Mr. Strong took time to give me the genealogical background of the family.

Stephen Towne, archivist of the State of Indiana who set me straight on how officers were chosen during the Civil War and who provided valuable information on Fielder Jones and the 8th Indiana Cavalry.

I would like to thank the librarians of county historical societies in Potter County, Pennsylvania and Macon County,

Missouri for their help in piecing together the story of a true citizen soldier, Brig, Gen. Fielder Jones.

Thanks to one of the Abbots of Mt. Angel Abbey, a Benedictine Seminary, serving the German and Swiss farmers who settled in and around Marion County, Oregon, during the nineteenth century. The Abbot was interested in the Civil War and left his own personal collection to the library. And to Patti Miller, one of the Abbey's longtime librarians, thanks for making my visits a source of joy.

Annette Lynch, volunteer historian at the Crawford County Historical Society, Meadville, Pennsylvania, who was able to identify the Congressman in whose office Fielder Jones studied for the bar exam, and who was well informed on the railroads that once centered on that city.

General Sheridan for the care he took in presenting in outline form the units and their commanders in his division, and to the Sheridan, Oregon, library for sharing with me an original edition of the General's *Memoirs*. Of all the memoirs by the great leaders of the Civil War, both south and north, Sheridan's epic is in a class by itself.

The Wyants, Bob and Kay, for their research on Evarts and railroad refrigeration, and for Kay's suggestion that I read *Father to Daughters, the Family Letters of Maxwell Perkins*. That led to a delightful contact with the great-granddaughter of William Maxwell Evarts, Bertha Frothingham, who still resided in one of the old family homes in Windsor, Vermont.

Since the age of the web has clearly dawned, recognition and thanks to the University of Rochester for the research done on the Erie Canal and Governor DeWitt Clinton. And to Western Reserve-Case University for matters pertaining to what was once a portion of Connecticut's westward claim in northeast Ohio.

James Driscoll, a great-grandson of Henry Dosch, for his willingness to open his home, Villa Eichenhoff, along with artifacts from the time Dosch had served as a one-man ambassador to the world. Two unpublished works of Henry's son, Arno Dosch-Fleurot, an overseas correspondent for the Pulitzer paper, *New York World,* covered two World Wars and the Russian Revolution, provided serendipitous information.

To Julie Cole of the Tidewater Barge Lines for the pictures of barge traffic on the Columbia and to Glenn Vanselow, Executive Director of the Pacific Northwest Waterways Association for reading an early draft of the chapter on river transportation.

Samantha Salenger, history exhibit director at the Wells Fargo Museum in Portland, and Robert J. Chandler, who both helped provide a wealth of material relating to the famous overland express company.

Librarians beyond counting have assisted in my research. The library in Newberg, Oregon, along with the inter-library loan network centered in Salem, the state capitol, has provided me with needed reference books. Thanks to the Oregon Historical Library for materials relating to Dosch and Ainsworth and to their photographic file.

My wife, Thae Reitzel Murdock, whose research into the genealogy of the McCully family strengthened the section on water transportation. And to my father-in-law, Raymond Reitzel, whose privately printed history, *All in a Lifetime,* gives us a glimpse of what it was like for some of the farmers who went west to claim a section of some of that "free land for the millions."

To Gloria Gonzalez and her assistants at Arnica Publishing Company in Portland. Norman MacLean in his forward to *A River Runs Through It,* writes, "Although it's a little book, it took a lot of help to become a book at all. When one doesn't start out to be an author until he has reached his biblical allotment of three score years and ten, he needs more than his own power." Gloria and her staff helped to supply that power.

Finally, I believe that in as many cases as possible, there should be some link between the author and the events described.

I have traveled on the Hudson. I have traveled on the Erie and the New York Central. I have made the Washington to Cincinnati run on the Chesapeake & Ohio. I have made the run from Washington to Atlanta on the Richmond, Fredericksburg and Potomac. There isn't a major rail line in the western states I haven't sampled. That includes the Great Northern, the Northern Pacific, the Union Pacific, the Western Pacific, the Santa Fe, and the three routes served by the Southern Pacific. I have driven coast to coast four times. On one of those trips I visited some of the Civil War battlegrounds in Tennessee and Mississippi. I have visited our National Parks more times than I dare count. I have made the trip to Alaska by ship twice.

I confess to being an Exposition junkie. My first visit was to the World's Fair in New York in 1939–40 and latest trip was to Vancouver, British Columbia, for their 1986 Fair. I have a collection of postal covers from other expositions held here in the United States. I hope the reader recognizes in the Age of the Automobile the love affair that I have had with the automobile. In my desk drawer I have dozens of ribbons that attest to the fact that I have entered shows or taken part in club tours.

ABOUT the AUTHOR

WILLIAM BARTON MURDOCK holds a Bachelor's degree from Hobart College, Geneva, New York, and a Master's in Divinity from the Virginia Theological Seminary. He worked for two years for the editorial department of the *New York Herald Tribune*, and he served in the United States Marine Corps from 1940 to 1946, holding the rank of major. From 1948 to 1980, Murdock was a clergyman in the Episcopal Church, beginning his service in Stanford, Connecticut, then moving to California and serving churches in Burlingame, San Bruno, and San Jose. For three years he served in the headquarters of the Episcopal Church in their Department of Christian Education.

Murdock's military honors include the Commendation Ribbon from the Commander of the South Pacific, Admiral William F. Halsey, for his service with the First Marine Division in action at Guadalcanal, and the Legion of Merit with Combat V for service during the assault phase of the Invasion of Okinawa.

Murdock was elected to the Chehalem Park and Recreation Board where he served three four-year terms. He has a life-long interest in American history with special interest in the Colonial period, the Civil War, and baseball. The author's infatuation with American-made automobiles is mirrored in one of the chapters in the book and extends from the Model T Ford, the Dodge Brothers Senior Six of the late 1920s, and the Studebakers of the post-war years. He and his wife live in rural Yamhill, Oregon.

To order additional copies of

WESTWARD LEADING

Contact:

Reverend William B. Murdock
PO Box 364
Marylhurst, Oregon 97036